Praise for *Contagious Culture*

Anese has tapped into something priceless about human nature and organizational behavior. In taking both a tender and powerful perspective, her approach helps people take more responsibility for their lives, their impact, and the culture they wish to create. Years after working with her and learning her methodology, her work continues to have ripple effects on my businesses, my health, and my relationships. To have her share this content and these principles in a book creates a tremendous opportunity for anyone to benefit from if they're willing to step in.

—Steve McPherson, founder PROMISE Wine, and former President
ABC Entertainment Group

Anese's methods, approach, and overall intuition about how people engage in and out of the workplace has had a profound effect on our organization. I think the principles embodied in IEP have broad appeal, are simple, teachable, and above all, useful. Challenging people to grow and to take responsibility for managing their own Intentional Energetic Presence is something I would recommend highly to others to apply.

—Paul Bennett, Chief Creative Officer, IDEO

In *Contagious Culture*, Anese introduces us to the myriad of intangible elements that have a very real impact on business success or failure. She reminds us that leaders exist irrespective of title, and how everyone shows up sets the cultural tone in an organization. Her practical advice for creating thriving cultures out of negative environments is invaluable, which is why we have sponsored so many of our employees to learn the IEP Method that she shares in this book.

—David Hassell, CEO, 15Five

Entirely inviting and approachable while being loaded with great ideas and actionable ways to help people become more effective in every phase of their lives, even if they don't know how to begin this important life-changing journey. Whether you want to be a more effective leader, parent, or team member, this book provides practical real-life experiences and tools to meet anyone where they're at.

—Jerry Calabrese, retired Corporate VP, McDonald's Corporation

Energy is the currency of culture and no one knows it better than Anese. Her principles and frameworks can shift it immediately. Her chapter on meetings alone could change how your culture operates. Start there, so you experience a fast shift. Meetings will be much more enjoyable and you can use that energy to apply to the deeper principles.

—Robbe Richman, author of *The Culture Blueprint* and former Culture Strategist at Zappos.com

This book is about truly and deeply realizing that your life and your world starts with taking accountability for the impact you have on yourself and others. It is about starting with YOU and is about making positive choices, coming to terms with each moment, and making the most of them so you can have a positive impact on your inner and outer worlds. This book has the power to transform people to become the powerful people that they have always been able to be; they just needed a little push in the right direction.

—Patrick Hoban, founder of Probility and Great Lakes Seminars

Anese Cavanaugh is a trailblazer in creating new strategies about what it means to be a courageous leader in today's market. Her fresh ideas are powerful, energizing, and address what companies need to do to create healthy and engaged workforces where people thrive. This book provides guidelines that all levels of an organization can implement and reap the rewards.

—Jenny Misirli, MAED, Director of Enrollment, University of Phoenix

Anese is brilliant to highlight intention as the key source of success in business. It's the secret behind great leaders, great teams, and great results. *Contagious Culture* is chock full of actionable and aspirational ideas and tools that anyone, at any level, can put into play to up-level their game and create a more effective dynamic at work. It's accessible, written in a playful yet powerful style that's easy to read, and inspiring. Reading it compelled me to highlight, bookmark, and write notes in the margins so I can page back and reexperience its many gifts.

—Kate Purmal, Angel Investor and Advisor, former SVP SanDisk Corporation

I work with some of the world's top thought leaders, founders, and visionary executives. In every case, Intentional Energetic Presence is key to their remarkable impact. Anese's ability to catalyze change is a unique superpower: I've seen her teachings transform rooms within minutes, and her presence in my life has profoundly influenced it for the better. Buy this book, integrate its wisdom, and watch change ripple out into your life and your culture.

—Alison Macondray, advisor and partner to thought leaders and professional speakers, presentation design expert, former General Manager of Wired News

Anese wrote the definitive guide for how to leverage your energy to have full power and control over your life. This book is a "must read" for any leader in business who wants more power and influence over their team, their customers, and their personal life.

—Andy Drish, cofounder, The Foundation

Who takes the opportunity to think about their intentions and the effect they will have on others? Anese, in her truly incredible work, has managed to simplify, name, and offer opportunities for growth in a world of leadership development that can feel so overwhelming. Her warmth, genuine insight, and brilliant strategic advice for what Showing Up really means have been invaluable. I constantly recommend her work to others and this book is the perfect opportunity to meet her. She is very much on every page.

—Heather Currier Hunt, Global Director of Learning & Development, IDEO

Anese shines a brilliant light on the intricacies of creating impact in our lives and organizations through the way we show up, in how we take care of ourselves, and how we cultivate leadership, inspiring others around us to lead. She's taking leadership and its impact to the next level using words like energy, presence, and vibration to get organizations to gel more effectively, to get people to come to work more fully, and to give leaders an extra edge that until recently has been difficult to "put a finger on." If innovation, culture, collaboration, and feeling good are important to you and your organization, you'll want to pick this one up.

—Nick Sarillo, founder, Nick's Pizza & Pub,
author, *Slice of the Pie: How to Build a Big Little Business*

Contagious Culture is a must-read for anyone looking to increase their business impact and performance. Cavanaugh offers you simple practical examples of how to create a culture that can inspire better results with lower costs, both at work and in life. Easy to follow, simple, and will connect with everyone who reads it.

—Henry Dziuba, President & General Manager, SMA

Anese Cavanaugh has just given you an amazing gift, a primer for leading your life and your business in such a way that you will be both successful and satisfied. Many people tell you what the ideal state looks like, but Anese gives you actionable steps to get there. Having worked with companies around the globe, I can tell you that the companies that are leading in this way are some of the most successful ones on the planet and by the way, people enjoy working for them.

—Karen Gordon, President and CEO, 5 Dynamics

I have to admit that I was one of the entrepreneurs who were skeptical about the IEP Method that Anese has developed. But after reviewing her work and hearing her speak, I realized that what Anese talks about is what all of us need most—a complete balance of mind, body, and spirit to be the best for ourselves and those around us. The message and method Anese has created must be shared with as big an audience as possible!

—Paul Spiegelman, Chief Culture Officer, Stericycle, author of *Why Is Everyone Smiling? The Secret Behind Passion, Productivity, and Profit* and *Patients Come Second: Leading Change by the Way You Lead*

The concepts contained within *Contagious Culture* are elementary, logical, and yet rarely connected in any academic approach, directly to powerful leadership presence. Cavanaugh's concept of creating an intentional impact through contagious energy is irrefutable.

—Thomas J. Walter, Chief Culture Officer, Tasty Catering

This book should be the precursor for every leadership class. *Contagious Culture* clearly identifies that great leadership starts with a leader who possesses great Intentional Energetic Presence (IEP). Anese challenges leaders to first optimize their energy, then use their leadership skills to achieve high performance, an excellent method that leads to success.

—Jamie Pritscher, cofounder That's Caring and nuphoriq

Illuminating and empowering, this book is an asset for anyone seeking to find balance in leadership and living.

—David Schonthal, cofounder, MATTER

This book is special. Anese bridges love, gratitude, and presence with leadership and culture in a truly unique and beautiful way. She invites us to step into more of ourselves in order to connect more authentically with others. This book will make you rethink what it means to show up as a leader.

—Agapi Stassinopoulos, author of *Unbinding the Heart*

Anese's book provides the tools you need to honestly "check-in" with yourself and strategically embrace and navigate anything life throws your way. No matter where I am in my life, at any crazy point—high or low, personal or professional, the IEP Method created by Anese Cavanaugh continues to be the driving force guiding me back on track. Through this work, you will discover your personal path to happiness and success, and you will gain the ability to make your dreams realities by learning how to start every day with purpose and intention. Anese is the best kind of contagious there is, her essence is truly inspirational!

—Diane Cooper, television executive

The health of your culture—within yourself and with the culture you create around you—is what ultimately determines your success. Anese's IEP Method gives you the tools you need to crack open communications, drive meaningful changes, and build healthy, successful relationships. Use the ideas in this book to set the tone and create a space where everyone, including yourself, can flourish.

—Mike Robbins, author of Nothing Changes Until You Do

Since life has become "richly scheduled" as a norm, who wouldn't be looking for ways to fine tune success and make their world easier and happier! Reading *Contagious Culture* is like having Anese with you, giving guiding ways to make yourself, your team, and your organization work in sync amid what could be chaos . . . if you let it be! Brilliant, easy, wonderful read!

—Cathy Mahoney, Sr. Vice President, Sales Operations, Freeman

Anese Cavanaugh distills in this one easy-to-read volume the wisdom of a lifetime spent helping organizations and people get better. Really better, not just "feel good" better and not just "better on the numbers." I started my career in tiny startups and am now proud to be part of one of the world's great business cultures. The lessons in *Contagious Culture* apply equally well in both circumstances, and provide practical steps for getting better no matter where you are or your organization is on the journey to greatness.

—Jonathan Nystrom, Executive Director, Big 4 Accounting Firm

Every start-up founder should be required to read this book! The ups and downs in the start-up world can be intense and so it's essential to have the right set of tools to stay focused and perform at the high level that is required to hold the vision, inspire the team, and execute. If you want to operate from a place of strength and stability in your professional and personal life, you need to run, not walk to get this book. I promise it will change you in ways you never could have imagined.

—Michele Serro, founder of Doorsteps

There is gold in this book. It changed my game. I've watched it change others' games. From kids to culture, from employees to executives, and everyone in between, this work has impact. Anese has distilled the art of Showing Up, and other complex intangible super powers into an incredibly simple guide you can start using from page 1. Easy to read. Applicable to anyone. Let her walk with you in words. You'll feel her in this book.

—Michelle Francois, Director, Foster Ed, National Center for Youth Law

In this book, you will find ideas that will enrich your life and transform your organization. Anese offers a practical and proven approach to defining and building a better culture from the inside out.

—Mark Bernstein, University of Michigan Regent and President of the Sam Bernstein Law Firm

As a business owner, it's easy to get wrapped up in your own world and forget that your team is taking cues from you. One negative comment or misplaced sigh can cause a cascading effect that demotivates your entire office for the day. When you multiply this across a team, the expense of negative energy is astronomical! Anese's methods give leaders practical tools and exercises that they can implement personally, and at the company level, in order to recharge their leadership and energize their company culture.

—Marisa Smith, founder, The Whole Brain Group

Contagious Culture shows how our presence influences others, the workplace, and ultimately, the vitality of our own lives. Anese weaves together wisdom that will, in the end, leave you in a better place than when you started reading the book.

—Shawn Murphy, author of *The Optimistic Workplace*

Self-reflection is one of the main ingredients to effective leadership, which is a theme peppered throughout *Contagious Culture*. As a leader in law enforcement, I continuously search for ways to transform individuals, so they can grow into successful leaders that will ultimately benefit the organization. Anese's book has created significant impact upon myself, thus inspiring all phases of my life and changing the way I "Show Up." I challenge those who are looking to enhance their leadership skills to read *Contagious Culture*, so they may perhaps experience a paradigm shift as well.

—Sergeant Rob Patton, Sacramento Sheriff's Department

This book offers a roadmap to individual as well as organizational success. I will definitely be incorporating some of the content into my strategizing sessions with my team.

—Ebby Antigua, Creative Services Director, Latina Media Ventures

"The culture is you." That is my favorite sentence in this great book. It summarizes perfectly the message that Anese is giving to all of us. It is a call to action, a reminder of responsibility, and a big opportunity to take action and create something exciting.

—Carissa Reiniger, founder and CEO, Silver Lining

CONTAGIOUS CULTURE

SHOW UP,
SET THE TONE,
AND INTENTIONALLY CREATE
AN ORGANIZATION
THAT THRIVES

ANESE CAVANAUGH

Mc
Graw
Hill
Education

New York   Chicago   San Francisco   Athens   London
Madrid   Mexico City   Milan   New Delhi   Singapore
Sydney   Toronto

1 2 3 4 5 6 7 8 9 0   DOC/DOC   1 2 1 0 9 8 7 6 5

ISBN   978-1-259-58457-2
MHID   1-259-58457-7

e-ISBN   978-1-259-58458-9
e-MHID   1-259-58458-5

Library of Congress Cataloging-in-Publication Data

Cavanaugh, Anese, author.
    Contagious culture : show up, set the tone, and intentionally create an organization that thrives / Anese Cavanaugh.
        pages cm
    Includes bibliographical references.
    ISBN 978-1-259-58457-2 (alk. paper)—ISBN 1-259-58457-7 (alk. paper)
    1. Corporate culture.   2. Organizational behavior.   I. Title.
    HD58.7.C388 2016
    658.3'12—dc23   2015028858

McGraw-Hill Education books are available at special quantity discounts to use as premiums and sales promotions or for use in corporate training programs. To contact a representative, please visit the Contact Us pages at www.mhprofessional.com.

To Gratitude and Impact.

And to Jake and Izzy, who teach me what it means to Show Up every day.

CONTENTS

FOREWORD

I have distinct memories of the very first time I worked with Anese. As she does with many of our clients, we began our collaboration with lots of conversations on the phone. But when we started working on a project for our organization IDEO, around leadership development, we arranged a working session together at our studio in New York.

It was one of those particularly hot summer days when the air felt thick and wet the moment you stepped out of the subway. Our studio at the time was in Soho, in a former dance studio with massive windows. On that particular day, Anese met me in our front meeting room, which basked in the sunlight. And on that particular day, the air conditioning wasn't working.

We sat in the conference room, which felt like it could more appropriately be used as a Bikram yoga studio. I wondered how we were going to make any progress when it felt like it was 105 degrees in the room. Anese took in the room, looked at me, and, her eyes smiling said, "Wow, it is really, *really* warm in here!"

Anese had a way of immediately acknowledging the situation and taking away the stress of it. Through her calm presence, we soon forgot about the temperature of the room and had an incredibly productive (and fun) day.

In that moment, I knew that there was something to Anese's approach that was more than just tools. And I wanted to know more.

And here we are today, years later. Anese has worked across most of our offices around the world, either directly engaging with our people through "IEP Leadership" launches, serving as an advisor and partner to our leadership to help us create an even stronger culture, or guiding us in the background to help build up our own coaching and development capabilities. When Anese asked me to write the foreword to this book, it made me reflect on the impact of our work together and all that's happened as a result of integrating this content into our culture.

A few things really stand out to me. One is the way in which the language and principles of her work show up in everyday interactions. For example, when teams get together to work on a new project, you'll often hear them "building agreements," or setting the social contract for how they work together. Or when there might be tension between people on a team, you'll hear someone "name" the tension so they can externalize it and look at it together to resolve their conflict. Or when people give one another feedback—both positive and constructive—you'll often hear them using Anese's principles and frameworks to make the feedback more human, specific, and actionable.

At this point, these behaviors are so ingrained that I really have to listen for them to remember that we did not always work in this way. So why does it matter? As an organization, we are built upon the success of our projects and relationships. What Anese's IEP methodology has been incredibly helpful at doing is unlocking greater collaboration for our project teams and greater leadership for our people, which results in better outcomes. And it doesn't stop with projects or project teams—people who have been through her programs at IDEO often say it impacts all of their relationships, inside and outside of work, because they are able to bring their best selves to their interactions.

To give a really tangible example, would you rather have a meeting in your organization where everyone is distracted by their phones, with an unclear agenda and unclear outcomes, not fully present and even worrying about anything other than what's needed in the room at that moment, or a meeting where there is a clear purpose and outcomes and everyone is present to listen and contribute and bring their best thinking? I suspect we'd all prefer the latter, but I equally suspect we've all been in the former more times than we'd like to admit. One very clear, practical application of the work in this book is to enable a shift from unproductive interactions to highly engaged and productive ones.

For companies that have never worked with Anese before, or done this kind of work, I can imagine it's a little unclear, if not intimidating. What on earth does intention, energy, and presence (IEP) have to do with my business? Why does it matter for leaders how leaders show up every day?

My answer to this is simple: you need to think about these things because you can't afford not to. From my work at IDEO, I have the privilege to work with companies across many industries. And a theme that unifies all of them is the quest to be more innovative.

We live in a time when new forms of competition can emerge practically overnight, with an ability to disrupt existing ways of doing business. And the big learning that we see again and again is that the key to innovation isn't isolated "innovation teams" working in a corner somewhere, hoping to find a silver bullet. The key is to elevate the capabilities of all leaders and all employees to spot new opportunities and to see their day-to-day work in new ways.

So I recommend taking some time to engage with the content of this book. Try it on for size in small ways—What's one thing you can try in your next meeting? Or in your reply to the next e-mail you get? Notice if you see a shift or feel a different impact. And I especially recommend this to leaders thinking about how their teams might use this content—don't give it to others without trying it yourself first. As leaders, we've all been exposed to various types of development and coaching, with varying levels of success. It's easy to say "I've got this already." Just remember that the best way to shift an organization is for the leaders to model the desired behavior, so doing the work yourself is incredibly valuable.

I've had the absolute pleasure to know and work with Anese for years. I truly believe this content is worth your time, and the impact is tangible.

Enjoy.

—Duane Bray
Partner and Head of Global Talent, IDEO

INTRODUCTION

Let's take a moment.

Wherever you are in your life, right now, I'm here to tell you that you are contagious. I'm also here to tell you that *you* have control. Likely more control than you think. I'm contagious. You're contagious. We're all contagious together, and what I share in this book is how we make "contagious" work *for* us versus against us.

The fun thing about all of this is that whether you want to be better for yourself, for your business, for your organization, for your culture, for your family, for your kids, for your making in the world, and/or for the people who trust you to lead them . . . you take *you* with you. So you've got you covered.

As we step into this next era of leadership, when we have more to do, more to care for, and more opportunities to make impact, there is a call, a demand even, to show up bigger, better, and more in service of others than ever. The most effective leaders listen to this call knowing that whatever they are sensing or feeling—frustration, joy, hunger, inspiration, even helplessness—has to be listened to and supported in order to lead forward and create impact in the world. The more we listen and honor this call, the stronger we become. When we lean into it, we ripple. We become productively contagious.

This book is about answering the call and setting yourself up for success. This book is about improving your leadership presence and your impact, not just on others, but on yourself, so that you can create the space you need to answer your calling. This book is about working you over — with love — from the inside out so you can become more of the leader you want to be. This book is also about learning to enjoy every moment of it (even when it's hard) so that you can contribute to creating a culture of leadership, "Showing Up," growing others, and answering the call every step of the way.

First, lest you think I have all of this figured out, let me set you straight right now. I am practicing and learning with you. I am a mom to two, a CEO, a speaker, teacher, writer, friend, sister, partner, advisor, coach, consultant, dog owner, thought leader, and creator of a methodology that's helped many. And frankly— in between bouts of holding it all together and feeling I might crash—thriving.

Yes, thriving. Absolutely thriving.

Am I busy? I'd say I'm richly scheduled and well used. Do I feel busy and overwhelmed? Sure, in my less intentional moments. Is it daunting at times? Yes. Am I complaining? No.

I am grateful. I have tools.

I share this with you not to toot my horn or diminish my credibility, but rather to share that I, like you, am another human being with a hunger to create positive impact in the world. I'm also keen on living a life I love and being a good person to the people in that life. Working the principles in this book is helping me do this, and my intention is to pass them on to you in whatever way most serves you.

Show Up and Up Your Game

In addition to elevating your leadership, this book is about up-leveling your game in general. It's about showing up for your life. It's about showing up for yourself. And showing up for the people you lead. It's about staying connected to purpose. To staying present to what counts. To nourishing yourself. And to using yourself to create a beautiful culture: at work, with your team, with your peers, and everywhere in between.

I'd love to say that just by reading the book, your leadership presence will take care of itself, but it won't. You will have to work for it. And at the same time you will have to just let it be and enjoy it. In this book I will walk you through a model I've developed called the IEP Method® and share many of the different components that are necessary to become the leader you want to be and to have the impact on the people around you that you truly want to have. Working your Intentional Energetic Presence® (IEP) is a powerful, pleasurable, and yes, sometimes daunting thing. And . . . you've got this! You're always just an energizing (or de-energizing) decision away.

I'm also going to talk to you about culture. Because while you may think that culture is something that's created by others, and just about your organization, it's much bigger than that. You are creating culture every day through your intentions (or lack of intentions), energy, and presence. You're creating the culture within your organization, with your team, with your clients, and in your meetings every day. You're creating culture within your family, with your friends, and at the dinner table every day. All of it is contagious. You are the contagion. This, by the way, is good news. You have power and influence here!

The days of being able to lead based simply on our titles, skills, competencies, and even our emotional intelligence are gone. The days of it being enough to just be a good leader and make cool stuff happen? Gone. In order for us to innovate to the next level of business and to solve the many, many problems that we want to solve, it's going to require a new kind of leadership. It's going to require that we create more leaders than ever. And it's going to require that we intentionally infect our cultures with impact-focused leadership, love, and care—starting with ourselves first.

I believe that the ideas, tools, and principles offered in this book will help you start to find what showing up and leading at this next level looks like for you personally and help you to find it in a way that has you feeling rejuvenated and engaged, versus burned out and busy.

This book is a work of love, crafted after 23 years of working with individuals and organizations, with athletes, executives, entrepreneurs, designers, teachers, parents, entertainers, CEOs, founders, and people in support and administrative roles.

The principles and tools shared in this book have been used by some of the most innovative and inspiring companies in the world. Organizations like IDEO, Zingerman's, and others have integrated components of this content into their talent development and design processes, customer service experiences, team meetings, leadership training, executive education, onboarding and exiting processes, and more. Executives from companies like Citigroup, McDonald's, and others have used these principles to help them enhance their executive presence, their leadership competencies, and their connection to meaning and purpose. Companies like Chevron, IBM, and others have used the concepts from this work to help them coach and be better leaders inside their organizations. Start-ups and small businesses have used this content to help them create healthy cultures of leadership and accountability from the beginning. Teachers have used it in schools to enhance their impact with students and each other. Physicians and wellness professionals have used it to improve their bedside manner and leadership in their practices. Designers and makers have used it to enhance their collaboration and communication skills. And nonprofits (including those working with high-risk youth and within the foster care system) have used it to empower youth and cultivate confidence in the kids coming through their programs. I even received a note this last year from an 11-year-old who was using it with her best friends to "get straight A's."

I've shared many stories to support the principles explored. I thank every single person who's ever worked with me for allowing me into their lives and for sharing their life's work, their challenges, their wins, and their pains, and for paying their learning forward by allowing me to share their stories. All stories have been tweaked to honor privacy and confidentiality; names changed, gender sometimes changed, details changed, but everything shared in this book is a true story, or composite of a story, from people who have integrated IEP into their lives in order to honor themselves, unlock their leadership potential, and grow others.

Some of this work will resonate for you. Some of it will hit you three weeks later in the shower. Some may become key for you five years from now. Some of it may simply not be for you but may point you toward something important that *is*. Whatever the case, be kind to yourself. Enjoy what you enjoy. Integrate what you want to integrate, and use this as a living work in progress.

May you find exactly what you need in this book. I love you already.

XO,
Anese

REFLECTION: PUTTING IEP INTO PRACTICE

Setting Intentions

In every section of this book I'll ask you to put this work into practice. You can do as much as you like with these queries. Let's start here.

I'm big on intention. You will be too soon if you're not already. I'll be giving you several tools as we build, and I'll be inviting you to try them on as you go. Consider this book a living document for your life and organization. Read it over and over again, skip sections, and come back to it as much as you please. All of the people I've ever worked with or had in one of my courses have shared that no matter how much they engage with this content, they learn new things every time. Due to what's happening in their lives and the personal work they've done, they're new, and there's a new place to step into. So make this book be alive for you.

I've also found that people get more out of our work together when they're clearer about what they want going in. So let's set some intentions *right now* for engaging with this book. Note that even that intention can change for you as you get further in.

Take a moment and consider the following:

1. What do you want to get out of this book? (List at least 3 things.)
2. Who are you now, and who do you want to become? (For example: What kind of leader, parent, maker, friend, entrepreneur, human, etc. are you now? And what kind do you want to become?)

3. What kind of agreements with yourself would you like to have in terms of integration? For example:
   - "I'll try one thing immediately every time something 'sparks' for me."
   - "I'll pick one new principle a week to keep working on until I feel it's a habit."
   - "When I start to think 'I know this,' I'll look for where this applies to my life and wisdom *now*."
4. Who else can you share this experience with? Who might be a good accountability partner for working through this? (You might do this with a partner or your team or an executive circle for even more impact and fun.)
5. Are you reading this book for *you* or for someone else? Tell the truth. (In other words, do you want someone else to understand this work, so you're reading it to see if you can find ninja tricks to change him or her?) If so, let's let that go, and go back to the first question.

That's good for now. We'll dive into more specifics as we go, especially as we go deeper into assessing and optimizing your IEP. For now, the invitation is to do quick intention checks as you read the rest of this book to see if you're getting what you've intended. If not, shift accordingly so that you do. Have fun!

PART 1

THE FUNDAMENTALS OF SHOWING UP

You simply must show up.

Whether you're the one who's impacted by everyone else's energy, or you're the one setting the tone, showing up with intention is where leadership starts. This is going to be fun. Ready?

A Couple of Important Things Before We Dive In

One, You're Contagious

You're creating a culture that is contagious. You're setting the tone. You're making it happen—or not. You are to celebrate for the success of your culture, or to blame for its failure. You—yes, you. How powerful is that? Whether you are the CEO, a supervisor, an employee, a janitor, or a parent, how your culture is right now is a result of how you've shown up, the decisions you and your team have made, your own personal relationship with accountability, and your willingness to create a life you love. Of course, if you are higher up in the organization, in an official leadership role, you have even more responsibility and opportunity to be contagious. Regardless of your position, you emanate the culture. The culture is you. This is great news because you're contagious and you have impact.

1

Two, You Have the Power and Absolute Right to Create a Life and an Organization That Thrives—or Not

You get to create awesome impact. And you get to feel wonderful doing it. Your success in creating impact will be highly related to how you show up, what you choose, and how willing you are to do the work to make things hum.

Three, Leadership Starts with You

Again, regardless of your role, position, degree, age, gender, sexual preference, clothing style, or if you're a cat or dog person, leadership starts with you. There are things you can do to lead well or terribly, to be happy or miserable, to pay it forward and share the joy or shut it all down and be a curmudgeon. This book is loaded with suggestions for you. In order for you to lead well and create the impact you want, we will need to take an inside-out approach that will include everything from protecting and nourishing yourself to nourishing and serving those you lead. You'll see.

And Four, You're Always Having an Impact

Positive or negative or completely ineffectual, you are having an impact—on yourself, on those you lead, on your peers, on your customers, on your boss, on your kids, on the barista at the coffeehouse. How present and intentional you are about this impact will be the difference between you being a rock star leader people want to be around and follow, or someone they tolerate or follow simply because you're their boss and you give them a paycheck. How you do this as an organization or team will be the difference between people wanting to work for your company because your culture rocks and people feel amazing, or because they couldn't find anything better, your organization was a default or third choice, or in some odd way this new job feeds their ego, not their purpose.

Showing Up

Let's talk about "showing up" in culture, regardless of whether that culture is you as an individual or your team, your organization, or your family unit as a whole. How you show up will impact everything. Showing up includes your intention, your energy, and your presence, which emanates from you everywhere you go. So regardless of which element of your life or which "culture" we're talking about, you're going to want to show up and show up well. It's a bit like dropping food coloring in water. It blends in and you can't separate it out. And just like you can't take food coloring out of water, you can't take how you show up out of life. Your presence creates impact on every level. Again, this can be a great thing.

The first part of this book looks at the fundamentals of showing up. We'll focus on how to start relating to yourself in this domain in a way that serves and honors you, the people you lead, and the impact you want to have. While I generally am speaking to you as an individual, I'll also be speaking to you inside a system, whether that means your team or your organization or your family. Just think of "showing up" as having multiple levels of impact—the most important one being *you* in the center of it, rippling out to everyone else. Why? Because we are contagious.

You

One last thought before we dive in . . . If you're reading this book, you likely already have a healthy dose of self-awareness and a desire to create an even better culture and to contribute more powerfully to the people around you. Great. This book will be about optimization and extra special self-care for *you*. This book will likely be most helpful to you in strengthening your leadership and in nourishing and protecting your own energetic field so you can do more—without feeling depleted or getting dragged into other people's stuff.

The content in this book is very possibly the missing piece you haven't been able to dial in for impact. It is often incredibly talented high performers who contact me because they can't figure out why they've been unable to get to the next level of impact. This work tends to shine a light on the blind spots and has a way of unlocking that next level. Little tweaks, quiet awareness, and subtle shifts in one's Intentional Energetic Presence (IEP) can make the difference between being the leader people *want* to follow, versus *have* to follow, the difference between *surviving* and *thriving*, the difference between being in *action* on one's path and feeling like a *passenger*. If you're already succeeding in your life but still aren't having the impact you want—you're not revered or promoted or inspired or as inspiring as you'd like—you'll be well leveraged in working some of the principles here.

You in Your Organization

If you are a member of an organization or a team reading this book in order to make your culture better—bravo! Know this: Your highest leverage move right now is to make sure that every single person reading this does the work for himself or herself *first*. (That includes you as the CEO or team lead.) In other words, if you do the work personally, show up more powerfully and compassionately, and take great care of yourself, you will be better for others, period. You're bound to feel better, lead better, and simply be better to be around. And you'll be better able to optimize or create the organization that thrives. Much like on an airplane, the flight attendant will tell you that if the airplane starts going down, you should grab your own oxygen mask first so you can be as helpful as possible to others. If you take care of others first, you pass out. You're no good to anyone. So take care of yourself, mind your own business, get your oxygen, own your impact, and get in here with me.

Triage or Optimization: Where Are You Now?

When I go in to work with teams and companies, I tend to put them into two categories: triage or optimization. Triage means there are serious issues: damage, wounds, unhealthy culture, high attrition, low energy, lots of busyness, and burnout. There's also likely lots of gossip, blame, and focusing on the wrong things. There's an overall lack of purpose, and HR may be a bit busier than it would prefer to be. It's not pretty. But it's common and very human. When a company needs help from a place of triage, there's a lot we can do, but it takes time. Baby steps are the name of the game. The key is to get every leader in the company focused on creating positive impact and doing his or her own personal work. When leaders are modeling showing up well, they are able to create a culture of trust and accountability that others can count on and be inspired by.

Optimization mode, on the other hand, is when an organization is already succeeding. The organization is known as a good place to work, where people are happy, getting great stuff done, and having solid impact, and its leaders want to be even better. In the optimization stage we're honing and refining purpose and values, team alignment, and personal fulfillment and transcendence. We're optimizing productivity and performance, unlocking new leadership and collaboration competencies, making things even better by their new definitions and dreams of what *great* looks like, and diving into building a stronger IEP Foundation in their company.

Regardless of where you are as an organization in terms of triage or optimization or somewhere in the middle, dive in with me now. As *you*. Look for where this information can serve you in new ways or take you to the next level. Step into curiosity and expand your range. Give yourself another level of insight.

One of the reasons I love this work so dearly is that there is no finish line. There's no "right" or "wrong." There is no cap on showing up big and brilliantly for ourselves and for others. The better we get at it, the more work we realize we have to do. How gorgeous is that? So lean in, dear reader. Let's create some impact together from where we stand. Our lives and cultures depend on it.

CHAPTER 1

Holding Your Fate

Are you doomed? It's up to you.
Will you thrive beyond your wildest expectations?
Up to you too. This will either depress or liberate you.

First, let's get one thing straight about your fate: You determine how you want to show up and what you're going to create in your life. You also determine the kind of business and culture you want, even if you're not the boss. You have impact. You have power. Your fate starts with taking accountability for what you're creating and for owning your impact.

I hear statements like this a lot: "It would be so much better if they did 'this' better or if they led better or if they were easier to work with, or if they weren't such jerks or if 'they they they' did something differently." It's a common sentiment. But the truth is that holding this stance is a little crazy making. It gives all the power to "they." Waiting for "they" to show up differently, to act differently, to do something differently, to *be* different is a waste of time and energy at best, and completely uninspiring. You have no control there. Sure, you can request. Sure, you can give feedback. Sure, it often helps. Sure, sometimes it works . . . but not always.

More often than not, in the most challenging of relationships and circumstances, waiting for someone else to show up differently so you can get something done, or have a relationship be easier, is a long, unproductive, soul-sucking, disempowering wait.

Here's the gift: You can change your culture, your team, your family dynamics, your satisfaction with your job, the amount of energy you have in the morning, anything. Why? Because you *do* have control of *you*. Yes, you. No matter how horrible your boss is, your employees, your sister, the stranger on the street who just yelled at you because he's having a really bad day, even your culture, *you* are in control of *you*. You have the power. With intention, presence, and action, you can shift it. And if all of these things are awesome, which they very often are, then you have the power to enhance, sustain, and optimize them even more. Yes, you.

The team member who's not showing up as you like, your boss not "seeing" or acknowledging you, your culture being restrictive, your kids who are fighting constantly, your spouse not listening to you—believe it or not, you have influence in all of this. And the influence starts with your awareness, your presence, your intention, and how you show up.

The fate of your culture—whatever culture we're talking about—is yours for the influencing.

Leadership and Cultural Contagions

Let's talk about your culture. I believe there are seven indicators that point to how healthy a culture is, and can be. These are also indicative of the levels of trust and connection that allow for optimal collaboration and innovation. I'll talk about these more specifically in Chapter 14, but for now they are *accountability and ownership, safety to show up fully, curiosity and vulnerability, the intention of contribution, the spirit of reciprocity, shared purpose and values*, and *intentional measurement and rewards*.

When everyone comes to the table honoring these, the culture works itself out. The culture becomes what it wants to become. Notice that all of these start with the individual's stance and mindset. If each member of the culture holds and honors these, then the system works better together.

Note that it does not matter if the culture you're referring to is your organizational culture, your family culture, your community's culture, or the crazy culture that lives inside your own head—you are creating your culture. And by the time you're through this book, your culture will be different.

On top of these cultural intentions there are two things I look at to help me determine what kind of contagions are being projected from leaders: how they "show up" and how they grow others. These two things are strong predictors of the quality of their leadership as well as the quality of the culture they're contributing to creating. The better leaders are at these two, the easier it is for them to be successful at the cultural "Super 7." The more intentional they are with the Super 7, the easier it is for them to be successful at showing up and growing others.

The first thing, showing up, involves the obvious: your presence, your body language, your tone of voice, what you say and do, and your ability to simply get stuff done—to lead. Showing up also involves the intangible, not so obvious things: your intentions, your energy, how you see people, your levels of accountability and ownership, and your ability to make someone feel seen and valued—to be.

The second thing that will highly influence the quality of your leadership and culture is your ability to grow others and the size of the "container" you can hold for people to step into. We'll talk about the "container" later, but for now, know that this basically boils down to your leadership in service of other humans, how you regard them, how you believe in them, what you believe is possible for them, and how you mentor, guide, and direct them.

I believe this all starts with belief in others, topped off by skills. Here's the rub: Your ability to grow others, hold space, and truly optimize impact is highly dependent on your presence, your own growth, and your relationship with yourself. So in order to lead others, you must lead yourself first.

If you want to enhance your executive presence, create your intended impact, innovate, collaborate, navigate conflict, lead better meetings, and simply build a happier life in which you feel turned on, tuned in, and on purpose, it's time to get to work.

So, how do you hold your fate? Do you focus on what you want? Take care of yourself? See the best in others? Take ownership for your impact (the good, the bad, and the ugly)? Show up for your life? *Or* . . .

Do you focus on what you don't want? Leave self-care on the back burner? Assume the worst? Walk through life in judgment, blaming, jealous, maybe competing, feeling threatened? Do you feel victim to circumstances and people (even yourself)? Do you wait for things to get better? Are you in a constant state of feeling overwhelmed?

These are two extremes: Where do you fall?

How do you create your fate? Where do you rock it like a rock star? Where do you need some TLC? Let's look.

Meet Jill

Jill, an executive at an LA marketing firm, needed a reboot. She'd been on an accelerated growth path over the last two years, knocking things out of the park left and right. But over the last eight months things had shifted. Things had gotten tough. Some big life changes, less time with her family, a shift in focus in her work with clients, some team dynamics she didn't love dealing with, all contributed to her feeling overwhelmed, stuck, and frustrated. She was tired, and everyone around her knew it. To top it off she was caught in the vicious cycle of busyness and the feeling of having "zero control over anything." While eight months before she'd been on a roll, now she felt powerless.

Jill spent a lot of time venting and listing all of the reasons these issues still had a hold on her.

None of them were "*her* fault."

Not a one.

Now before you think I'm picking on Jill, I assure you I am not. As a human being, I'll bet you can empathize with almost any of the things that were stressing her out. Jill is not a bad person, or leader, or mom, wife, whatever. She's amazing. She'd simply gotten on a path that had turned into a perpetual and contagious state of negativity that she kept feeding. Every time she told the story, and especially if it was validated by others, she fed it. Here are just some of the things she was grappling with:

- She and her husband had bought a new house. The process was very stressful and very busy. Her presence communicated that it had happened *to* her and had her hostage. She had turned something beautiful and amazing and a big accomplishment into something absolutely stressful, painful, and "horrible."
- She'd been "put" on one project too many. Her company was thriving, and for now, clients needed her in the room more and her direct reports needed more direction and mentorship. She was exhausted. Her focus on feeling pulled in so many directions completely clouded her ability to see how this was good. Instead she stood in the place of suffering and martyrdom.
- Her husband didn't "see" her, understand her, or support her in the way she wanted to be supported, her kids were whiney and disrespectful, and she was chronically sore, sick, or coming down with something. Everything hurt. She didn't have time for workouts or even eating well. She felt like everyone wanted a piece of her. It wasn't pretty.

11

What Jill hadn't been able to see, until this point, was that she was hurting herself more than anyone in these scenarios. She'd been crafting her story and her experience. She'd been holding her fate.

What she hadn't been able to see, until this point, was that she had choice and power. She wanted a "do over."

Decide to Shift

The first steps in creating a "do over" are in recognizing—authentically—where you are, taking ownership for what you're creating, and then deciding to create something different.

Jill recognized that she'd been in a cycle of judgment, blame, victimhood, abdication, and shame. She'd been so "in it" that she'd been unable to take any accountability for it. Deep in this cycle over the last eight months, she realized she'd been contagious—and not in the ways she intended. Her husband was responding negatively, her kids had caught her outlook, her team avoided her, and even her boss was exhausted by her.

So she gave herself a break, realizing that beating herself up for this would do no good. She took a breath. And she *decided* to reboot. She decided to get help and create a plan.

Can you relate? Either for yourself or for someone you've led? If so, there are a couple of things you can do to help yourself (and those you lead) better hold and shift your fate.

Discover What Lies Beneath: Beliefs, Needs, and Other Tricky Things

After Jill got present to what truly was and how bad it all felt, she got to work. With the help of a trusted friend, she identified three things that were lending themselves to her state.

First of all, *she wasn't feeling heard*. Every time she'd try to talk about how scared or overwhelmed she felt, she was met with people trying to point out the "good side" of her situation. She didn't have space to complain. So instead of getting an awesome well-witnessed, well-cared-for, vulnerability-laced, loving *vent session*, she did mini ones that not only didn't pay off for her but also exhausted the people around her and resulted in a continuous leak of "blech." Her needs to be truly heard and witnessed weren't being met, so they manifested in unintentional ways—by a series of slow-leaking complaints and cries for help that exhausted her and everyone around her. She needed to develop the skill to hear and be heard.

The second thing contributing to her state was that *she had no space for herself.* She wasn't prioritizing her well-being or personal time. She was eating poorly. She wasn't moving. She had poor sleep habits. Not even a morning tea time for herself. With a life as richly scheduled and engaged as hers (and yours), if this stuff is not marked out, it doesn't happen. Jill could see how she was creating this dynamic in her life by not taking a stand for it. She needed to develop the skill to create time and space to take care of herself.

And the third thing that was causing trouble for Jill? *Her habits and beliefs.* Complaining and seeing the "bad" side had simply become habit. Originally influenced by fear, resentment, and a feeling of being overwhelmed, it had become just a natural way to see things. And her whole presence had adopted the stance. Not only was this a habit, she'd actually begun to believe all of it— "Life is hard," "This is bad," "This is not fair," "It *should* be stressful to buy a house," "My husband *should* change," and one of my favorites, "This is just how it has to be." These beliefs impacted everything she did and projected out in her presence as contagious blech. She needed to develop the skill to identify beliefs and habits that were getting in her way.

The combination of not being heard, low self-care, and practicing old habits and beliefs had landed her in a cycle that's really difficult to break if you can't see it. So now that she could see it, Jill decided to break it. There were a couple of things she did immediately.

Start by Creating Space

Jill knew the way she was working wasn't serving her. She needed TLC. She needed space. She needed to be heard. So she dove into each of the things that were stressing her out with a responsible "thinking partner": someone she could trust, who would listen and hold space for her without piling on, judging it, making it worse, or invalidating it, *and* while holding her accountable for her own contributions and leadership. Her colleague gave her space to explore without worrying about looking good or being a great leader, allowing her to be exactly where she was and to authentically explore what was up.

A responsible thinking or venting partner can help a person unlock the ability to move through an issue or complaint in a genuine, productive, and sustainable manner. This stops the cycle of continually repeating the same complaint, behavior, or situation. It also ensures that learning and new best practices are captured. An *irresponsible* partner will often collude with the negative thinking, making matters worse, sending the person even deeper into his or her drama, perpetuating the cycle.

Break the Cycle, Create Structures to Make Your Life Hum, and Get into Action

First, Jill asked one of her teammates and a personal girlfriend to serve as "responsible" venting partners. Despite being inclined because of her previous attitude to walk the other way when they saw her coming and let her calls go to voice mail, they obliged. Something had shifted in Jill; she wanted to get better at this, and she needed help. They agreed. Their job would be to hear and witness her and love on her in all her glory and fear. Their job was also to hold her accountable for shifting out of it and being the author of her life. This would be the key to Jill's growth.

Jill started a journal in which she focused on three things: gratitude, ownership, and impact. She drilled down to the following seven quick questions to ask herself every day:

1. What am I grateful for today?
2. What relationship do I want to nurture or celebrate?
3. What is the thing that's bugging me or scaring me or whatever? (Jill called this her "ick.")
4. How am I contributing to it, or what am I assuming?
5. What am I going to do about it—even the littlest thing?
6. How am I going to take care of myself today?
7. What is the impact I want to have today?

Finally, she decided to start focusing on what she wanted as well as noticing her complaints. Before a complaint fell out of her mouth, she'd consider if it was really something worth complaining about, and if so, she'd turn it into a request or suggestion. Notice that her shifts did not require a lot of effort to create movement.

Jill had awareness. She had someone to witness and reflect with. She was willing to look at and explore her part in creating the "ick." And she chose to change. The initial changes came down to space, self-care, self-awareness, and attention on where her attention was.

Change Your Story

As time went on, Jill's story changed even more. Congruently and sustainably. It began to look a bit more like this (some of these changed faster than others):

"Bought a new house, wow! So the contractors messed up and it's not perfect. Yeah, there is extra financial pressure now. And? *And* wow, we bought a new house. We worked really hard for this. We don't have to do it all at once or even now. There is time. Thank you. Wow." Breathe.

Too many projects? The company was succeeding. It was breaking records. Celebrate and appreciate. *And* what did she need to do to shift her perspective, create some leverage, and redefine some boundaries? Digging deeper and using the IEP Method, which you will learn about in this book, she found places where she could carve out more time in her schedule and where she could be more of a leader empowering others to step into roles and tasks that grew them.

Her direct reports? She had an opportunity to create impact here. Truth be told, she felt insecure about her bandwidth and ability to inspire them—it's difficult to lead and inspire from burnout. So what to do? Well, first, telling herself the truth was essential. As she explored her situation, she finally admitted, "I'm not confident that I can mentor and lead my team members. I feel resentful that I have no time. I don't even like two of them." (Now we're getting somewhere.) So she found someone else to work with the two she couldn't believe in while she did her own work to resolve what it was about them that didn't work for her.

Her husband? She realized she'd gotten into the trap of passive-aggressive waiting behaviors with her beloved, and they'd both jumped into the game. One of them had to shift, so Jill ran with it. She went home that night, put the kids to bed early, and had a heart-to-heart talk with her husband. What changed? Did he? No, she did, and that shifted his state.

And her self-care. That was tough. But it was key to all the areas she felt powerless in. Once she had a bit more space and awareness, and once she started to see the impact of movement and food on her body, she took another step. She set herself up with the simplest thing she could do *now* that wouldn't take a lot of time. She committed to drinking more water and eating more vegetables and protein. She also committed to cutting soda, watching her sugar intake, and intentionally increasing pleasure and delight in her life.

What Jill did here was hold her fate on a whole new and productive level. She couldn't control a lot of what was happening—things were moving fast for big and great reasons—but she could shift her mindset and the way she stepped into each piece. Her game continued to change. And she became contagious in other ways—ways that inspired people to engage with her, get curious, and follow her.

Now, of course I share Jill's story as if she were able to make these adjustments in two seconds. In some cases, lifestyle changes can be that quick. But sometimes they take a lifetime and an overhaul shift in our mindset, our relationship with ourselves, and our accountability for our lives. The great news is that you have all of this *inside* you. I'm not going to give it to you—no one can. But I'll point you in the right direction. And man oh man, if you decide to grab onto even a few of these concepts in taking accountability and leading your fate, your life is going to expand.

Your Turn

Your job here? Get *big*.

When you turn and face the stuff you don't like, when you finally admit to the things that you're not loving, where you're falling down, where you're miserable, the skies open up. Things can breathe. You can shift them. Only you. There is no cure for feeling down, broken, overwhelmed, or victimized by your life or circumstances or relationships like turning inward, giving yourself a bit of TLC, taking the situation by the horns, getting into action, and asking for help where needed. Another powerful cure is gratitude and contributing to someone else, but we'll get to that later. Let's take care of you first.

Of course, as always, all of this is contagious. Just watch. Have you ever been inspired by someone grabbing life by the horns, choosing to lead, or just simply choosing to show up differently? Yes, it is contagious. For good and for bad, we're contagious.

Reflections: Putting IEP into Practice

How Are You Holding Your Fate?

Here are five steps to help you get clear on what's going on and what you can do next. If possible, get a "thinking partner" as you work through these steps.

1. **Be aware.** Are you aware of what's really going on and how happy or unhappy you are?
2. **Decide.** Do you want to shift? Have you truly decided to make changes? (You will likely need to ask yourself this question for each change.)
3. **Create space.** Allow for full expression and unpacking without judgment and without denying any problems.
4. **Mine for gold.** Explore issues by asking the following questions:
    a. What's not being heard? What are the requests under the complaints?
    b. What beliefs and habits are getting in the way and keeping you stuck?
    c. Do you have space for reflection and self-care?
5. **Get into action.** What needs to happen to create even tiny shifts? Go there.

A Couple of Other Places to Look

What do you have to celebrate? Where are you doing things well? For example, "I just rocked that project/bought that house / had a great parenting moment."

If you're not happy right now, and stuck in your unhappiness, what is the supposed gift of that displeasure? For example, the "gift" might be "I'm miserable, and my misery is giving me an excuse to not work harder" or "I love my story of struggle, and I take pride that it has to be hard."

What are you focusing on? What do you want to focus on? For example, trade "I'm not having this impact" for "This is the impact I want to have," or "This guy is a pain to work with" for "Here's how I'd like to work with this guy."

What's the littlest thing you can do, right now, in this moment, to shift your situation? Little or big, what's the next thing? Get present, tell yourself the truth, and you'll know.

Fate Game Changers

Here are some quick game changers that will allow you to create your own fate. Do one or do all—each of these will shift your state so you can get into a better position to lead.

1. Do your work. Be accountable for your choices.
2. Stop complaining and start resolving.
3. Ask for help—admit your glorious imperfections.
4. Surround yourself with good people.
5. Practice gratitude, even for the stuff that hurts. You don't have to be grateful for everything, but do be grateful for what you learn from everything.
6. Eat well. Really well. Move your body. Drink water.
7. Love your kids. Love your friends. Love your people. Love yourself. Remember who you are.

Are you holding your fate? What's your next step?

CHAPTER 2

You Are Contagious

For good or for bad, for better or worse,
your presence has impact—it is contagious. You are contagious.

You know "that guy" (maybe you are that guy). He walks into the conference room, one that was previously humming with discussion and people feeling engaged, safe, creative, and inspired, and the minute he walks in, the energy shifts. The room gets quiet. It gets "hard." It shuts down.

Or maybe you're one of the people in the meeting having a lively positive experience, and you have two teammates who just seem to glom onto the negative. They seem absolutely devoted to staying down, sinking the room, focusing on what's not working. And then bam! While it started with two, it's now four, and the team begins to sink.

Or maybe you're on stage, leading a client presentation, or doing a huge talk, and you can feel that guy. That guy (or that woman), sitting there in the audience, eyebrows furrowed, scowly face, arms crossed, shoulders slumped . . . his entire presence communicating, "I don't want to be here. You're wasting my time." And while he may be truly feeling this, more often than not, he's completely unaware of the impact of what may be his "default presence," completely unconscious to how he's showing up. His presence is sinking the room—and *you*. *But* only *if* you let it.

Or perhaps you're the friend who calls another friend with a piece of good news, all excited to share it with her. You share your delight, and then you feel her negativity (and maybe jealousy or concern). You feel deflated . . . she might not have even said anything, it may be just the vibe she gave off. All you know is that you went in flying high, and now the wind is out of your sails.

Do any of these scenarios sound familiar to you? Either on the giving or receiving end?

How is it possible that we can have such an impact without even saying a word?

It's because we're *contagious*.

We pass our energy onto each other without even thinking of it.

We talk about how busy we are, and then the person we're talking to feels busy and depleted.

We talk about how hard it is, and then it gets harder.

We hope not to hire or date the wrong people, yet we keep hiring and dating the wrong people.

We focus on creating something great and having a good conversation, and we do.

We set an intention to get a great workout in, and we do.

We decide to attract awesome people, talent, dates, and opportunities, and we keep attracting awesome people, talent, dates, and opportunities.

You set the tone for your culture.

You set the tone of your life and relationships.

When it comes to culture, everyone around you is feeling whether or not you believe in yourself, your people, your organization, your clients, your products and services. They're sensing it on a level they can't likely even point to . . . but they sense it. And you're powerful, so guess what? They're likely to adopt some of it as their own—especially if you're their leader.

Consider the leaders who inspire you most, who feel the best to be around. What makes them contagious?

Consider when you're at your best. What's present? What's going on? A likely common denominator is that there is a rich quality of energy and presence that *feels* good to be with.

It's contagious.

And so are you.

This is great because it means you can create the culture you want . . . if you're intentional about whom and what you want to infect.

It also means that you can decide whether or not to "catch" someone else's attitude. Yep, it works both ways. You're contagious, and so are others. Your power to decide what you take on and what you don't lies in your own level of intention, energy, and presence.

And guess what? This isn't just about leadership and culture and impact, this impacts your sales and client relationships too. Go into a meeting to sell something you don't fully believe in? It's going to be in the room in some way. Walk into a client meeting with tension on your team or not liking the client? They'll feel it.

When the Lowest Energy in the Room Tries to Bring You Down

The gentleman was sitting down to my left in front of the stage— arms folded, brows furled, a look of boredom and disdain on his face. He was the lowest energy in the room. And he was winning. Despite the other 224 people in the room who were "in it" and giving me warm fuzzies . . . my attention was on *this* guy. You know him. He's the one who can sink the energy of the room without saying a word; the one others look to to set the temperature in a room, yet avoid at all costs any kind of interaction or stare down with him. And here he was. In my room. At my talk. Glaring.

I felt tired just knowing he was there.

He was messing with my jam.

Ironically I was in LA delivering a keynote on the power of using your presence to optimize your impact. He was having none of it. In fact, not only was he having none of it, he seemed to be throwing it back at me, testing me to see if I could hold my space. Feeling the lack of love that seemed to be emanating out of him, I questioned this myself; his energetic field was so strong and negative that I wondered if I'd be able to pull it off.

And while I had shining faces, smiles, woots, "amen, sisters," and "I love your boots" being yelled out at me from the audience, this guy had me. Of all the awesome people in this room, I was giving this guy my attention and energy.

He was *ruining* my talk. Throwing me off my game. I swear his negative energy was messing with my audiovisual. I felt a bead of sweat on the left side of my face.

The irony was that this guy probably needed my message more than anyone else in that room did. This guy was probably brilliant but couldn't understand why people didn't love working with him or find him inspiring. Then I realized I was doing what I coach people not to do. I was giving him *my* space. I realized that at this rate this man would win. He'd have me, he'd have my whole talk. And he'd have validation that this work was not impactful. I'd create the opposite of my intended impact. All because I couldn't hold my space.

I really didn't want that to happen. And there were bigger stakes at play, namely the other 224 who wanted and needed this talk . . . .

So on stage, I stopped. I took a breath. I pushed my hair back and wiped my brow. I smiled. I gave him my biggest grinny smile, sent him a little dose of love. Said "Hello." And then looked out at the rest of the room that was smiling and open. And I rebooted in a matter of a minute.

He shifted, oh so slightly. And while I didn't win this guy over, I didn't give myself away, either. The talk finished well, and the people who were there got some of what they wanted and some of what they needed. And this guy . . . well, I'll never know. And that's okay.

What I learned from this guy was priceless.

First, don't be that guy. Just don't.

And second, thank him. He lets you know that you're alive and you still care. He's your greatest teacher right now. So thank him, acknowledge his impact, but don't surrender to him (or her). Don't catch his (or her) schtick.

What should you do instead? Show Up.

When Your Colleague Has "Had a Day"

After my talk I headed to the airport. And as I sat there at the bar, I got a whiff of the conversation happening to my left. Three colleagues were having drinks after an apparent meeting with a prospective client. They were deep in it, and they were loud. What was interesting to me was that before I could *hear* what they were saying, I could *feel* it.

It started out as an exciting and happy conversation—their field was positively magnetic and contagious. But over a short period of time, it shifted to ick.

This was the gist of it: Two of them thought the meeting had gone well; they really liked the client, they were optimistic, they were happy. The tone of the conversation was of celebration. Their flight was delayed, but that was cool; they were laughing and ordering food and drinks. (They sounded like fun; I kind of wanted to join them.)

But as the conversation went on, the energy and tone took a turn. The third person apparently was in a funk. Despite it going well, he was irritated they'd had to work that hard to get a meeting with the client, that they'd had to travel in to meet the client at this stage of the process, and that they were sitting in a bar at LAX at the end of a long day, delayed.

"We shouldn't have to run around the country proving it. Those guys should have just taken us at our word on our call. There was no way we needed three of us to fly out to meet with them. Ridiculous," he snarled. The deflating impact of his words wasn't so much in what he said as it was in how he said it and the energy and presence he said it with. The other guy said something about building a better connection and that this would serve them in the long run, and that since the company valued being true partners to clients they'd done the right thing. Besides, now they got to hang out. Despite the temptation, the two stayed "high" vibration, while the one guy continued to stand his ground. For a bit.

I watched as the energy and tone of that triad went slowly from jovial to sober. They finished their drinks in silence as they waited for their flight. The lowest vibration won.

Ever seen this? Experienced it? Been the instigator of it? It happens all the time. It happens at conferences and in conference rooms, in one-on-one conversations and in team huddles, at PTA meetings and at the dinner table. It's likely happening in your culture right now. Contagions abound. And when you notice it's happening, or even get a hint, *that* is your choice point. You can shift your contagions in a moment. And you can decide whether or not you want to be infected.

Bottom line? Don't go there. Stay clean and clear. Stay in your space and hold it. You do not have to adopt their negativity. You don't have to let it in. You get to decide what gets in and out of your energetic field. Here's the trick and part of the secret sauce:

The better your presence is, and the stronger your energetic field, the easier it will be to decide intentionally who and what gets in and stays out. It's your call.

The Common Denominator and Some Science

In both of these stories, there was a person who had impact. In the first story, the guy said nothing, but he had huge impact. In the second story, the guy said something and had impact, but his impact was even more in his tone and the way he "showed up."

Our impact is often not in what we say or do; it's in our presence and how we show up. Albert Mehrabian, the author of *Nonverbal Communication*[1] and *Silent Messages*,[2] conducted a study years ago at UCLA that found that as little as 7 percent of people's impact, in the communications of feelings and attitudes, was in the words they said; the other 93 percent was in their body language: tone of voice, physical presence, and more. (Specifically, in his study 7 percent was in words spoken, 55 percent was in facial expression, and 38 percent was in the way words were said.)

In my experience, that 93 percent also reflects people's energy, their posture, how they're taking care of themselves, their attitude and beliefs, and their intention. These internal workings are just showing up in their presence, tone, and body language. Consider how much of your impact is getting lost (or worse, leaving a negative imprint) in your presence and how you show up. Whatever that is for you, it's shiftable.

You've also seen this, I'm sure.

You've been given feedback from someone who was supposed to be awesome and helpful (and maybe it was), and the whole time you could feel the blame and judgment seeping out of his or her being.

People tell you they're happy for you, but you feel their jealousy.

Your partner gives you a compliment, but you sense the "conditions" under it, or the hesitation.

You tell your kid you're listening to him or her, totally "there" . . . but you're not.

You sit in a meeting feeling lost, chaotic, and confused as to what you're doing there because the energy of leadership is amiss.

All of these examples are reflections of intention, energy, and presence—someone's IEP (Intentional Energetic Presence)—gone awry. IEP affects the way people show up. Whether we're talking about your organization, your culture, your team, or any of your relationships, your presence is at play—and it is contagious. It also compounds, meaning your energetic field and resilience becomes stronger or weaker depending on how you nurture and hold your own space and Intentional Energetic Presence. And this all contributes to the culture you create.

Organizations often think that the way to optimize their culture or fix their problems is to do more. Simply more. They'll have meetings and initiatives, seek out feedback training and leadership skills building, hold strategy sessions to "address this thing" and off-site events to build trust and create the culture they want. And then they'll put people together in a room to do more of the same—more doing. This is all good. But what they often don't realize is that no matter how many problems they solve or skills they give their people or strategy sessions or off-sites they have, if they don't address the "being" of people and what creates the most contagions, they've left a huge opportunity on the table. In addition, all the great results they've worked so hard to achieve are likely not going to be sustainable. This is ironic because when we focus more on the intention and "being" and how people show up together, the doing becomes much easier, and we don't have to work that hard in the first place. So what is it that creates the most impact in how people show up? It's the intentions they hold, the energy they bring into the room, and how alive they feel. It's their presence.

A Contagious Meeting

Thirty partners convened in a beautiful retreat setting for their annual meeting. They had a great set of outcomes they wanted to achieve—and a very specific way they wanted to achieve them. The agenda was solid, the venue was beautiful, logistics set, and all systems go.

This was a high-stakes meeting. There was a lot of work to do, much of it falling in the category of what I call "the Tender Agenda." The Tender Agenda is the stuff "underneath" the stuff that's often getting in the way of organizational progress and needs to be addressed. It's usually scary, prickly, and vulnerable, and it requires a tremendous level of care and safety to unpack. Fortunately they felt they were in especially great shape because they'd recently gone through communications training together and they "knew how to put the issues on the table." It looked like they were good to go. But they weren't. They started the meeting, got about an hour in, and stopped.

Despite their new communication skills and all they'd done to prepare, this group—even with the best of intentions—had dug in in a way that would have left dead bodies everywhere by sundown. While initially half the room was "in" and ready to roll, the other half was not, and their energy, being contagious, had an impact. Arms were crossed, body posture slumped, brows furrowed, defenses high, phones fidgeted, and an energy of carefulness, "let's just get it done," and "it's not my fault" took over the room.

So they started over.

Over the next two hours they threw out the agenda and game plan and rebooted, setting the space for honest and productive communication. They spoke to what was happening in the room. Despite their best intentions for impact, they asked, what was actually happening? And was that what they wanted? That got them started. Over the next couple of hours they did three things that changed the trajectory and outcomes of their two days together:

1. They spoke to what was actually happening in the room, naming their fears and dreams for their time together and speaking to what was getting in the way.
2. They set their intentions for what they wanted to get out of the day for themselves personally and as a team. What did they want to walk out with? How did they each want to feel? And how would they have to show up to create those outcomes?
3. They created agreements for safety as a team, including confidentiality, "no one gets to be wrong," and "let go of looking good," that would help them show up authentically, contribute to the room, and achieve these outcomes.

Their meeting was a success. Not only did they achieve their objectives, they also walked away feeling honored and supported as collaborators. When they got into tension points, they simply honored their agreement to be responsible for how they were showing up. Was their intention, energy, and presence contributing to things going better, or worse? Were they focusing on the right things? With a new level of intentionality and responsibility for how they wanted to be contagious together, they were able to put their new communication skills and awesome agenda to better use, authentically and effectively.

Where Do You Stand?

What's happening in your life right now? In your organization?

How much appetite and energy do you have to dive into this stuff? How open are you? How hungry? Anywhere is perfect. In order to create more impact, it helps to know where you are right now.

Through client work, I've discovered several types of people who are ready to create a practice and awareness in their lives to be contagious in a positive way. Here are five common types (of course there are more and these are not gender specific). See if any, or the combination of any, resonate for you.

The Optimizer

The optimizer wants to be better, lead better, make better, and create better results. She's easy to work with, hungry, and quick to pay it forward. She's commonly looked to as a role model for others. She's committed to contribution and helping others succeed. Ironically, she's the hardest on herself: occasionally getting struck by "imposter syndrome"; "How did I get *here*? I'm not that good. When will they figure out I don't know what I'm doing!?"

If this is you, consider your intentions for diving into this work. What's the dream outcome? And also, how can you "pay it forward"? Notice if you are being hard on yourself. Notice your internal language, catch yourself being cruel, and shift accordingly. That's your first assignment. One of the best ways I know to shift from self-beatings and the "need" to be better (not just the "want") is to focus on contributing to another human being and helping that person be better (truly in service of him or her, not in service of your ego), while practicing intentional care and compassion with yourself. And the "cure" for imposter syndrome? Honor your feelings, learn from them, find your true edges, and roll with it. Learn to trust your awesomeness.

The Projector

This guy is all about his people working on how they show up— just not him so much. He thinks, "I don't need to work on this, but my people do." (Of course, this often means he needs it more than his people.) This guy has done some kind of leadership development at some point—maybe even a lot—and he thinks he's mastered all he needs to know.

If this is you, cool. Listen to the little whisper that nudges at you saying there's more work to do here. Maybe you're scared or you don't have the time or your ego is done with "personal development." Just listen and notice, and then consider what might be possible if you dive in. Even just a bit. As Marshall Goldsmith says, "What got you here won't get you there." I consider good leaders those who are always on their edge, always looking for blind spots, and always willing to step into the dark in order to step and lead into the light.

The Sooo Busy Staller

This person has no time for development. Just no time. Busy-busy-busy is the name of the game. Sleep? Downtime? This person thinks, "I'll sleep when I'm dead." "Work-life balance is for those who can't handle working hard." Exercise? "Who has time? I'll get it on the walk through the airport." Good eats, "I'm on the road all the time, no time for that." Or "My kids need me." She can't stop. There's work to do. And deep down, she fears that if she gets into it, she'll lose her focus (or worse, she'll find things that *aren't* working, the gap will become more painful, and then she'll have to address it). She wants to grow but doesn't even know where to begin. She needs small steps, very easy to integrate, with immediately actionable and tangible steps and outcomes.

If this is you, be kind to yourself. Remember that the Sooo Busy Staller has had her purpose—she's a taskmaster, and she's helped you get "here" . . . But she's also the greatest robber of peace and health and quality of life. If you're afraid you might unearth some tough stuff, I applaud you for reading even this far. It's common. When you dive into this work, you often find that seeing yourself as the common denominator for problem relationships and scenarios is quite liberating. You can change them because *you* lead you.

The Hard Scientist

This guy is tough but lovable. And he can also be a big advocate for this work, but only once he's experienced it himself for a day or two. If this is you, your hesitation and the way you decide whether something will truly work for you and/or your organization is honorable. Intention, energy, presence, and showing up can be hard to hold onto and quantify, which is why it's secret sauce and why we can't buy it off the shelf. It will take a leap of faith and trying a couple of the things in this book to experience what's possible here.

But there is no pressure. I'm going to invite you to suspend judgment, take what serves you, toss what doesn't, and allow yourself to reflect. How do you put a number or measurement on someone being nicer or happier or more inspiring to work with? How do you quantify joy and feeling aligned and energized and in control? How do you put a perfect scientific measurement on the feeling you get when you have a positive impact on another human being? Or when your direct report overperforms and gives you the extra 10 miles because he wants to, because you've inspired him? So why not give yourself and the science a break and allow yourself to enjoy this?

The Hater Naysayer

Did you know there are actually people who make a sport out of hating? They get huge mileage out of it. And they get even more excited when their hatees hate them back. The haters teach you gratitude, determination, and perseverance (but don't tell them that). They teach you to keep going, to appreciate the good, to learn from the bad, and to focus in the right places. For the haters, the ideas in this book won't work—until they want them to.

If this is you, cool. And here is an invitation to consider what it is that you hate. What truly is up for you? Look there, get curious, lean in, and embrace—in there lies likely one of your greatest teachers, liberators, and points of personal power in your own impact and relationships. By the way . . . if this is you, and you're fed up with this, yet still reading, I applaud you. Stick with it. There's magic and learning here for you too.

Whichever type, or combination of type, describes you today is perfect. And wherever you'll be tomorrow—also perfect. There is no finish line to this work. At all. It's an ongoing process, never done. And each stance will teach you something.

The Cost of Contagious Negative Energy in Your Organization

We've all experienced contagious moods and energy and even physicality (ever notice yourself mirroring the way another person talks or accidentally mimicking someone's accent?) We've experienced feeling deflated, feeling agitated, and feeling energy and emotions that are not ours.

You probably have an idea of the energetic cost of this for yourself, but what about the financial cost? There is one.

People ask all the time how to quantify a contagious culture. That's tricky. How do you quantify the value of someone not being a jerk to work with anymore? How do you quantify the value of people bringing all of themselves, their creativity, their best thinking and innovation to the table because they feel good, like working with you because you have awesome IEP, and they want to have it also? How do you quantify feeling happy every day or being in alignment and integrity with yourself?

It's tricky to put dollar signs to. Some would say these factors are priceless.

Waking up feeling in flow and on purpose and in alignment? It's impossible to price. Working in an organization where your people love to show up every day, bringing their best selves to the table because they feel seen and honored and valuable? Priceless.

And when these things are not happening? Impossible to price as well.

One way to measure the cost of energy in your organization is to look at your employee attrition, retention, and lost time rates. Why are people leaving? Why are they staying? Look at the data there, the exit interviews, and the employee satisfaction surveys.

Most often people leave because of the culture, their manager, they're not feeling seen, valued, or meaningful, they've become disconnected from purpose, they don't feel trusted, and more often a combination of all of the above. If you can lead your organization to proactively practice IEP and the principles shared in this book, your chances of growing, nurturing, attracting, and retaining top talent rise.

The Cost of Team X

Team X, a team of eight, was having some issues with collaboration and productivity. There was tension, stuff wasn't getting done, and the company had had an abnormally high turnover rate in the last six months. The team members wanted help, they wanted to fix it, but they didn't know what to do, so they kept tolerating the situation.

The majority of their issues were coming from two people— let's call them Julie and George. Both were brilliant and talented; however, they were also completely committed to snarkiness, judgment, blame, and basically bringing everyone down.

Here's what would happen. Everyone would get started, and the room would feel good (though with a bit of tentativeness coming from the rest of the team). People would be happy, and then Julie or George would make some Debby Downer comment that would put a bit of a stink in the room. The other would climb on. And down the whole team would go.

Here' the thing: It wasn't so much what they said, it was more how they "showed up" in that meeting. Body language, tone, facial expressions were all at hand. Even more powerful, though, was their energy and intention. You could *feel* them in the room, and you could *feel* that it wasn't a positive thing. The lowest energy would win as the air got sucked out of the room, people climbed onto the doom wagon, and all the momentum and positivity that could have resulted in a killer meeting was deflated.

So now they have another unproductive meeting on their hands. What's next?

Well, they all leave feeling less than inspired, a little or a lot frustrated, already dreading the next meeting. Not Julie and George though—they feel great and validated, "See, these meetings suck, they're a waste of time." Yep.

The impact after the meeting is worse. The other teammates feel drained walking out of there; they're not as creative or productive. The two negative colleagues start to debrief and gossip about the meeting with their teammates, their colleagues, and likely even their spouses that night. The story expands in dramatic prose.

And in the meantime, the company's results are showing it, and people are quitting because they're not as inspired and energized as they'd like to be. People report, "Our culture is just bad."

The good news is that this is all fixable. But first you have to identify the problem and the cost.

I'm not saying that this is entirely Julie and George's fault, not at all. They're a catalyst but actually just a symptom of the bigger problem. The bigger problem is that the team and company are not taking a stand for focusing on results, being intentional, and showing up well. And the leaders are not holding people accountable for doing so (or themselves in many cases). So, let's circle back to the question we asked earlier. What is the financial impact of not showing up?

Do the math:

8 people × 1.5 hour/day (conservative!) wasted time/energy/productivity/gossiping/etc. × $100/hour (average hourly billable rate per person in this group) × 5 days/week × 49 weeks (giving them all 3 weeks of vacation) = $294,000/year

So $294,000 a year is being lost in low energy! This doesn't even include lost opportunity costs or hard costs or anything—just the cost of negative energy dragging people down.

While this number isn't exact, you get the idea. What would this number be for you alone? Just you, in your own life—forget the organization. Even one hour of lost time each day? There is a cost. Consider that with your team, ripple it to your organization, and the impact and cost multiplies.

Reflection: Putting IEP into Practice

Do the Math

What's contagious negative energy costing you in your organization?

____people × 1.5 hour/day (conservative!) wasted time/energy/productivity/gossiping/etc. × $_____/hour (average hourly pay per person for this group) × 5 days/week × _____weeks (52 weeks minus designated weeks of vacation) = $_____/year.

Remember, this is a conservative estimate; we just want to get an idea for you.

Quick Start Tips

The following tips are especially useful when you're sure it's "all their fault." How can you be intentionally contagious for positive and not negative impact? Here are a couple of places to look.

- What is my intended impact? How do I want people to experience me?
- How am I contributing to this situation or dynamic? Am I helping things go better or worse?
- How am I showing up?
- Is this in service of others or the organization?
- What do I personally need right now to improve my impact?

CHAPTER 3

The Leadership Trifecta: Impact, Self-Care, and People-Care—You Need It All

To create impact you need
people, purpose, and personal nourishment.

We've hit an interesting time in history where we have greater ability than ever to do more, be more, strive harder, and push further. But with this ability to do more, there is a downside. Compromise of health and relationships is on the rise; burnout and substance reliance high. Comments like "I'll sleep when I'm dead" are pervasive. There is a disconnect of purpose, presence, and intention in our daily lives as business moves fast and demands for attention hit hard. Sometimes it's all people can do to keep their heads above water. Despite some big business impact being made for many, the people and leaders in the company are not thriving. It's not sustainable. It's doable, but we have to do it better.

On the other hand, there are people who are great at taking care of themselves but they're not creating impact. They're not growing other leaders. They're not driving results. These people are self-focused and not using their super powers for the good of the organization. In a world where we need to be creating impact, growing leaders, and doing great stuff, this model is not sustainable either. It's doable, but we have to do it better.

Impact but No Self-Care

Colin was the CEO of an Inc. 500 ranked company. His company was in the 300s. He and his team were ecstatic when I met him at an Inc. conference a few years back. He was caring, had lots of drive, a great guy, funny, and . . . tired. Oh so tired. In his terms, "completely fried."

When we met, Colin shared all the wins the company had experienced that year. It was almost too good to be true. People were tired, but it was certainly fun to be on the list this year.

Behind the scenes, however, there was a different story. In all his pushing and pulling and winning and creating awesome impact in his company, his life and self-care had fallen apart. He and his wife had separated, he saw his kids infrequently—relying on Skype and FaceTime for the majority of their interactions. He took one vacation a year, where by his own admission he used the hotel babysitting service more than he'd like to admit so he could get his work done. His health had also declined; his personal relationships had fallen off, his workouts were nonexistent. He was not the man he wanted to be . . . but his company was "killin' it."

Partial win.

This is one of the greatest challenges we have as leaders doing cool stuff. To push the company, the team, the product—make it shine. Win. Celebrate. *And* balance it all with quality time with our spouses and kids and friends—oh, and make it to boot camp, hit up yoga, and cook up a batch of brownies for tomorrow's class party, help our kid with homework, and prepare thoughtful productive feedback for someone who's not even our direct report. It's a bit daunting, and frankly, most often, completely unrealistic. When push comes to shove—especially as the leader of an organization or team or in start-up mode—business often "has to come first."

Approaching our lives this way has a cost. And it can be done better. Through presence, intention, and choice. It doesn't have to be hard; it does have to be intentional.

Self-Care but No Impact

Matt, a manager of a tech products and services team, was a model for work-life balance. He left the office at 5 o'clock every night. He didn't respond to e-mail in off-hours. He exercised daily. He ate well. He took more vacation than anyone else in the office. He often left in the middle of the day to go for a walk. He was, by his own admission, "highly selfish." After all, he had to take care of himself first in order to serve others. He would be a model for self-care and leadership *if* he actually created impact through leading. He did not.

While he was humming along and bright-eyed and bushy-tailed, no one was inspired. People didn't feel led; they actually felt repelled and in some cases insulted. They didn't trust him. He was nice, but he had little credibility. He was not someone they could count on. Despite having a lot of energy in front of the room leading meetings, his presence was unfocused and unintentional—nothing to anchor the room in. Though he was a great starter with all that energy, he finished few initiatives, brought in little business, closed few deals, and did not follow through on performance reviews or his people's development plans. Ironically, none of this was intentional; his focus was just in the wrong place and his self-awareness pretty much null.

When he honestly thought about his focus, he realized it was simply on himself, his own career, and being a "leader" in the company. That's all well and good; however, he was missing the leadership piece. He rarely contemplated the impact he wanted to have on others or how he might serve them better. He never stuck around with the team at the eleventh hour to lock something in for a client. He did not lean in on leadership challenges. This didn't make him a bad or inconsiderate person; it just made him an ineffective leader.

This has a cost. And it can be done better. It needs the same solution our first challenge needed: presence, intention, and choice. And in Matt's case, leadership skills.

Impact Through "Leaving Dead Bodies Behind"

Ted was a young whippersnapper CEO. His company was even higher on the Inc. 500 list, in the 200s. He wore a hipster hoodie and cool horn-rimmed glasses, even to more formal events.

Ted's problem was that he had a habit of yelling and throwing phones at people.

This is an example of a leader who's probably brilliant. Leading a cool company. He's got the "cool factor." They're getting results. But he's leaving dead bodies all around him in order to do it. This doesn't work either. In the land of energetic karma, or just treating humans like humans, or having a business that people feel good about doing business with, this is a fail.

If you want to create impact, sustainable positive impact, you've got to bring your people along with you. With intention. You can push them, pull them, inspire them, challenge them, even give them "the talk" . . . but it has to be done with presence, care, and intention. In Ted's case I'd add desire as well—the desire to lead by inspiration, to be in service of people, and to focus on the long game instead of solely on quick wins.

So What Do You Do?

All three leaders in these scenarios were contagious. Colin's people, in order to keep up with him, took busy to heart and compromised their own well-being. Matt's people, to deal with their frustrations, talked behind his back, spreading more frustration. And Ted's people, to cope with the tension, compared stories of outbursts amplifying cultural fear and drama. Fortunately, all three of these scenarios are fixable. They simply require presence, intention, and choice.

In the Case of Impact but No Self-Care

First, to handle all you are doing, you need to eat really, really well (you have to eat either way, might as well choose it to fuel you). And then you do what you can. You do 10 push-ups five times a day in between calls. You get the team out for a beer or a quick stand-up meeting outside. You send your spouse a love letter and say, "Thank you, I love you, I see you." You buy the brownies for school from the store (gasp!). You get an extra hour or two of sleep. You stay present—if even for two-minute segments of connection. You make everything about quality versus quantity. And you plan mini vacations, and hold boundaries to protect them, in advance and with rigor. And you breathe. (You also check out Part 2, where we'll go deep into building your own energetic field and well-being.)

In the Case of Self-Care but No Impact

You consider others. Period. You consider the impact you truly want to have. You look to the things *outside* yourself that you want to be a contribution to. You notice your impact on others. You get feedback. You decide to lead. You decide to change little behaviors here and there, and even big ones that will give you the most leverage. You connect with your team and your colleagues as human beings. You align with them on the impact the team

43

wants to have and how you all have to show up. You make agreements for staying till the eleventh hour when that's truly what's needed. You follow through, honor your promises, and go the extra mile. Do the work to be better. You keep working out and taking care of yourself, but you use that energy and fuel to pay it forward and serve others. You contribute to things outside yourself. You hone in on your skills through the lens of service. (You also check out Part 3, where we'll go deep into leading others and creating impact.)

And in the Case of Impact via Dead Bodies

If it's working for you and you're attached to it, you might just keep it and come back to this chapter when you have a change of heart. However, if you want to be the kind of leader whom people follow and give their best thinking and creativity to because they *want* to, and you want to lead a company whose culture thrives and people love being there . . . well, then here's what you do. You see the humans working for you. You make requests. You get curious. You include them in what's happening. Numbers low? You're concerned? Cool. Get curious, make it a team effort. Find the way forward. Pay attention to impact: How do your people feel working for and with you? Be accountable for being their leader and leading in a way that inspires. Get feedback, hire a coach, have your assistant follow you around and give you on-the-spot feedback for how you're showing up. Do whatever you have to do to lead and inspire and love these awesome people who make your products what they are and your customers happy. (You also check out Part 4, where we'll go into creating a culture people want to be a part of.)

Intending and Leading Forward

For any and all of these scenarios, take a step back. Get clear on what's needed here now. Find out how you have to show up in order to feel good, help others feel good, and create the impact you want to have. Once you do this, then you move forward. You can still have impact. You do have to do the work.

Intention is the name of the game. When you intend how you want to show up and how you want your life to go, you get to happen *to* your life instead of it all happening to you. If you do not have a conscious intention, the default intention will win. The default intention will often be other people's needs and demands and intentions *for* you *or* bad habits, old behaviors, or unconscious ways of being that create damaging impact (like poor results and leaving dead bodies behind).

If the default intention wins, you're in the soup. (And not the good soup.) Don't let the default win.

Intend, lead, and take great care of yourself. After all, you are contagious.

Reflection: Putting IEP into Practice

Ask a few trusted people for feedback on the following areas:

- How would you describe my leadership presence? What's one thing I could do (*or be*) to show up more effectively?
- How effective am I at creating results and impact? What's one thing you'd like to see me do (*or be*) to increase my impact?
- How do I make you feel? What's one thing I could do (*or be*) to make you feel more valued/seen/led/etc.?

Notice that you'll have feedback that has to do with action ("Do this; give better feedback, acknowledge people more, finish on time, stop yelling, etc."), or feedback that has to do with "being" ("Be more curious, be more present, be a better listener, be more rigorous, be more empathetic, etc."). The *doing* is speaking to your actions and is pretty tangible, while the *being* is speaking to your presence and a feeling you create for others. It's worth asking for both as you'll invite people to "look" in different places to access the best feedback for you. We'll talk more about this in Chapter 4.

Once you've gathered your feedback, you'll find themes. Pick the ones that resonate the most for you and that you want to put your attention on. For the themes that don't resonate, just put them in your back pocket. If you find a theme that you don't "see" but it hits a nerve, look for the gold in that one. That's one that likely needs some attention.

Bonus: To make your feedback productive, identify one thing you will do every day to get better at it. (Little steps and leapfrogs all count.)

CHAPTER 4

Showing Up with Intentional Energetic Presence

Who you are, what you intend, and how you
show up speaks louder than any brilliant thing you might do.

Now that you have a strong sense of where you are, it's time to dive into how you show up well and how you set yourself up to do so. In this chapter you will learn how showing up well allows you to create a positive impact around you while feeling good and energized.

What Is IEP, and Why Does It Matter?

Most people think their skills and capabilities are what create their impact, but in reality a much larger part of their impact lies in their presence, or what I call Intentional Energetic Presence (IEP for short). At the end of the day, your IEP is about how you show up in the world. I think of it in two ways: (1) being intentional about the energetic presence you project, and (2) setting yourself up for success to show up well through intention, healthy positive energy, and solid presence.

Let me break it down a bit more. The first one is simply being intentional about the energy you put out there. That's it. The second frame is more about setting yourself up well to show up well so that energy is helpful. Attending to all components of IEP allows us to do that more easily. For example, I've found that the more intentional people are about the impact they want to create, the easier it is to have that impact. The more leaders take care of themselves and are responsible for the energy they bring to the table, the easier it is for them to have the energy and stamina to show up powerfully and keep leading. And the more intentional and in tune people are to their presence—both in how they show up and in how present they are in the moment— the easier it is to experience the now, access greater intuition and knowing, and project a strong presence. Any way you slice it, when you put this all together, you have Intentional Energetic Presence, or your IEP.

As to all the stories shared in this book, you can have the best skills and even the best of intentions, but if your intention, energy, and presence are not aligned or right, you miss it. Your IEP is infused in your actions and behaviors and makes the difference between people wanting to be with and follow you because they want to, or because they have to. But it's not just about being in service of someone else. It's also about infusing yourself with nourishment and presence so you have more sustainability and joy in the process of leading your life.

As we've discussed, it's not enough just to have great impact or take great care of your people; it's essential that you take exquisite care of yourself as well so that you can sustain and optimize that leadership and care. Taking care of *you* is a foundational part of the IEP Model—it allows for greater access to personal energy, creativity, wisdom, and intuition. Working your IEP for *you* (and later for your organization) is secret sauce for not only having more intentional and positive impact, but also doing it in a way that you get to thrive.

As a leader, you have a ton of people who want things from you. People needing things, pulling at you, needing nourishment and direction from you—all important. And the stronger your IEP is, not only do you have more to give them, and a better perspective to give it from, you have more of you as well. I've found that so often when people are struggling with impact, or having a hard time with their attitude or mindset, it's due to neglecting their own self-care and need for nourishment. They're out there giving, giving, giving and sending energy out for others, but they're not receiving it back. And more important, they're not creating the space for themselves to receive it.

Consider a time (maybe now), when you're feeling overwhelmed, exhausted, maybe frustrated or even resentful about a relationship or something you're leading. If you drill down, it's likely that there is a place where you are feeling depleted and you're not filling your own reserves. When we take the time to stop, breathe, and look at where we ourselves need that nourishment—and we honor it—more space and patience opens up to be there for others. Check it.

Having Intentional Energetic Presence is deciding consciously how you want to show up, what impact you want to have, how you want people to experience you, and what you want to create—in this moment, or in the arc of your life. It's about deciding—consciously—how you want to create space for yourself and honor your own needs so you have the strongest base to lead from. It is the difference between you happening to your life and results, versus them happening to you. And the great news is that you don't have to wait for anyone else to give you good IEP—it's yours to lead and create as you wish.

Meet Joyce: Brilliant Skills, Subpar IEP

Joyce is a growing leader in a service organization, evolving her leadership daily. She is often on her edge and out of her comfort zone working on getting better at what she does. She has big dreams: She wants to be a partner in the firm, she wants to be known for creating a lot of impact, she wants to make a lot of money, and she wants everyone to like her—especially the other partners in the firm.

She does everything she can to make all of these things happen. She works till the wee hours of the night, has impressive credentials, speaks up, and jumps right in. She has lots of coffee with people to "get to know them." It seems she's doing it all right. This gets reinforced when she gets promoted to a new level of leadership. She's delighted.

Joyce has three desires in her new role: to be the best leader she can be, to get officially put on the "partner track," and not to get swallowed up by the beast of "busy and burnout" that runs so rampant it's become a badge of honor in the organization. She has a marriage and personal life to attend to as well, though she's up for compromising them for a while in service of her career. After all, the other partners seem to have done that, why shouldn't she? It's almost become a cultural expectation.

Joyce's first instinct is to focus on her skills; most people do when they first try to optimize their strengths and opportunities. She wants to be better at leading meetings, giving feedback, having difficult conversations, inspiring others, bringing in new business, strategizing career paths, and managing her people. She's all in. Then she gets set up for a round of feedback. The feedback from her employees, peers, and business leads shows where she shines and where she needs help. It stings, bad. The places she needs help are not where she thought she needed help.

High Leverage Opportunities

Her feedback boiled down to three themes. The first, the *doing*, was all good. The second and third themes were what stung. They boiled down to her *impact*—how she made people feel, and her *agenda*.

Doing. Joyce was *brilliant at the "doing"*; she worked with clients well, she was organized, wickedly talented, she got the job done. People wanted her wisdom and brain in every room. The things she thought she needed to get better at—the skills—were already pretty strong.

Impact. Despite wanting her brilliance and wisdom in the room with them, her colleagues didn't want the rest of her. She projected an energy of rigor and a "get it done" approach, without connecting with them—often mowing them over. Through her demeanor in the way she spoke and interacted with them, people sensed she thought they were her personal "minions." She "managed up," showing up differently in the room when clients or "someone important" was there. People walked away from interactions with her feeling dismissed, small, disconnected, pushed around, and often angry.

Agenda. She had an agenda. She talked frequently about her career path and wanting to become a partner. This aspiration wasn't what hurt her. What hurt her was the feeling people got that this aspiration was what drove everything rather than having *being in service of* the work, the people, or the client as her primary motivators.

She was devastated. First she was crushed, then angry, then in denial, and then resolved. The feedback had been given in themes after being collected and synthesized responsibly. While her impact was unintentional, she sensed the feedback that stung the most had some truth to it. She also knew that if she wanted to be better with people and move to the next stage, she'd need to show up differently.

The tricky thing about the feedback was that it focused mostly on the "soft stuff" instead of hard-core leadership skills. So what could she do about it? It boiled down to her intentions, her energy, and her presence. And there was something she could do about it.

Putting Feedback into Action: Lessons from Joyce

Joyce's first step after processing her emotions was to accept the feedback and see it as a gift. The fact that people were brave enough to give her honest feedback about what was getting in her way was a big deal. Once she could see that, she could receive it and get into action. So she did.

To kick it off, she created an "advisory board" to help her process and integrate the feedback. Then she did three basic things that changed her internal game.

Tap into Gratitude and Humility

First, she thanked the people who gave her the feedback. She apologized for making them feel anything but positive through how she'd shown up with them. She shared the themes with them, owned up to the feedback, and told them she'd be working on it, and specifically how. She also asked them to let her know how it was going—she needed help. This alone was huge. This connected them with her as a human being with humility and authenticity. Tension disintegrated, and compassion was generated because her listeners saw that she was sincere. (If she wasn't, and she was doing it to get ahead, they'd sense it and she'd have just made it worse.)

Connect with "Why"

She reconsidered her "why." What was really truly motivating her in her work? Was it truly to become a partner? And if so, what was important about that? Why did she work here? This was gold. What she realized was that yes, partnership was important to her, and it would be a nice acknowledgment of her efforts, but even more importantly it was an opportunity to have more impact and do more good on a broader level. She worked for the company because she believed in what it was doing; she had a heartfelt connection to helping it be successful. The health and medical related services it was providing were important. When she shifted her focus to her "why" in service of others, having more positive impact and doing more good, her energy and attention shifted. Now in a room she could focus on creating impact and results with people in service of their collective why. Her shift in intention and focus showed up in her presence. It was no longer about "me looking good" or "getting to a certain point," it became about "us doing good" and "getting somewhere together."

Tackle Three "Being" Behaviors

She chose three behaviors she would consciously get better at to help her show up better: *curiosity*, *contribution*, and *acknowledgment*. Every morning, and before every conversation or meeting, she set her intention to show up in service of her team and to acknowledge people for who they were. For *curiosity* she simply listened and gave space to the question, "What else was in the room?," and when she felt hooked or "right," to "Where might I be wrong?" For *contribution*, she looked through the lens of "How can I contribute" and "Does this serve?" And for *acknowledgment*, she looked to catch people doing things well, to thank them, and to reflect back genuine awesomeness.

All of these states required her to be more present and intentional in her interactions. They also became easier and easier to tap into as she practiced them. And she noticed something else in the process: Part of the reason she'd been showing up as she had stemmed from the fact that she'd been compromising her own personal life, self-care, and attention on her marriage. This had put an extra level of unconscious urgency into her career goals. Joyce began to carve out more time for herself and her personal life. Oddly, more space opened up. She relaxed. She still rocked it at work, but her presence was different, and people felt it.

One year later she'd made it to a higher level of leadership in the organization and was on track for partnership. (Ironically now it wasn't as big of a deal.) People had seen marked improvement in her leadership and presence. And perhaps most important, she was happier in her role and now able to pay it forward.

Universal Lessons in IEP

In addition to Joyce's experience and the learning we can pull from it, here are three critical IEP lessons I've found helpful to help people ground themselves in this work.

How you show up matters. Regardless of your pedigree, your MBA, your PhD, or your talent, your presence and intention with people can undermine any smarts. If you are unapproachable or unkind or don't care or if your presence just stinks, at best, your brilliance will only get you so far.

You are the common denominator. You take yourself with you wherever you go. If something is showing up in one place, it's likely infecting other places. If you don't like something, look at how you're contributing to it. And if you're convinced it's not about you, look for the themes in other relationships—they're likely there. As the common denominator, *you* are your fastest path to creating contagious impact in the rest of your life. This is high leverage, my friend—if you change one thing in you, you will change a ton.

External motivation is exhausting. Being driven by money or a job promotion or looking good takes a lot of energy and most often doesn't get you there in a happy and thriving manner. People see right through it and run from it anyway—especially if it's at the core of your leadership agenda. Check your motivation, and be honest about it. And then find something internal that fuels you, and go for that. Want the promotion, want the money—want what you want—but want impact and your "why" even more. The promotion and money will follow.

The Art of Showing Up

The art of showing up is a dance between being there for yourself and being there for others. It's not enough to just feel good. It's not enough to just create amazing impact. You have to have both.

I know people who are amazing at getting things done, they're rock stars in the organization—great business developers, awesome visionaries, brilliant entrepreneurs (a lot like Joyce)—but they don't have the people and self-care thing down. They leave dead bodies behind. People follow them because they *have to* not because they *want to*. And they eventually burn out, get into trouble with their organization, or leave—often because they're exited.

And then there are those who have the people and self-care down, they're loved by all, inspiring, their chakras are all in alignment, they may even be the epitome of health and vitality (a lot like Matt in the previous chapter) . . . but they don't have the impact thing down. They're not getting the job done, and they're not getting the results they want. As I discussed in the last chapter, we need to have all pieces of the puzzle—self-care, people, impact—in order to be the most energized, healthy, vital person possible.

The best way I know how to have all the pieces (at least most of the time) is to *show up* for your life.

We all have the power to show up, and it's free.

Showing Up Is a Choice

Showing up is a choice. It's that moment when you're moving along in your life, or in that meeting, and you have the urge to do something, say something, to step in, to take the high road, to swing out, to be accountable, to say yes! or no!—it's that moment. And stepping in is the difference between whether your life moves forward and you drive it and big awesome things happen, and you feel tuned in and turned on, *or* your life moves forward (or maybe backward or not at all) and it drives you, leaving you feeling left behind. Showing up and stepping in makes the difference between power and hope, passivity and hopelessness, adventure and big, . . . or beige. It's the difference between leadership and abdication, inspiration and force. It is the difference.

So there's "the moment." That precious moment. What will you do with it?

You must decide to show up.

What Does It Mean to "Show Up"? Your Credo

Some people intrinsically have the ability to show up; it's inborn in them. And some people have to grow it, nurture it, practice it their whole lives—work at it every day.

The people who already have it, their life's work is to keep stepping in bigger and bigger, staying on their edge to create more impact. These people need to work at keeping themselves sharp, growing, and accountable, while helping others to do so as well. Their job is to lead, teach, and pay it forward.

The people who are learning how to show up, and maybe even struggling with it, their job is to just do it, to surround themselves with the right people, and to focus on the bigger vision for impact for what they want to create and make to help them move through it.

No matter where you are, I believe your job is to continue working on it, showing up bigger and bigger, using your super powers for good, and expanding your range for leadership and joy in your life.

Showing up might mean that you do all you can to lead your life. You take really good care of yourself. You consider at all times whether you're contributing to things going better or worse in situations—especially the ones you can't control.

It might mean that you take risks, swing out, fall on your face, and all the while practice self-love and compassion.

It might mean you show your vulnerability as a leader and ask for help.

It might mean that when these things don't add up, or you completely forget about them, you quickly recover and climb back on—not making yourself wrong and bad for forgetting, but rather practicing that compassion and mining the precious learning that's come from all of it.

It might mean you say "I'm sorry"—but only in the moments you truly have something to be sorry about.

It might mean you partner with your life, your challenges, your problems, and even your nemesis to move forward in a way that feels right.

It might mean you're there for your organization, your clients, and your team in a way that honors all of you and does good.

It might mean you look at the culture you have and the culture you want to create—in your organization, your family, or in your own being—and you create it . . . starting with you.

So, what does showing up mean to *you*?

Make your list—make your own "Credo of Showing Up."

The Five Components of Showing Up (The Good, the Bad, and the Ugly)

So let's break down Showing Up, shall we? You know what it is. You have your own version of it, whether you are aware of it or not. But how does it really break down?

Showing Up breaks into five main components: intention, energy, presence, action and skills, and impact (Figure 4.1).

Creating leadership that thrives (and therefore a culture that thrives) requires that you "Show Up" first. The five components of showing up and creating impact all work together. Enter at any point. For best results, start with "Intention" as it fortifies and accelerates every single component.

Intention is what you want to have happen, a desire. It's what you plan to achieve, a determination. You have to own that intention and be clear on it. It's also about the intention and regard you have for another human being. How do you see this person? What do you believe is possible for him or her?

FIGURE 4.1 **Five Components of Showing Up**

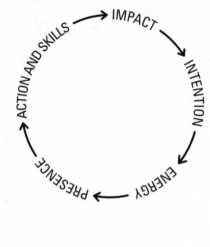

Do you see this person as another human being? It serves big time to own this intention and be clear on this as well.

Energy is how you take care of yourself as well as what you bring to the table. It's how you set yourself up to be the most thriving, sustainable, powerful instrument of change possible. You have tremendous control here. People often underestimate their power in this component of showing up—this is low-hanging fruit!

Presence is how you show up, how people experience you, how present you are to your life right now and to the person in front of you. It's right here, right now, in this moment. Presence also includes the more traditional forms of presence like stage presence, appearance, charisma, physical presence, and leadership and executive presence.

Action and skills are what ensures that you move forward and accomplish your goals. These allow you to show up and create positive impact and pleasure in your life. Action is where you make things real. Your skills and action are always being impacted by your intentions, energy, and presence. In fact, your presence often speaks louder than your actions or words (but you know that already).

Impact is what you make happen. It's what happens over-all as a result of applying great intention, energy, presence, actions, and skills to what you wanted to create in the first place. We're always having an impact—good, bad, ugly, pretty, negative, positive, ineffective, rockin'. Impact, done extra well, starts with an intention. It's a cycle.

The better you do these five things, the stronger your leadership presence and the more effective your impact.

You combine action and leadership skills with your IEP, and you have a powerful force for impact. You could do the action and skills alone of course, but without the IEP, at best you're leaving opportunities for impact on the table, and at worst you're leaving dead bodies behind, risking negative impact and your own personal burnout. Of course you could just have the great IEP, alone, but then you're likely not getting a lot done. It's like a Möbius strip, never ending with everything impacting everything else. You need all of it. Now, let's dive deeply into the IEP Method.

The IEP Method and Model

What is the *IEP Method*? The IEP Method has three primary components. All three operate and build upon one another at all times, dynamically. And you can call upon each (or all) when needed. Ready?

1. **Reboot your presence.** The first component of the method is the Presence Reboot. The ability to reboot your presence in the moment and choose your impact and how you *want* to show up is key. Later in this chapter, you'll learn how to do a Presence Reboot in 30 seconds or five minutes. This is a quick way to integrate IEP into your life instantly.

2. **Create intentional impact.** The second component of the method is the ability to create intentional impact. If your impact is not intentional, the default impact often ensues; this is where you get to lead, and do it intentionally. In Chapter 5, you'll learn the Five Steps to Intentional Impact framework that will guide you in doing this.

3. **Build a strong foundation.** You are cultivating the strength of your IEP by using the principles in this book, practicing self-care, taking care of yourself, and building the strongest energetic field possible. This is not a one-time deal. Your IEP is building and strengthening (or not) in every moment. The stronger your foundation is, the easier it will be to do reboots and create intentional impact. You'll use the *IEP Model* to build and strengthen this foundation.

The liberating news is that you never have to actually *do* any of these three components. It doesn't have to be daunting or hard. Your foundation is being built daily. You're rebooting as you go, moment to moment, day to day, week to week. And you're setting intentions and working your Five Steps to Intentional Impact for every meeting, conversation, even workout. The more you live these three components, the easier and more dynamic they become. Until one day you forget you're even doing your Five Steps and your Presence Reboots and building your foundation as they have all just become a normal part of your leadership practice! You'll also find you've increased resiliency when you have a tough day, a rough room, or the sky just seems to be falling. Embracing IEP in your life is a lifelong practice, like brushing your teeth. It constantly changes and shifts and grows. Some days you kill it, and some days it kills you.

Let's dive into the actual model.

The IEP Model

The IEP Model in the context of leadership is depicted in Figure 4.2. While people often think they need to work from the outside in—focusing on skills and abilities first, working from the inside out allows for more optimal, sustainable, and energizing impact (making those leadership skills and competencies easier to master and more effective to use).

FIGURE 4.2   The IEP Model

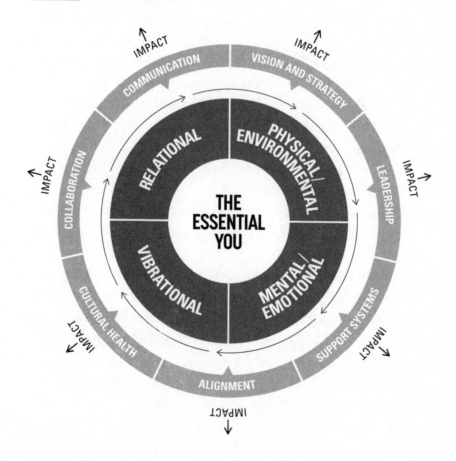

There are basically four layers of the IEP Model. These ripple from the inside out:

1. The Essential You (at the core)
2. Energy and Presence (layer 2)
3. Skills and Competencies (layer 3)
4. Impact (layer 4)

When first learning the IEP Method, it's critical to start by focusing on you, your Essential You. A lot of people who learn the IEP Method want to start at skills and competencies in order to create impact. While it's important to address these, they're just not our highest leverage impact point. If we focus just on skills and competencies, too much is left on the table, and it's not necessarily sustainable. So I'm an advocate for starting with you. This will give you stronger roots and awareness, a better sense of what tools and competencies are actually needed, and likely a richer, more purposeful, effective, and meaningful experience.

So instead of starting on the outer levels, we start in the middle. Here's my favorite route:

First, get grounded in the **Essential You** (values, purpose, authentic you, this is all about you, baby!). We'll cover *how* in the next part of the book.

Next, clarify and intend for **impact** (what impact *do* you want to have, anyway?).

At the same time, nurture **energy and presence**, take great care of yourself, set yourself up for success, show up really, really well, and be intentional about it all.

Now, combine this with your **skills and leadership** prowess, and you have a much better chance of creating your desired impact. Oh, and guess what? You can do it without burning out and actually feel good. And when you're having an off moment, you just reboot. Please note: This does not have to be hard or take years or send you into a tizzy. The principles of IEP are intuitive.

We'll be diving into all of these in the next parts of the book. You'll see as we get deeper into this book that energy and presence covers a lot of ground. I can't stress how much impact this has not just on your ability to lead but also on your personal fulfillment. The energy you bring to everything—your intention, your presence—it all counts. It counts for you, your people, your team, your organization. Your intention, energy, and presence are creating a culture that either thrives, simmers, or fizzles out. Let's play with it, shall we? But, first, let's take a time out and reboot . . . we'll come right back.

Presence Reboot: The First Component of the IEP Method

Let's do a quick reboot, right now in this moment as you're reading this chapter. Here I give you the official IEP Presence Reboot framework. You can play with this throughout the rest of the book and for the rest of your life. For now, let's do this in real time.

First, start with getting present to what *is right now* from an IEP perspective.

> **Intention.** What do you want to get out of reading this chapter? What do you want to get out of this experience? How intentional are you being with absorbing and making this real to *you* as you read versus just reading yet another book?
> **Energy.** How are you feeling? Need water? Need a stretch? A snack? Something to fuel your brain? Tired? Want a quick nap/break/run/dance break? Hop to. Pay attention to your energy and act accordingly.
> **Presence.** How are you showing up right now reading this? Check your face, your breathing, your posture, your mindset.

How mentally present are you? Is your physicality supporting you in being present? If your presence is not where you want it to be, what do you need right now to shift it?

IEP Presence Reboot

Now reboot as needed. No matter where you are, heading onto a stage, about to lead a meeting, engaging in a feedback conversation, dialoguing with a customer, in a fight with your spouse, ordering your dinner, or reading this book, you can reboot your presence in a moment.

1. **Get present. Notice where you are.** How are you? What's your presence right *now*?
2. **Intend. Intend where you'd like to be.** How would you like to be? What do you want your presence to be?
3. **Take care. Note what you need.** Water? Breathe? Move your body? Clear your mind? Take a nap? Let go of a judgment? Shift your state?
4. **Breathe +.** Take a deep breath, wiggle your body/shift your posture/whatever. Do it, and do whatever you need to take care of yourself. Maybe you can't get that nap in at this moment, but you can promise yourself more sleep later.
5. **Step in.** See that intended presence again . . . . Step in. Just do it. You don't have to go meditate, take a hike, disappear on a mountain, or go to yoga. This would be grand. And in the moment, you're just going to step into your intended presence.

And from here? Rinse and repeat. You've lost presence? Gotten distracted? Completely checked out? No worries—reboot. (Note: This can all happen in 30 seconds or less, or 5 minutes or more, up to you! It just depends on how much time you have and what you need.)

Internal and External Energy and Presence

Okay! Back to energy and presence. I break energy into two components, internal and external.

Internal energy and presence is all about how you set yourself up for success with a strong internal foundation. You control a ton of this. This is all about what's happening for you physically and mentally. It's how you treat your body, the kind of environment you create for yourself, your intentionality around creating an energetic field that serves you. It's also all about being aware of and conscious of your mental energy and giving yourself full permission for emotional authenticity. You have a ton of power here—the better you do at setting this up, the stronger everything else is.

External is all about how you show up externally for others and in your relationships. This has a huge impact on your executive and stage presence, credibility, and reputation. You have control over this one as well, but not as much. The better you are at using intentionality and setting yourself up using Internal IEP, the easier it is to get this one humming. External is all about how others experience you. It's about the quality of energy and dynamics in your relationships, and it's about how you make others feel.

Internal is about creating impact on yourself. External is about creating impact on others. You need them both.

The wonderful thing about this work is that it's not linear—everything impacts everything. Address one area, and just like the butterfly effect, other areas shift as well. We'll be diving deep into both of these areas, and the rest of the method and model in Part 2; for now, know this:

You Are an Inspiring Force

Showing up is a choice. You get to choose. The quality of your IEP and how well you set yourself up with your IEP will hugely influence how easy it is to show up, how much you actually want to show up, and how others feel about the way you show up. It's worth noting that even in the most difficult of circumstances when life is flailing about or you're not being an effective leader, having strong IEP will help you get through. It may even be the saving grace you didn't realize you needed—or had all along.

If you're thinking about how this applies to your colleague, someone on your team, or even your life partner, I promise we'll get to them. But for now, let's focus on you. Your highest leverage is first learning how impactful showing up can be; this will only serve and inspire your partner, spouse, and team. One caveat: While this may inspire you, it may also temporarily frustrate the people around you as you step more and more into your power and get clearer on who you are and how you want to show up. Stick with it. It's temporary. And if it's permanent, the arc of that relationship may be complete.

So how do you show up? Think back to a time that was tough for you: maybe a relationship, a tough decision, a career move or fail, a big organizational change, something big . . . and you came out stronger and wiser and better. Got it? What did you do? How did you get through it? My guess is you showed up. You may not have felt like you were showing up. It may have been a horrible time that felt miserable and dragged you down to your knees, but you got through it. Consider the following situations:

- Lola felt a pull to do something about an industry that she saw wasn't working. She stepped in and started her own company. The company rocked it and had big impact.
- Thomas felt dissatisfied that he wasn't getting to dive into his craft enough. He leased a design studio and started making. He's still making and happy.
- Carrie was fired from her company. She made the next year about owning her stuff and figuring out what she really wanted to do. She changed industries, twice.
- Charles sat in a meeting and watched his team move into muddy ethical waters. He stopped the train and challenged

the team members to go back to their roots and values. They accelerated their purpose (and avoided a lawsuit).

- Ashley's husband passed away when their son was only six months old. She created a 21-year plan for him to get to know his dad a bit better every year. He's now four and feeling loved and connected to his dad.

These are all real-life examples of people showing up in different ways—some big, some small—to move through challenging moments in time. And they were all contagious; each one of these had a ripple effect.

So what's your moment? How will you show up? In that moment, what will you choose? Decide to show up now, decide to be present, and let your wisdom inform you what to do next.

You're a force for making things happen in your organization, a force for inspiration, a force for inviting others to show up as well.

How confidently you decide to do this will determine the difference between:

- People following you because they want to instead of because they have to.
- Creating the results you want versus unintentional results.
- Feeling aligned and clear versus ambiguous and wishy-washy.
- Being decisive and driving versus unsure and abdicating.
- Your team killing it or killing one another.
- Your culture being abuzz and inspiring versus complacent and surviving.

As always, it starts with you. When you step in and show up, you give others the lucky combination of an invitation, a demand, and permission to do the same. You show up, they show up. Because, yes, you are contagious.

Reflection: Putting IEP into Practice

So . . . *What* does showing up mean to you, and *why* is it important?

Here are three exercises to help you get clearer. Do one, do all, make up your own, but do something before we dive into how we make this all happen for you.

Your Showing Up Credo

Write your "Showing Up" credo here. What does it mean to *you*? Look back earlier in the chapter for sample declarations and create your own.

Showing up means . . .

Your Five Components of Showing Up

Of the five components of showing up, *intention, energy, presence, action and skills,* and *impact,* which one—intuitively—do you sense is the easiest for you? Which one is the toughest? Which one would your peers say is highest leverage for you to start working on?

Are You Clear on Why?

Now that you've gotten this far in the book and have completed Part 1, "The Fundamentals of Showing Up," how is this work going to be important to you?

Write yourself a quick letter; you might share your intentions for yourself, what you'd like to get out of this work, how you see this serving you, your organization, your family, your partnerships and relationships, your kids, your impact on the world, and why this is all important. Go big or go small—it could even be a haiku. Your mission: Anchor this chapter in before we head into the "how" in Part 2!

CHAPTER 5

Crafting Intention and Creating Impact

Your desire is yours for the intending. Your impact is waiting.

You want something? Go get it.

Don't wait for it; though patience (or procrastination) sometimes is wisdom in waiting.

Don't abdicate it and hope some leader, parent, or prince will bring it to you; though receiving is a lovely thing.

Don't complain about not having it; there's a reason you don't have it yet.

Do make sure you really want it; The right reasons will help speed the process up.

Do claim it, and share your desires and intentions with others; good stuff happens in collaboration.

Creating what you want—be it a great organization, a thriving culture, an honest conversation, a healthy relationship, a strong body, or a really great meal—all starts with a desire and an intention to make that desire come true.

Crafting intention thoughtfully, and doing the work to make it a reality, allows us to happen *to* our lives, versus our lives happening *to* us. The more present and intentional we are, the more we set ourselves up for success with strong IEP, and the more "in service of" the bigger picture we are, the easier it is to work with whatever comes our way.

So what do you want?

And are you willing to move toward it intentionally?

That is a major step. The want is the steam that propels the train forward, the gas that fuels your mind, body, and spirit.

The intention is a proclamation to the universe: "I want this to happen," "I am going to achieve this," "I am going to behave this way." And you believe it. In fact, your energy, belief, rigor, and solidness infused in that proclamation is so strong, you'd be shocked if it *didn't* happen. This belief is what fuels your intention.

We underestimate the power of intention because it's often intangible. But we're creating impact through our intentions or lack of intentions all the time. And without being clear and awake to intention, it's very easy for the default intention to win. The default intention is often unconscious and driven by other people's needs, requests, and intentions. It's also contagious. And it's huge in creating culture.

If I'm not intentional about what I want to create, or how I want to show up, and I'm just coasting through life or a conversation or a relationship, other people's intentions and agendas win. They take over. When we're all intentional, we get to create together.

Maybe you've seen it. Someone's life is "happening *to*" him or her, and the person gets frustrated because someone else's agenda got attention, or someone else got the promotion, or was recognized for his or her work, or got to have dinner with a hotshot. The other person often just seems lucky or privileged or favored. But more often than not, if you really look, you'll see that other person was intentional. He or she stood up. Asked for what he or she wanted. Led. And if the people that person was leading didn't have their own agenda or intention or stake in the ground, it's very possible that the "lucky" one's intention became a reality.

Don't be a victim to your lack of intention or the power of someone else's. Show up. Intend for what you want, hold your space, and do the work to make it happen. Lead.

So How Do You Set an Intention?

Intention setting is truly one of your greatest super powers. You likely are already doing it, everyday—possibly unintentionally. However, when you put more focus behind your intention, you accelerate it and amplify its power. Enhance your presence, take care of yourself, clear unwanted energy out of your space, get more intentional with intention—these all support and build upon one another. Do one or all of these things and accelerate your effectiveness as a present and impactful leader.

Here are five steps to setting a powerful intention. Don't skip any of them. When these become second nature for you, skip them, but until then, wear them out.

Step 1: Get Present and Feel into What You Want

Allow yourself to dream and want what *you* want. Just like a dream is a great access point, a complaint or something that frustrates you is a great place to access this information as well. What's the request or dream living underneath the complaint? Intend something different.

Step 2: Be Clear and Claim Your Intention

Do you want this thing? Really? Claim it. It's yours. Be as specific as possible here, and state it in the positive of what you want, not the negative of what you don't want. Be clear.

Step 3: Make Sure the Desire Is Truly There

Make sure that your energy is congruent in wanting this thing. It's something *you* want, not something you think you should want or your mom wants or your boss wants. You're looking for a "full body yes," not a "yes" that comes with the energy of "maybe" or "I should." If you find the desire is not truly there, that's cool— be honest about it with yourself. Is there a tweak on the intention that will make it truly yours? Do you need to ditch it altogether? Or if it's something you really have to do but aren't super keen on, how can you find alignment? What's the littlest place of alignment you can lean into? Truth is really important here. If you trick yourself on this one, it's going to be harder to make that thing happen. If you're honest, even to the point of "I don't actually really want this, but this is important for X," you're in the right relationship with yourself and this intention and you'll be more likely to make it happen.

Step 4: Share It—Surround Yourself with the Right People

Don't do this stuff alone. You can, you're welcome to, and sometimes you need to do it alone. Sometimes it actually works better to make this a very personal trek. But more often than not, it's more effective to do it with someone. Get support. Once you've set your intention and you know you want this thing, share it with someone, or several someones.

There are a couple of reasons for sharing your intention with someone. First, speaking it aloud creates a new level of energy and accountability and ownership for this thing you've now claimed. Second, support is a great thing. Having people who care about you and who can give you feedback will accelerate your process and make it much more enjoyable. And third, when you announce something, people now know how to help you. They know what to look for, they know to connect you with opportunities to help manifest your intentions, and they become aware of extra points of leverage that may serve you, your organization, your clients, and others. And be intentional about whom you share your intentions with. Depending on what's up, you may have different people you share with, different allies, different devil's advocates, different collaborators—but either way, be intentional here. Look for people who will support you and hold your intentions with care, especially for the tender intentions that have to do with who you're becoming or any vulnerable edges.

Step 5: Make a Plan, Set a Timeline, and Get into Action

Your next step, possibly in partnership with your crew, is to make the plan and create a timeline for when this will all unfold. How will you do it? What allies do you need? What do you need to let go of? Who do you need to be to make this happen? Revisit this plan and this intention every day. Keep it alive by connecting with the "why" of the intention, the feeling of it, the vision of it becoming a reality, and the intention of who you have to be and what you have to do to make it so.

The Quick and Dirty Intention

This may seem like a lot of steps, and you may need all of them, with time and attention and planning, or you may just need a quick intention. If so, here's what that looks like.

You become aware of something you want for yourself, for a project, or for another person. Simply claim that that is some-thing you want to have happen. For example, you're heading into a meeting, and your intention is to be present and to have fun. Done. Go do it. Just the claiming of that has now changed your awareness and what you'll focus on in the meeting. You can hold onto that intention as you go.

Set your intentions, be passionate about them, want them with your full heart, *and* be flexible when they don't turn out exactly as you planned. Show up as best you can, do all you can to manifest the outcomes you want, and enjoy it. But becoming too attached to getting your exact outcome manifested is the recipe for disaster. You can't control situations or other people, you can control you. Go in with your intention, show up, and let things unfold. Following are some tips that will help.

Seven Ninja Tricks That Make Intention Better

1. **Make your intention in service of something bigger than you.** For example, "I want to show up as a better leader for my team because I want the team members to feel able to bring their best selves to the table so we can do meaningful work together." This is a much stronger intention than "I want to be a better leader so I'm more powerful, more recognized, and more respected." The first intention is about you in service of your team, the second is about you in service of you. It won't sustain, others will sense it and feel you're about you versus them, and your impact will be blech at best. Make it "in service of."

2. **State it in the form of what you want.** For example, "I intend to lose weight" is not as powerful as "I intend to be fit and lean so I feel strong and powerful, have more energy, look great in my jeans, can run around with my kids, and have more mental bandwidth for doing great work in the world." Claim what you want, loud and proud.

3. **Make it specific.** Years ago my little sister set the intention that she'd get a car by her high school graduation and that it would be gifted to her somehow. She got it. She got an old, broken-down car that didn't run! I'll never forget that one. This is where I learned about the power of specificity. A stronger intention would be that by the end of her senior year she'd get a beautiful, well-functioning car that was safe and felt great to drive. Be specific.

4. **Have a "why" that's not about feeding your ego but rather feeding others.** For example, "I want to make a lot of money so I can be respected and important and admired for my nice stuff." This is one of the things people usually do not say but that often lurks underneath these kinds of intentions. It is not as powerful, compelling, or sustainable as "I want to make a lot of money so I can have security, provide my family with security, have more freedom for creativity and doing things that are meaningful to me, be comfortable, give more people jobs, and contribute to more causes I care about." Find the "why." The more heartfelt your intention is, the easier and more compelling it will be to manifest. (Off-topic, bonus ninja move: If you're looking to make more money to gain respect, you want to look at other ways to feel respected, and even more so at how you're doing at respecting yourself and others.)

5. **Make it a collaborative intention.** When it comes to relationships or building culture or creating a team that rocks, pull other people in. Set the collaborative intention together. What do we want to create? How do we want to feel? What do we want to be known for? How do we want new hires to feel walking in the door? What does leadership look like for us? How will we have to show up to manifest these intentions? These are all powerful places to look and dive into. Do it together.

6. **Create a tribe.** Create an advisory board of people who believe in you, can see you and what you're up to, and can hold intentions *for* and *with* you. I've had many people do this as part of their leadership work. Whether it's a circle of CEOs or designers, parents or teachers, or a combination of many, I find one thing is consistent: Intentions get bigger, and because of this, so do the people in the circle. A different perspective can be gold. It's incredibly helpful to have someone who can not only point out a new perspective, but help you hold it, and then hold you accountable for stepping into it and

making it happen. You'll learn more about this in Part 3 when I talk about "containers" and your "posse." Get your tribe.

7. **Stay awake.** There will come a point when you'll take this intention stuff for granted, or you'll think you don't need it, or it's too hard, or too much work. And then you might get on the slippery slope of having no intention, leading to no intention for action or how you're showing up. And it may be fine and even great for a while until that moment when you've just had a really bad meeting or something you'd really rather not have had happen goes off the rails and makes you realize you checked out. Recover and get back in there. Notice when you want a break from intention (the intention to give yourself a break from intention can be powerful in itself). In my experience, intention does not take away from spontaneity and pleasure at all but rather creates a greater field for one to enjoy it in. Stay awake and enjoy it.

Creating Intentional Impact in Five Steps

You know this scenario. You're heading into a meeting, *another* meeting. You feel your blood pressure spike just thinking about it. You are already thinking of the 18 other things you need to do right now, besides this meeting. You think about the other people in it. You think about what you're all going to be doing. The doom and gloom energy that comes with feeling overwhelmed or ambiguous about what you're about to give up a chunk of your life for starts to build. (You hate meetings. Ugh.) While that builds, you feel your life force drain.

You walk in, a few minutes late—only to be followed by others who are even later (drain, drain, drain). You sit down for the meeting, you get up, grab some coffee, shuffle your papers, put your phone on vibrate (so much commotion for little old late you), and then you are "there." Maybe you've missed something, so you ask "What did I miss?" slowing everyone down and adding to the drain. And then, you guys all celebrate that you're actually getting started only 12 minutes late. And then, with everyone there, and kind of caught up, and coffee in hand, and now only 48 minutes left to work with . . . you jump in.

This is a scenario I see often, all too often. If my little vignette irritated you, no worries, that's common. That usually means you play this part (or some form of it), or you're surrounded by people who play this part and even the thought of it stresses you out. Chin up, I've got your back.

Since we're having so much fun here, let's do one more scenario.

You have a big conversation coming up with your *partner* (insert: spouse, colleague, direct report, kid, parent, landlord) today. You have three ways you may be going into this; clear, clean, powerful, tuned in—you are ready to roll. *Or* nervous, unclear, defensive, scared—you'd love to postpone. *Or* you haven't even given it a thought, it's just another of 50-plus conversations you have today—you'll figure it out when you get there.

Are you with me?

Think about it. Think about the meetings or the conversations you have planned today. How clear are you on what you want to talk about, the impact you want to have, how you want to feel, how you want others to experience you, and what you want to make sure you all walk away with? This one is totally in your control. And this is part of your leadership IEP.

How you enter and your state of being entering these meetings and conversations will have a big influence on how easy and effective each conversation is. It will also influence whether or not you get the outcomes you want and whether this meeting or conversation or whatever you're up to was a great use of your time, with solid next steps and a plan, or just another thing to trudge through.

Here is the framework or formula that I like to use to help create intentional impact. This is a core component of the IEP

Method as mentioned in Chapter 4. I've used it for myself in conversations with clients, my team, my partners, my kids, my vendors, my leasing agent, you name it, and I've used it very effectively with teams and sessions I've facilitated to help people create the most powerful interactions and meetings possible.

Five Steps to Intentional Impact

Step 1: Outcomes. What are the outcomes you want to get out of this interaction or meeting? What do you want to have as a result? What do you want to walk away with? It is essential that you give this some thought.

Step 2: Impact. What's the impact you want to have on these people or this person? The emotional impact? How do you want them to feel? How do you want them to experience you? How do *you* want to feel?

Step 3: Presence. How will you have to show up to create the outcomes and impact you want to create? What will your body language be, your energy, your vibe, your intention? What will others have to feel from you? This one is golden.

Step 4: Beliefs. What will you have to believe in order to show up this way? What will you have to believe about this person, the project, the company, the meeting, your kid, your partner, your dog? This step is where people often go off the rails.

Step 5: Action. This is often a two-parter: What will you have to *do* in the meeting or conversation? And what will you have to do afterward to move it all forward? Very often simply nurturing steps 1 through 4 will set you up beautifully for presence and impact, but more often, if you do just steps 1 through 4 but don't do any action, you are missing the good stuff that will make this all real in the world. What are the next steps?

Here are some scenarios for how these steps might play out.

Scenario 1: The Team Meeting

In order to avoid the painful scenario in the beginning of this section, we're going to want to be more intentional, individually and as a team, as to what we're going to create together. Of course, ideally this is all done ahead of the meeting—whoever "owns" the meeting sets the pace and direction on this one. In fact, before the meeting even happens, it's already been set up nicely: All logistics are taken care of, food is handled, people are reminded to be on time, out-of-office notes are on e-mail to allow for full mental and emotional engagement, the space for meeting is life giving and not soul sucking. Set your space right. It will pay off.

Here are the five steps applied to our scenario:

1. Outcomes. All participants in the meeting receive a framework of intended outcomes for the session so they're clear on why they're there, what they can contribute, and any prework that will help them be even more effective. Send these out before the meeting, and review them at the beginning of the meeting.

For example, here is a sample list of intended outcomes:

- *The plan for the first quarter is complete.*
- *We have three core projects prioritized and have identified the owners and supporters of each project.*
- *We have a wish list of potential focus areas for the second quarter.*

2. Impact. Consider this ahead of the meeting, and make sure to focus on your desired impact together at the beginning of the meeting. That way, each person is intentional about how he or she wants to feel and to make others feel. For example:

Our intention for this meeting is that we all feel connected, that there is safety in the room, and that we inspire one another. We want to feel good and excited about what's next.

3. Presence. In the meeting, have everyone consider how he or she will need to show up to create these outcomes and this impact and what might need to be done to create the space to show up that way.

You could do an energy check here to help get everyone present to what's here now. (I talk about leading energy checks in Chapter 13.) Then everyone does his or her own intention setting and reboots. Ideally they would have already done this before even walking in the door, but this is an opportunity either way for the group to regroup and do this together. Have the group members consider how they'd like to feel and how they want others to experience them. And then ask them to "step in." It's also helpful to set agreements as a team to help create the space. For example:

> *In order for us, and for me, to create these kinds of outcomes and impact, I will need to show up as open, listening, present, attentive, creative, and as willing to take risks. I'll also have to take ownership for the things I want the most. I'd like to feel connected and powerful. To support us in doing this, some of the agreements we might need are direct engagement, suspend judgment, assume good, look for what works, build don't break—and if you must break do so with care, phones down, time integrity.*

4. Beliefs. What will each of you need to believe about this meeting or initiative or one another in order to show up that way?

Beliefs and assumptions are running all the time in the background and will influence your presence and impact whether you like it or not. So what are the beliefs that will support you here? What are the beliefs that won't? And how do you shift and honor them if need be? For example:

> *In order to show up fully, take risks, and create the outcomes we've set, I have to believe I can trust my team, that these three projects are worth doing and will impact the right people in the right way, and that we may not have it all figured out perfectly, but if we work together well, we'll find the right path forward.*

5. Action. What needs to be done during the meeting and then after the meeting to make sure this all moves forward?

Consider the things that need to be addressed during the meeting, any content that needs to be introduced or discussed, exercises as a team, talking points shared, research that you'll need to interject to support decisions, and so on. And then make sure you have next steps for everyone to bring it home, even if these next steps are "We didn't get this item done in the meeting, put it on the agenda for the next meeting."

For example, during the meeting:

- *Set agreements as a team at the beginning of the meeting to create safety and alignment.*
- *Bring the 10 potential projects to the room. Blow them up on poster board and have someone present them as a stakeholder.*
- *Review last year's numbers and outcomes to ensure the projects we pick this quarter support us and move us all forward.*

For example, at the end of the meeting:

- *Create a master Google document for all of us to build our plans into—Julie, by December 12.*
- *Compile highly energized teams for projects—each lead with his or her direct reports, by December 13.*
- *Communicate with direct reports who the teams are and what the next steps are so they're in the loop and aligned—all leads by December 16.*
- *Come back together to solidify the plan and ensure we're set for next year— all leads, by December 19.*
- *Set agenda and schedule the next meeting—George, by December 4.*

This process may look lengthy, but it's actually not. It starts out heady and linear, and the more you practice it, the more it becomes second nature and you won't even realize you're doing it.

The bottom line is, although there is a benefit to spontaneity and being present to each individual moment and *this* moment, by adding intention for how you want to show up, you will not only save a ton of time and energy before, during, and after your meeting but actually make the process enjoyable.

Reflection: Putting IEP into Practice

Your turn. Let's set some intentions.

Meetings, Conversations, and Project Intentions

For your meetings and your conversations—either quick engagements or big projects—revisit the Five Steps to Intentional Impact in the last section and set yourself up right here:

1. The outcomes I want to have are . . . .
2. The emotional impact I want to have is . . . .
3. In order to create these outcomes and impact, I will have to show up as . . . .
4. In order to show up congruently, I'll need to believe _____ about this person or situation.
5. The actions I'll need to take in order to make this happen are . . . .

Following are different questions that serve as entry points to these areas. See which ones resonate most for you and run with them. There are no right or wrong answers here. You can do these for yourself personally; you can also do many of them as a team or organization.

Identity Intentions

Who do you want to become?

What do you want to be known for?

What's the impact you want to have on every person who comes in contact with you?

Relationship Intentions

What's important about this relationship?

What do you want this relationship to look like? Feel like?

How do you want your partner in this relationship to feel?

Cultural Intentions

What do you want your culture to be known for?

How do you want it to feel in your organization?

How will you show up to help create this?

Desire Intentions

What do you desire more than anything in the world?

What's something you want to make happen?

What's something you'd like more of or less of in your life?

Body Intentions

How do you want to feel in your body?

What do you want your body to be able to do for you?

How do you want to relate to your body?

PART 2

SHOWING UP FOR YOU

You lead you.

Now that we've established what being contagious means, we're diving into *you*. You as an individual leader. This next part of the book focuses on building your strongest IEP foundation and being contagious so that you can help others grow. In this part be prepared to learn *how*. We'll break the IEP Method down further into three primary components, and you will understand how what you do for yourself (often perceived as "selfish") is actually the most generous and loving thing you can do for others you lead. In this section you'll work a lot as I invite you to reframe your relationship with self-care, energy, impact, and how you show up. It doesn't have to be hard, and this section will be highly valuable to you if you want to lead well, create a healthy culture, and enjoy your life in the process.

First, here's a quick reminder that the IEP Method consists of three primary things:

- The ability to reboot your presence in the moment.
- The ability to create intentional impact for whatever you're stepping into.

- The ability to build a strong energetic field and leadership presence every day.

Rebooting your presence in the moment? We did that in Chapter 4. Creating intentional impact? I gave you that formula in Chapter 5. Building a strong energetic field and leadership presence every day? We're doing that throughout this book, especially in this section. As we dive in, keep showing up, keep doing your reboots, and enjoy the hike. We've got lots to do.

Let's Start with a Reboot

We'll start with a refresher from Chapter 4. You're about to walk into a meeting, you've got to be "on," but you've got all this stuff whirling, you've just had a fight with a colleague, and now, you've got to show up. But you're in the weeds. What to do?

Do a Presence Reboot.

Before you walk into that room, notice your energy. What is your presence right now? What are you bringing into the room? Then, decide *if* that is indeed how you want it to be. If it's not, then you move on to the third step, which is to notice what you need to do in order to take care of yourself. Then you keep rebooting. Here are the steps:

1. Get present and notice your energy.
2. Intend and decide if that's what you want it to be.
3. Take care and notice what you need to support yourself.
4. Breathe and envision your intended presence and how you want to show up.
5. Step in. Become it. And then rinse and repeat.

It's that simple.

Now, this could take as long or short as you want it to. And you can go through all the steps almost instantaneously, or you can take your time with each. You can do this before an important call or even at home in a conversation with your kids. Take five minutes before any meeting to do it as well. So take whatever time you need for it. Do it as often as you wish. And let it be easy.

The intention of the Presence Reboot is simply to show up intentionally.

This is important, so let's break down each step in real time. This is what it might look like:

- **Get present and notice.** As you're about to go on stage, or walk into a room, or step into a conversation, notice your posture, how you're feeling, what your energy is like, what you're putting out there, and your attitude.
- **Intend and decide.** If you're not where you want to be, own it. Envision what you'd like instead, and decide to shift. Notice what's in the gap between where you are and where you'd like to be instead. What's missing? What's present? What do you need to do to take care of yourself? This is where you'll start feeling into yourself.
- **Take care and notice.** You might notice that you just need to breathe and shift your posture. You might need a quick attitude adjustment. You might need to access the state of gratitude or curiosity. You're going to actually take care of those things as best you can in this moment.
- **Breathe and envision**. Again envision how you'd like to feel and show up instead. What experience do you want to have? What is your desire? What is your desired experience right now? How do you want others to experience you? Envision that in your mind's eye, feel it in your body, and then ...
- **Step in and reboot.** Keep doing this over and over again anytime you check out or lose presence.

It's a practice. It's quick. It takes awareness and intention. And you've got to decide. Fortunately, the more you practice your reboots, the easier they become.

Now! For the rest of the book (and the rest of your life), I invite you to integrate the Presence Reboot as you go. It will serve you not only in your impact on others, but in your impact here as well in how you engage with this work and create your ultimate experience!

CHAPTER 6

You, Yes, You

Engaging the Essential You

To lead others well you must know thyself,
lead thyself, and continuously become. The size of your vision
and the impact you want to have will determine who you become.

The Essential You is *you* at the core of it all (Figure 6.1). This is the authentic you, not the you that your boss or partner or organization or society or even your mother thinks you should be. Just you.

You at the center of the model, because leadership starts with you. Consider this "home base."

This is where we dive into your core values, your purpose or "why," the vision for your life (or your culture or organization if you're applying the model to your company), your beliefs and desires, and your natural state. This is also where we explore how to work with your space as a contagious leader. We'll call this space your "bubble."

FIGURE 6.1   The Essential You

Why start here instead of anywhere else in the model?

Leadership requires self-awareness and energetic hygiene. In order to keep your leadership clean and clear, you have to know yourself. The more connected you are to yourself, and the clearer you are on what kind of impact you want to have, the easier it is to hold your space and lead intentionally. From intentional space, you can stay grounded and on track despite external forces and demands. Grounded and on track means you lead in the direction and manner that's congruent for you. Grounded, on track, and congruent means people feel it, trust you, and follow you.

And when it all falls apart and you get knocked off your path, the more grounded you are in your Essential You, the easier it will be to recover and climb right back on.

When you have a big decision to make, whether personally or as an organization, coming back to your core—your why, your values, and your vision—can bring you home and provide direction. The more grounded and present you are here, the more permission you give others to shine in their own Essential You. As with everything else, your being grounded in your Essential You is contagious.

In this chapter I'll walk you through some of the core components of the Essential You and how to apply them to your personal and organizational life. These elements are foundational to clean leadership and cultivating a healthy culture. Like the rest of the IEP Model, the Essential You is dynamic and constantly evolving. It's never done. So be where you are, notice what you notice, and let's start with that bubble.

Get into Your Bubble!

What? A bubble in a leadership and culture book? Absolutely! You have one now; it just might be all over the place or really weak or crowded or solid and you don't even know it. Either way, you've got an energetic bubble (Figure 6.2). And if used intentionally—and with love and care and appreciation and some serious cultivation—this bubble will nourish, support, and drive your ability to lead effectively.

FIGURE 6.2 **Your Bubble**

With everything you have to engage with every day, it's essential to be able to "Bubble Up" so you can create space for yourself to breathe and lead from. Your bubble is a sanctuary and an important first step in grounded leadership.

I've shared this concept with some of the most brilliant, creative, discerning, and even skeptical people, including engineers, executives, creatives, teachers, tech geeks, and more. Even the most analytical of minds have benefited from this concept. So, what is "the bubble"? We all have our own energetic space. I like to posit that I have 18 inches all the way around me; front, back, side to side, above, and below. You can let your bubble take whatever shape resonates and feels great for you. It might be translucent, pearlesque, solid, glass, steel, glowing, whatever you wish. Inside the bubble is your stuff: your hopes, dreams, fears, energy, creativity, power, lightness, darkness, beliefs, presence, all of it.

Outside the bubble is the rest of the world's stuff: their hopes, dreams, fears, energy, lightness, darkness, projections, demands, and to-dos for you. Their stuff is their stuff—especially the stuff they want you to do or be.

The external world will do everything it can to get your attention. People will do all they can physically and energetically to get your attention: to ask of you, influence you, bring you into their world, and to meet their needs. If they're in a bad place or feeling overwhelmed or negative, they'll sometimes "offer that up" for you to heal for them. And guess what? You'll do the same to them. We all do it. We project. We get into each other's bubbles, into each other's space. As human beings who care and are vulnerable to energy, no matter where someone is coming from, it's easy to step right in and take it on. We can be contagious for good or bad.

It can be easy to think that it's all about protecting ourselves, or that in some way we're victim to another's energy. But the main reason we want to nurture our bubble and hold our space is so that we stay clear and aware of what energy belongs to us and what doesn't. For example, suppose you're in a great mood, and you connect with a colleague who's not. You feel the person's energy and negativity—will you take it on as your own and lower your energetic vibration, or will you hold your space and stay true to where *you* are? You can be compassionate and caring *and* still hold your space without taking on another person's energy.

By using the concept of the bubble, we make it easier to stay true to our own authentic energy without changing it to match someone else's. This works both ways. We want to hold our space in order to be responsible for the energy we project upon others as well. No need to get caught up in who's infringing upon whose space—simply own your space.

So here's how to do it. Plant your feet on the ground, or plant yourself in your seat if you're sitting. Feel your body. Breathe. Imagine a bubble all the way around you. You might notice it's really big or really tight, transparent or made of steel. Whatever it is, it's yours. Ask it to come in to about 18 inches around you, or whatever feels right for you. When you "Bubble Up," notice how you feel: powerful, clear, strong, positive, solid? Connect with *that*. Anchor it.

This can be a quick process when you're in the heat of it (remember in Chapter 2, my nemesis when I was on stage giving that keynote—I tapped into my bubble and did a quick reboot), or you can take your time and let it be delicious and rich (the more you do this when you have the time, the easier it will be to do it on the fly).

The newer you are to this practice, the faster your bubble will refill with outside energies and demands. If you find yourself not feeling clear or strong, take a moment to refill your bubble with your own energy. If there's anything holding you back, or if it feels like other people's negative energy keeps getting in there, no worries; let that stuff go. Notice it, and release it back to its rightful owner. The bubble is a practice of intention, and the more you do it, the stronger your bubble becomes.

The idea here is to create space for yourself. Focus on keeping yourself in your own space and out of the space of those around you. You're responsible only for what's in your space: you, your energy, your goods. Everything outside your bubble (bills, world, traffic, crazy calendars, other people's energy and demands) is outside your bubble.

From here you get to decide *how* you want to interact with each of these things (bills, world, traffic, crazy calendars, other people's energy and demands). This does not mean you abdicate and don't deal with other people and energy and life. This does not mean you're off the hook for being a jerk. This does not mean you bury your head in the sand to problems and all the stuff that's going on around you. *This simply means you've created a space for yourself to be intentional with how you want to interact with all of these things.*

This space can make a world of difference in the quality of your energy, your presence, your decisions, and how other people feel in dealing with you. Without your bubble, the alternative is to get completely overwhelmed (and busy! Oh so busy!) by the demands of everyone else—often so much so that you can barely hear your own voice. Your bubble is a sanctuary. And it is an important first step in grounded leadership.

Values and Purpose

Your values are the things that drive you. They're what's important to you, what you stand for, what you hold dear. They're you. You wouldn't be you without them. Your purpose is why you get out of bed in the morning. It's what you want your life and your impact to be about.

Your company attracts people to it because of its core values and purpose; like attracts like. When you've fired people or they've quit, it's likely there was some misalignment of values or purpose in play.

When you are on track with purpose, there's energy and inspiration. Burnout does not exist. When you are disconnected from purpose, burnout and resentment build, sleepiness occurs, you hear a lot of "I'm tired. I'm in a funk. I need to be inspired." When values are dishonored, they flare and deflate and create disconnection. Finding fulfillment and congruency in the moment, and for the long haul, can be as simple as identifying, claiming, and realigning values and purpose. Feeling the ick, feeling out of integrity, and getting triggered by the littlest things can all tie back to misaligned and dishonored values and purpose. It's all related.

So how do you identify these things? How do you honor them? How do you stay on track with purpose? And what do you do when values compete?

First, good news, you do not need to go meditate on a mountain for 10 days, or take six months off to find these things (though it's lovely if you can). You do, however, need to be present and pay attention to what's true for you. Your body and intuition, your friends' reflections, the questions you ask yourself, the stories you tell, and what you do all point to your values and purpose every day. Here are some exercises you can do for yourself or with a partner right now to explore. Don't go to your head, go to your heart. Have fun.

Exercise 1: Your Body Knows, and So Does Your Intuition

Take a deep breath. Get present in this very moment. Bubble Up. Connect with your heart and your true you and tune in.

What do you think your core values are? Off the top of your head. Try to come up with a list of at least 10.

What do you think your purpose is? Why are you here on this planet? What's the impact you want to have with your life? Again, just off the top of your head.

Exercise 2: Your Friends Are Brilliant—They See Right Through You

This one's easy (and fun) and can be applied to purpose work as well. Ready? Simply ask your friends and colleagues what they believe your core values are and what you're up to. They'll tell you. Ask five people, pull your themes, and see if they line up. (Hint: If they say something that hits a nerve, you've hit gold.)

Exercise 3: Questions That Make You Go "Hmmm"

Let's take it a bit deeper. Here are some questions to reflect on. You don't have to share your answers; all you have to do is tell yourself the truth.

1. What delights you? You feel joy when you do this or see this or experience this thing.
2. What upsets you? You feel sadness, resentment, restriction, frustration, or even fury when you see or experience this thing.
3. At the end of your life, what's the impact you hope you've had? The dent you left on the planet? Or in your company? Or on the people you served?
4. Look at your calendar. How are you spending your time, and whom are you spending it with? Why?
5. Look at your bank account. How are you spending your money? Why?
6. Look at your relationships. What do you talk about most? What's important about that?
7. Look at your health. What were your last three meals? Did they serve and nurture you?

Look at your answers: All of them point to your values and drivers. Don't get grandiose here, just look for common themes. It may be surprisingly simple.

Values and Purpose in Action

Here's how this all plays out. If I say that vitality, freedom, and security are values of mine, but I overeat and drink too much, I make little time for sleep, I work in a job I hate, and I'm spending too much money on shoes and not saving, something is out of whack. There's something I'm valuing more than vitality, freedom, and security. Or I'm simply not aware that I'm out of alignment. No biggie. It's just information and a choice point—once I see that my actions don't support my core values, I can adjust.

If we say that work-life balance is important to our organization and culture, but we expect our teams to work until 11 at night, give employees energetic guilt trips when they leave to be with their families or get a workout, or we honor the badge of busy and reward burning the candle at both ends, something is off. Again, this is just information. If work-life balance is truly a value, we need to shift and get into alignment.

For any of these, you may find yourself out of alignment with good reason; values can compete. It's possible that I choose the values of "play," "creativity," and "freedom" this month over "vitality," "financial responsibility," and "security" as I decide to nurture my friendships, my spirit, and my soul with some good old-fashioned letting loose and letting go (and buying great shoes). It's possible that our values for excellence and financial responsibility may trump our values of work-life balance this week as our team gets ready for a big product launch.

This is all just fine. The goal here is to be aware and to choose. The more aware you are of your core values, and the more in alignment you are with them, the better, clearer, stronger, and more grounded you'll feel. And the more solid your leadership and message. It doesn't mean you're honoring them perfectly—it means you know where you are, and you take full ownership for them.

In the Reflections Section at the end of this chapter, I've provided you space to identify and rate your top 10 values. I highly encourage you to play with it. Do it for yourself, and do it for your organization. See how they align.

"But It's Not My Fault I'm Not Accountable"

Holding yourself accountable for honoring your values and living your purpose is one of the greatest gifts you can give yourself. It's also one of the most compelling and powerful leadership qualities you can embody. And it's contagious. Whether we're talking personal or cultural, accountability breeds more accountability, just like victimhood breeds more victimhood.

Where we get into trouble is when we think this is all happening *to us*. We think we're not contributing to our situation in some way, we're a victim to it, or we simply don't have a choice—so instead of standing up, we abdicate or make it worse. The truth is, there's always something we can do to be more in alignment with ourselves. Even if that thing in this moment is simply owning your choice: "I'm not honoring my values right now, and I'm good with that." Or "This thing that just happened was horrible, and I'm going to figure out how to get back on track."

Sometimes stuff happens that is out of our control. And we're still at choice.

For example, let's say financial security is a value of mine. And I hit a financial bump. What's the littlest thing I can do to honor that value of financial security? Perhaps I can get more intentional with my spending, or I cut back on my lattes, or I work with a friend or financial planner to help me craft a plan, or now I start that savings account (even with the 20 bucks I have in my wallet). Other powerful places to honor this value may be to ask, What can I learn from this situation? How can this experience inform my future so I'm set up better should this happen again?

Or let's say vitality is a value, and due to external circumstances and other people's schedules and needs, I am no longer able to find time to work out. I feel victim to others' needs, and "It's not my fault," so I eat Cheetos and check out. That's one way to do it. *Or*, what's the littlest thing I can do to honor the value of vitality? Might I be able to do some push-ups at home? Stretch? Take my kids for a walk? Hit the stairs more? Maybe I can be even more intentional with the food I put in my body.

Or, let's say we hold direct engagement as a team value, which means if there's an issue, we go directly to our colleagues, and they come directly to us with it; no sidebars, no gossip, no talking behind one another's backs. And despite that value and agreement, *someone else* is gossiping behind your back, making life really tough for you. What's the littlest thing you can do to set this right? If you join the gossip wagon and jump into the drama, you're just adding to it. The gossip is contagious, and you've caught it. And now you're contagious and you're likely to pull others in with you. So clean it up. This may mean you go straight to the offender and make a request. Perhaps you redesign agreements for the next time something like this happens. Perhaps you get stronger in knowing that you can't control others. Perhaps you get into your bubble and reboot. But just because someone else stepped on one of your values or your organization's cultural values does not mean you have to compromise your own.

Stay accountable. Own it. And do the littlest, simplest thing you can do to get back in alignment.

Vision, Your Desired Impact, and the Intention for Who You Want to Become

Where are you going? What's the impact you want to have? And who will you need to become to make it all happen?

I am a huge fan of visioning. I created my business using visioning, before I even knew what visioning was, using a pad of

Post-its, a Sharpie, and my dreams, sitting in the front seat of my Dodge Durango in the parking lot of my gym while I waited for my 15-month-old to wake up from his nap. If you have kids, this may be a familiar scene. Sitting in that front seat, knowing that I only wanted to do work that would light me up and have me feel well used, and that would be worth pulling myself away from this little guy for, I envisioned the future.

I mapped out all the things I'd done in my career that lit me up and made me feel on fire. I felt so good doing these things; if I could do them all the time, mmm . . . watch out. These thoughts were all pointing to core values and purpose. Of course at the time I didn't know that; I just knew they made me feel inspired and on track.

Then I mapped out what a job would look like that would allow me to do all these things. It was a good job. Then I took it a step further, I had a high value around freedom and creating. What if this job was not a job, but rather a company? Could I make a company out of something I loved to do? Sure.

So then I mapped out what it would look like. If I could have anything I wanted, if my company could be what I wanted it to be, what would it be?

This all happened in the Durango in about 90 minutes. And when my son woke up, I was pumped for a great workout. I went home and couldn't stop thinking about it. It woke me up, got me out of bed early. And I dove in.

This visioning session, on Post-its, was the beginning of my business.

Visioning is powerful. Notice that with this vision, I had values and purpose built right in, which really made it hum. Also implied in visioning is impact, the impact you want to have through your vision. I've used visioning for projects and for creating relationships, building relationships, and completing relationships as well.

When you vision, and you believe in it, you've basically just placed an order with the Universe. You've also just made yourself clearer, more focused, more compelling and inspiring, and way easier to support.

Visioning in Business and Culture

David Schonthal, an entrepreneur and professor at the Kellogg School of Management, had a vision. He envisioned an organization of a pod of entrepreneurs focused on healthcare that could do more together than they could alone. What if they could design density and as a result engineer serendipity that would result in collaboration within an industry that would create technology in service of making people's lives longer, happier, safer, healthier, and more comfortable? What if they joined forces, put their resources together, and created one community in service of something bigger than all of them? What might be possible? Hungry for reaching more people and having a significant impact on health-related issues, he started a small organization. When people found out what he was up to, they climbed on. It happened. Three months later they had 70 start-ups as members and had raised $10 million in funding. That community today is called MATTER.

Thirty-three years ago, Ari Weinzweig and Paul Saginaw envisioned a deli that served awesome food, made with tons of love, and that people would come from all around to enjoy. People told them they were crazy. They opened up shop in Ann Arbor, dove in, and ran with it. People loved it and asked them to open shops all around the world. They said no, it wasn't in alignment with their vision. Today that organization does $55 million a year, employs more than 700 people, and has nine businesses doing all sorts of magical things all under the name of Zingerman's.

These are just two examples of vision and purpose coming together to create something cool. We're surrounded by them.

The organization you're in has its own vision. The more intentional that vision and purpose, the more inspiring the organization likely is. (By the way, if you haven't in a while, especially if you're working on creating an awesome culture, your vision and your "why" for originally starting your business is very much worth revisiting.)

Rarely does a business "just happen." If you look at any business around you, there was a seed of vision, and a seed of hunger and purpose that got it started. The more intentional and specific the vision and purpose is, the more quickly and efficiently it unfolds.

Culture, on the other hand, just happens more often than not. Despite people saying they'd like their culture to be a certain way, it either happens by default or leaders put things in place to "force" culture. What we need to remember is that the people *are* the culture, and the more intentional everyone in your organization (not just the founders or executives) is about what they want that culture to be, the more likely that culture will unfold in a healthy and contagious manner. The goal is to emanate, not dictate, the culture.

Brad and Sara and Their "Cool" Culture

For example, Brad and Sara wanted to create an awesome culture for their start-up. They had about 80 people in their San Francisco–based tech organization. When they started, they just knew they wanted the culture to be "fun and cool." They also wanted to get on one of the "best places to work" lists. They were pumped.

So they put up Ping-Pong and foosball tables, a basketball hoop and video arcade, and lots of espresso machines around the building. They catered lunches at least once a week, sponsored weekly bonding opportunities ("beer and chips" after work), and a more significant monthly culture event (karaoke, movie night, comedy night).

When you walked in, it was colorful, fun, it looked good. Brad and Sara were pretty happy about it. They'd invested a lot of time, energy, and money into getting culture right. But people weren't humming. Why? They felt like culture was being done *to* them. People felt the culture and values had been forced upon them. Instead of just having a culture they loved and that felt good and was positively contagious, they felt that the activities were contrived. Resistance spread.

What? The intentions were good. The actions were good too. But Brad and Sara had missed a couple of things. While they had met with a small group to create their vision and values, they didn't include others in creating the culture or rolling it out. Instead, they just told people how they should show up to honor those values. This hurt the culture. No Ping-Pong table would make up for feeling forced to show up in a way that wasn't congruent for them.

The fix was fairly simple. At an all-hands lunch meeting, Brad and Sara named the challenge, shared how and why they'd done what they did, and asked the community to help them make the organization and culture what *they all* wanted it to be. They stated their intentions, their dreams, and their fears that they'd failed. They also shared that they didn't have the answers—they wanted help.

The cool stuff stayed, and the values got tweaked collectively. They designed agreements for how they wanted to show up together as a team (more on this in Part 3), monthly events still remained but were coordinated by different teams, and weekly bonding occurred organically. These were easy shifts.

When you're visioning for your organization, especially around culture, don't do it in a vacuum. Feel free to start it, create an outline of dreams to build upon, and get people involved. The more your team members are included, the more they'll own it.

To apply visioning to your business (whether currently in existence or something you're dreaming of), consider the following: What does it look like? What impact does it have? What do you want? What do you not want? How do you want it to feel?

How do you want to feel leading it and building it? Who does it attract? These are just a couple of places to look. The clearer you are here, the easier it is to create, and the easier it will be for others to know how to help you make it happen.

And then you can create the plan. Ironically, the plan comes last.

Back to You . . . So What's Your Vision?

You can do this for anything. Here are some questions you might ponder to get in the frame for visioning.

What's the timeline? I find people like one year, three years, or five years. Pick the timeline that resonates for you. (If you're visioning for tomorrow's meeting or next week's leadership retreat, then you have a shorter timeline.)

What do you want "it" to look like? What does your day look like?

Who is in your life? Who are the people you surround yourself with? How inspired do you feel on a daily basis?

How are you showing up? How's your health? How does your body look and feel? What are you known for? What do people know they can count on you for?

What work are you doing? Is it your own company? Are you part of an organization? What's your team like? What are your revenues? What's the impact you're having? What awards have you won, or what has your company been recognized for?

Write your vision out in the present tense as if it's happening right now, even if it's a three-year vision. Feel into it. Become it. Let yourself run wild.

Once you've claimed your vision, it's time to get into action. This means you need to work for it, show up, and also relax into it. Don't be attached to exactly how you get there or what it looks like. Do be attached to the original purpose. Don't be attached to doing it perfectly. Do be attached to showing up fully.

Who Are You Becoming?

Your vision is just a very big intention for impact. It's an intention of the biggest kind. Your intention on a day-to-day basis will drive that vision. How you show up will drive how fast and powerfully that vision manifests. *The size of your vision and the impact you want to have will significantly influence who you become.*

You might want to read that again.

I believe that you can set an intention for who you want to become, do the work, stay awake, allow it to unfold, and you can become that person tomorrow, a month from now, a year from now, five years from now. It's your call—your intention.

Who will you need to be in order to make that vision, and the impact you want to have, happen?

How will you need to show up?

What will you need to believe?

What relationships will you need to cultivate?

What habits will you have to release? Adopt?

Who will you become? Write a vision for that.

Pulling It All Together

Once you've got this, you're going to want to visit it every day, if even for a moment. You want to stay awake.

You'll notice that on the outside of the IEP Model is "Impact." This represents the impact you want to have, which could be on another person, with an initiative, or with the culture you're creating. In this case, as you look at who you want to become and the impact you want to have, use this model to build that.

When you're present and grounded in the **Essential You** (your bubble, your vision, your values, your purpose), you're working your **Internal and External IEP** to set yourself up for success, and you're working your **leadership skills and competencies** to get done what you want to get done, you're better set up for **impact**.

Reflection: Putting IEP into Practice

This whole chapter is about you, with exercises for reflection built throughout. Let's anchor some big ideas here. Apply these to yourself personally, use them for your team, and/or work them over with your organization.

Your Bubble

Build your bubble. Nurture it. Use it in conjunction with the Presence Reboot. Enjoy.

Your Values

What are your core values? Make a list of your top 10 right here and rate how well you're honoring them from 0 to 10. Lower than you wish? Identify one thing you can do to elevate.

VALUE	RATING	NEXT

Your Purpose

What's your purpose again? What's the impact you want to have with your life? What's one thing you can do every day to bring you closer to honoring that purpose?

Your Vision

Where are you going? Choose your timeline. Be specific. Go big and dig in. Write it out, draw it out, map it out—whatever works. Set your vision.

Your Becoming

Who are you becoming? How are you going to need to show up to make all this good stuff happen?

Setting Yourself Up for Success

Physical and Environmental Energy

You are an instrument of change.
If you are to create the impact you want to have
in this world, you must nourish and take care of yourself.

Now you've got your bubble, your purpose, your values, your vision, and your intentions for becoming. It's time to create a stronger physical and energetic foundation to support all of it.

In the next two chapters, we're diving into the two quadrants of Internal IEP: Physical and Environmental Energy (Chapter 7) and Mental and Emotional Energy (Chapter 8). These are two of the most important chapters in the book as they dive into your internal workings—things you generally have a lot of control over and can shift as you please. Please don't take these chapters for granted. In my work with business leaders and organizations, I've found that these two quadrants are often the first to be neglected or completely overlooked. Ironically, they're also often the most foundational, offering the quickest and highest leverage in optimizing one's presence and impact.

The stronger you are internally, the easier it becomes to be positively contagious in your leadership and in the culture you're creating. Not only are these chapters about you holding your own space to show up well for yourself and others, they're about creating a solid energetic field that protects you from others' energy and projections, whether intentional or not.

The Physical and Environmental Energy Quadrant includes things like self-care, food, hydration, closets, calendars, wellness practices, healthcare, travel wellness, hygiene, the people you hang out with, your home, your office space, and other things that have a huge impact on your internal energy.

The Mental and Emotional Energy Quadrant includes things like beliefs, self-talk, intentions, assumptions, busyness, your stories, complaints and requests, intuition, intention, where you put your attention, and the decisions you make.

These all contribute to nourishing your energetic field or depleting it.

How We Got Here

I spent the first part of my career working with athletes. I'd studied Kinesiology (the science of the body and movement) and was fascinated by the potential of what people could do if they worked hard and took really good care of themselves. I enjoyed working with athletes and quickly realized that it wasn't so much the game I loved as much as I loved the people and the craft of preparing *for* the game. When the players' intentions, energy, and presence were aligned, winning the game and good sportsmanship were simply outcomes.

After athletics, I worked in corporate America in a number of roles related to health and productivity, disease treatment and reversal, and leadership. I found a similar theme. Winning the game wasn't as inspiring as what happened when the human beings took care of themselves, showed up, aligned, and worked well together. When peoples' intentions, energy, and presence lined up, healthy collaboration and great business results were simply outcomes. The positive energy that got produced and the contagiousness of it was what inspired me.

No matter what industry I was in, I noticed people with super powers. And when they practiced self-care, optimized their skills, and used those super powers for good, big things happened. Potential and impact they didn't even realize were possible opened up. These super powers transferred to business results, organizational culture, family health, and the individuals' personal levels of happiness. It all started with the individual, but the impact was contagious.

My hunger and passion for helping people unlock their super powers and optimize their impact eventually led me to create my company, and to build out what's now the IEP Method.

Why We Start with the Internal Stuff

I noticed over and over again that no matter how great people were, how talented, how successful, if they didn't take care of themselves, treat people well, and own their life, they could only go so far. It often fell apart. They burned out, they burned other people out, they got stuck, or they lost their edge.

What created the quickest, highest leverage impact on all of these individuals—whether they were athletes, executives, doctors, designers, teachers, parents, or employees—was taking care of themselves. When they nourished their bodies, their minds, their emotions, and their environments, they could do more. They could tap into more personal power, they had more to give others, and ultimately they could create more impact. The first step in doing this, where they had the most control and could create quick wins, was in their Internal IEP.

So let's dive into Physical and Environmental Energy (Figure 7.1).

FIGURE 7.1 Quadrant 1: Physical and Environmental Energy

Your first quadrant for nourishing and optimizing your Energetic Presence. This quadrant is part of your "internal energy" which means you have a ton of control over how you manage it.

Ask, "Is this serving my Physical and Environmental Energy, or is it hurting it? Is this contributing positively to my power and my energetic field, or is it depleting it? Will this make me feel better or worse?"

These three questions are your anchors in making sure your body and environment support you. Nourishing your Physical and Environmental Energy is one of your quickest and highest leverage ways to build a strong Internal IEP foundation. Anything you put into your body, do with your body, or surround your body with has an impact on your Physical and Environmental Energy.

It's as simple as that.

You have a ton of control here.

Let's talk about the physical side. First, get present. How are you feeling in your body? Think about the last thing you ate: Did it serve your energetic state? Do you feel energized, clear, good? Or do you feel tired, foggy, achy, depleted? Were you tired after lunch because the food you ate snuffed your energy? Or were you alert because you set yourself up for a great afternoon with good eats? Knowledge is power here, and you want to know how the food you eat impacts you as well as any stories you have around it: "I'm supposed to be tired after lunch." "I deserve doughnuts for breakfast because life is stressful." "I have no control over my food because I'm traveling." These are all common. Do they sound familiar?

People often don't realize how what they put in their body impacts them until their attention is on it. But food is fuel, and it affects how our bodies and brains perform and react. Now before you think this is about restriction and discipline, know this: I'm all for ice cream cones and chocolate and even that occasional ballpark hot dog. I'm also all for being conscious and intentional and setting yourself up to feel good.

We've become much more in tune to the impact of food, sugar, gluten, and inflammatory foods (and so many other things) on our bodies and brains over the last couple of years, especially with people like Dave Asprey (BulletProofExec.com[1]) and others leading the charge on cleaning our systems up for optimal performance and biohacking. And with people like Dallas and Melissa Hartwig (Whole30.com[2]) bringing us back to basics and healing our bodies through food and intentional eating. We've come a long way, and we have a long way to go.

If you think of your body as an instrument for impact and as a partner that you are in a very important relationship with, things open up. You can be more intentional with eating food that fuels you, supports the relationship, and gives you a stronger energetic field.

Ignorance Is Not Really Bliss

"I didn't know how good 'good' could feel, and then when I got there, I found even better." I hear this often—frequently followed by some version of "But now that I know, I notice when I feel bad faster and have less patience for it. But now I also know how to get back on track quicker."

It's easy to trek through day-to-day life, busy, trying to get through, a million priorities competing, walking around feeling good, maybe a bit tired, but good. In survival mode the bar for "good" is pretty low. This low bar has a big impact on your ability to lead in the energy you have, the way you process information, and how you show up with others.

When people take a step back and pay close attention to what's serving them (or not) energetically, they get a ton of information. From here, even making one small change to take better care of themselves brings them to a new level of good. This new level of good becomes the new norm, until they up-level again.

Of course, wherever you are right now is perfect! (Yes, even if you're living on Cheetos and think that exercise is getting up to get a new bag of Cheetos.) Simply notice how food impacts you. Notice the relationship you have with your body. Are you partnering with yourself? Do you feel the way you want to feel? Do you have the amount of energy you want to have? Notice where you are. And be kind.

You get to decide what to do about it. *You must be your own advocate and driver for feeling good.*

Here Are Some Other Things to Pay Attention to with Your Physical Energy

Food

- You have to eat; you might as well do it intentionally. Be present. Eat your food with intention. Enjoy that ice cream cone.
- This is not about deprivation: This is about pleasure and consciousness and fuel and being aware of how food impacts you.
- It takes just as much time to eat poor food as it does to eat good food.
- Fast food may be fast, but the amount of time and energy and brainpower you lose, and the cost of feeling subpar, more than

trumps the amount of time and energy it will take to order or make something thoughtful.

- Work meetings and travel are not an excuse for poor food choices. You can apply all of this to your off-sites, your on-sites, and your lunch meetings. Make requests or lead the charge. Fuel your team well.

Exercise

- Move your body regularly and in ways that resonate for you. Pay attention to your preferred (and even adored) form of exercise. What feels good to you; what do you really want to do?
- Great exercise is not necessarily about hitting the gym every day at 5 a.m. to pummel yourself, or doing yoga seven days a week, or running marathons. It's about doing what you want to do, being in your body, doing what makes you stronger and more grounded, and doing what gives you pleasure.
- Your exercise may be being in the gym every day, taking walks, doing impromptu dance breaks, climbing rocks, hitting the ballet bar, or kicking it up in Haganah training; it's up to you.

Sleep

There is so much information out there in the world right now about sleep. Arianna Huffington has done a beautiful job of making sleep cool and important again. I will leave it up to you to decide how you want to manage your sleep. As with everything in this book, to each his or her own—you are a unique creature with your own unique needs and combination for what will serve you most. But here's what I do not want you to leave this book without:

- Your sleep is essential. Do not "sleep when you're dead." Do not put sleep on the back burner. Do not take for granted the power of sleep on your mind, body, spirit, presence, and impact.
- When I was working on this section I came across studies and videos and articles and all sorts of stuff touting the different

elements and different sleep requirements. Some people need 10 hours, some 7, some say 5; if you hack well, maybe 4. Again, your call, but know that the information is out there. And know that it's having an impact.

- Your sleep impacts your energy levels, your hormones, your cortisol levels, your weight, your brain function, your mood, and with all of this I'd add from an IEP standpoint your levels of gratitude, generosity, presence, compassion, and power as well as your ability to rebound and recover when something comes up or knocks you down.
- Quality sleep is the name of the game. Intentional sleep can change your life.

Here are a couple of things to consider in setting yourself up for intentional sleep:

- Set the intention to "go to bed at *this* time" and "get up at *this* time."
- Turn off all glowing pixelated toys and electronics an hour before you crash.
- Make sure your bed is comfortable and serves you and that your sheets are clean and cozy.
- Make sure the noise is right (crickets, frogs, noise machines, city sounds—whatever floats your boat—hook it up).
- Lock your doors, kiss your kids, cuddle your partner, snuggle your dog, say your prayers, do whatever you need to do to feel safe and connected.
- Eat quality food at your last meal before bed.
- Breathe and relax into gratitude for what's happened that day (even crappy days), and set an intention for the next day.
- Set an intention for sleep and how you want to feel when you wake up.
- And then sleep. Well.

Self-Care

Doctor's appointments are high leverage—you address your physical, mental, and emotional energy when you address doctor's appointments. Seems too easy? Don't take this one for granted.

Anything that's clouding your energy or your mind, anything that's on your list around your physical well-being, that you're not taking care of, is draining your mental energy as well, so let's just get it taken care of. Every time you have that flinch of "Oh! I need to do that, or schedule that," consider mental energy and bandwidth compromised.

Another essential place to look when it comes to self-care and health is your hormones. Your hormones have a huge impact on your physical, mental, and emotional well-being. They impact our energy, our sleep, our weight, our moods, everything. I've found that many women don't consider this as a factor until they're older, and men often don't consider this at all, when in fact our hormones are impacting all of our systems, all of the time.

If you are doing everything that you can—eating well, sleeping well, exercising, surrounding yourself with great people, etc.— and you still don't feel right, get your hormones checked. Listen to your body. Partner with your doctor. Take care of yourself.

Travel

Despite what some may say, and as much as I can empathize and have definitely experienced compromised IEP on the road, traveling is not an excuse to throw your IEP out the window. In fact, you need your IEP more than ever when you're out of your element in different time zones, dealing with international flights, jet-lagged, sleeping in foreign places, and away from your rituals, people, and comfort. Do not leave home without a plan.

When I travel, here's how I do it. I bring my coffee and any shakes or supplements with me. I always travel with "emergency food":

A couple of avocados, almonds, water, protein, and anything else that's easily portable and serves my body.

At restaurants, don't be afraid to ask for the kind of food you want. They are usually happy to accommodate requests, especially if you're clear and ask politely. If you have something you love, like a certain oil or salt or butter, bring it with you.

When it comes to accommodations and your environment while traveling, you can be proactive about that as well. Make sure your hotel has a gym (if you use one) and that it's in a good location and you feel safe.

If you're on stage or performing or facilitating or in a service profession or leading a pitch and you've got to be on, on, on, time zones don't matter—you still have to show up. Take extra good care of yourself and ask for what you want. Make requests in service of giving others the best version of you, and if for some reason they can't make it happen, roll with it and do what you can to create it or make it happen for yourself.

You serve everyone when you take care of yourself. Set yourself up for success to serve well. Especially when you travel.

Surround Yourself with the Goods

Environmental energy is *big*. The things we surround ourselves with—the environment of our office, the food, the people, our calendars, even the way we situate our desk—has a big impact on our energy and either supports or detracts from our physical and mental energy. You have more control of it than you may think. And it doesn't take a lot to make a big difference—often the subtlest of shifts can completely change the game.

Sure, there's lots of stuff we can't control like what's in the air, open office layouts, the weather, the unexpected flight delay that's got us grounded in Chicago. However, all is not lost—you always have some kind of influence around your environment. It's about how you interact with all of it, and even more so, how you set yourself up proactively on the front end with the big things you *can* control, so that when the little things go off the rails, they're not so bad. Don't like your office building? Bring in some flowers, put up a picture, grab some headphones, and make a request. Hating the weather? Find something that you can appreciate about it, have a lazy day inside, stay in bed. Delayed in Chicago? Grab a good book, put on some tunes, make a new friend, eat your canned oysters. You can always do something to make it feel better for you. You decide.

Those are things that are often outside our control. But what about the stuff we *can* control? It's golden.

Is your environment and the way you're taking care of it setting you up for success?

Little things as simple as unsharpened pencils, ugly things in your house, that piece of garbage you keep walking by, that cluttered desktop you have to search through every time you want to find something—these are all little things that put a chink in your energetic field, slow you down, and waste mental energy, too.

And then there are the big things, like your calendar and schedule, where you live, your home, your closet, your computer desktop, what you wear, even how you organize you coffee cans and clutter. It all counts. Check in and see how each of these makes you feel, and if it's anything but great, adjust.

Your People

Whom are you hanging out with? Who are you becoming? Jim Rohn said, "You are the average of the five people you spend the most time with." Who are your five people?

If you surround yourself with people who exhaust you, who make excuses, who complain a lot, who have bad relationships, who don't take care of themselves, who don't care about other people, who have bad spending habits, who are entitled and selfish, whatever—guess what? You're bound to adopt some behaviors.

If you hang out with people who are purpose-driven, who want to create positive impact, who do great work, who author their own lives, who love their jobs, their relationships, and their marriages, who take really good care of themselves, who are grateful and generous, whatever . . . Guess what? You're bound to adopt some behaviors.

You get to hang out with whomever you wish. You are the captain of your fate. You get to decide how you want to show up and who you want to become. The people you hang out with are a big part of your environment; be intentional here. I call these people your Posse, and I'll talk more about them later in the book.

For now, let's keep rolling with our Internal IEP—more specifically, how you set yourself up for success in that beautiful mind of yours.

Reflection: Putting IEP into Practice

Internal IEP

Time for some reflection!

Go through each section in this chapter and write yourself a note with how you're doing (rated 0 through 10) and what your next step will be (a little one and a leapfrogger) to optimize that area of your Internal IEP. When you've done that, come to this page and give yourself a clean and prioritized path to address each section.

Quadrant 1: Physical and Environmental Energy

- List your top three areas that could use some TLC.
- How do you see these things impacting your leadership?
- What's the cost?
- What would the benefit be of partnering with them to make them better?
- What are your next three steps?

CHAPTER 8

Setting Yourself Up for Success

Mental and Emotional Energy

You become what you believe, decide, and act upon.

Intentionally nourishing your Mental and Emotional Energy field is another quick and high leverage way to build a strong Internal IEP foundation. While your Physical and Environmental Energy was all about setting yourself up for success physically, now we're addressing matters of the mind and heart.

Your second quadrant for nourishing and optimizing your Energetic Presence is shown in Figure 8.1. Part of your "Internal Energy", much like your Physical and Environmental Energy in the first quadrant, you have a ton of control over how you manage it.

There are four questions to ask to set yourself up for success mentally and emotionally so that you can be at your best: "Is this serving my mental and emotional energy, or is it hurting it? Is this contributing positively to my power and my energetic field, or is it depleting it? Will this make me feel better or worse? Will this make me be better or worse?"

FIGURE 8.1   Quadrant 2: Mental and Emotional Energy

Mental and Emotional Energy includes things like your thoughts, assumptions, and beliefs, your focus, your complaints, and how much space you leave for authentic emotion. Anything you think, feel, or make up has an impact on your Mental and Emotional Energy.

You also have a ton of control here.

So much of what goes on in this quadrant is impacted by what's going on in Quadrant 1 and vice versa. If you make shifts in either, both benefit.

Mental and Emotional Energy bleeds into everything: your level of productivity, how you show up, how you feel, your presence, how you navigate conflict, even the tone in which you respond to email. What you think impacts how you feel, which impacts how you show up.

You can probably relate to these situations:

• You have a misunderstanding with a colleague, and instead of cleaning it up immediately, you let it linger. This colleague seems to get worse; every time you talk with him there's more tension. Now he's on your mind—taking up precious brain space and bandwidth, and the more you think of it the more careful and unsettled you become. This energy now clouds every interaction and conversation, impacting your presence with coworkers. You lose sleep. You enter a cycle of mental and emotional doom as they mirror back more of the same.

- You're nervous about your board meeting, thinking some of the key players aren't fans or simply don't like you, so you show up differently around them: Careful, quiet, nervous, you're just not you. They don't get the full effect. Now they're really not fans—but they *were*, going in.

- You get really angry or hurt, but you don't want to feel that way (or "shouldn't"), so you swallow it and push it aside. And then you blow up over something little, or your frustration leaks out in weird passive-aggressive ways impacting innocent bystanders everywhere. You didn't honor the emotion, so now it's having you for lunch.

All of these things tie into your Mental and Emotional Energy: assumptions, beliefs, decisions (or a lack of them), focus. All of these things are contagious—either internally for yourself or externally with others, and usually with both. And all of them are your choice. You get to decide how you want to interact with every single scenario. So get into your Bubble, eat something fuel worthy, drink something delicious, take a deep breath, do a presence reboot, and let's dive in.

Assumptions

The assumptions you have tend to design how you show up and who you become. Who are you becoming?

Here's my stance: Don't make assumptions, and if you're going to make them, at least make sure they serve you.

When I am going in to work with a group or to speak, if I'm assuming the group members are going to be tough to work with, or they're going to hate me (like the guy in the boardroom example earlier), walking into that room my energy and presence is going to be low and I'm more likely to create that response. But if I assume that they're going to be wonderful, they're going to love having me in, and we're going to have a great session together, I walk in with a stronger presence and more likely to create that response. I get to choose.

Now of course, you may have your assumptions totally wrong. You walk in thinking you've got a room of happy people and it's a tough crowd—whoops. But here's the thing: If you walk in in a strong and positive state, it's going to be much easier to manage yourself, show up with what's in the room, and hopefully help create a shift.

Similarly, if you go into a meeting with a colleague and you're assuming a positive outcome, but your colleague is not, you at least have a clearer field to work with him or her in. If you go in assuming the worse and you're projecting the energy of careful-ness, dread, resistance, or fear, it's going to be rough.

When all else fails, here's some food for thought: What people think of you is really none of your business. Unless you are intentionally requesting feedback that will serve your growth, other people's judgments and projections are way out of your bubble domain. So at a minimum, be aware that you're mak-ing assumptions in the first place, be aware that they're con-tagious (both for you internally and for what you project to those around you), and then either don't worry about it or make assumptions that serve.

Checking Assumptions to Clear the Field

You can always check assumptions. This is a quick path to clear-ing the field and also building intimacy.

You can make transparent assumptions with your team, your clients, and your colleagues. For example, imagine clearing these assumptions at the beginning of a project: *I assume we all want to do this work, we want to be here, we're going to honor one another's time, we'll make the work a priority, and if there's an issue we'll address it directly instead of gossiping about it.* This does wonders at the beginning of a meeting or a group session and goes nicely with agreements (more on this in Chapter 13).

You might also check assumptions with a friend or colleague, especially if it's "getting in the way" for you with them: *Hey, I have this assumption I'm making about you/us, am I right or am I way off base?* The most important part of this conversation is your intention, your energy, and your presence when you're having it. If your presence in conversation is laced with blame or irritation or anything icky, your colleague will feel it, and not only will you likely not get closer, you'll probably get farther apart.

And then, of course, there are just the simple less charged assumptions you can clarify when you're working together as a team or on a project: *I assume Julie is responsible for this, I'm assuming we're going to honor agreements, I assume we'll make time for workouts and breaks, I assume we'll give one another feedback responsibly.*

Notice the assumptions you make about others, about events, about projects you're involved in, even about yourself, and decide if you really need to be making them. If you do, simply make sure they serve you. And if you want a bit of peace and clarity in dealing with what's real now, get "in front of it" and clarify them.

Beliefs

A close cousin to assumptions are your beliefs about yourself, other people, the world, your organization, what's right and wrong, and pretty much everything else.

My favorite body of work for unpacking, busting, and working with personal beliefs is by Byron Katie, who created "The Work." I also love, respect, and appreciate those in the Arbinger Institute for their work in this realm and how it impacts relationships and how we show up with each other. I'll talk about them more in the Vibrational Quadrant (Quadrant 3), but I wanted to mention them here because their work serves this quadrant as well.

There are a couple of different ways to think about beliefs. The first is the beliefs you hold about other people, projects, and even your culture. The second is the beliefs you hold about yourself.

If you believe that the world is not safe, people are bad, work is supposed to be hard, life is supposed to be hard, you're supposed to be less attractive or fit as you get older, your organization is not supportive, or your culture is lame, and that the world owes you, you'll likely act accordingly, show up accordingly, and create situations in your life to prove you right. Your decisions and behaviors will be filtered through this lens.

If you believe that the world is beautiful, people have positive intent and are valuable beings, work is supposed to be life giving and purposeful, life is supposed to be meaningful and joyful, you can be your best version of fit and healthy and energized and attractive at any age, your organization wants you to do well, your culture is cool, and your life and results are yours for the creating, you will act accordingly, show up accordingly, and create situations in your life that prove you right. Your decisions and behaviors will be filtered through this lens.

We choose daily, moment to moment. We often are not even aware we're doing it. Which do you choose? What are the beliefs you hold about your world, your life, your organization, your culture, and the people who work with you?

How energizing are these beliefs? How life giving, inspiring, and propelling? How do they impact your presence?

And what are the results you're creating—or not creating—in your life because of these beliefs?

If you and your team or organization aren't getting the results you want, look back to what you actually did to get that result.

What were the beliefs that drove the actions and behaviors that got you there? For example, if you believe that you have to do it all by yourself or no one else can do it as well as you or you can't trust someone to get the job done, then the behavior you're likely to model will be working alone, not asking for help, not delegating, and working till the wee hours of the morning. The result might be that you burn out, end up feeling resentful or overcommitted, and end with a subpar outcome that could have been way better if you'd challenged some of your beliefs and allowed other people in.

Now let's work backward and find a result we loved. Let's say your team just created an awesome tool for your clients. You finish the project and people are happy. You're bringing out the bubbly. If you look backward from your stellar outcome and identify the actions you took, you'll likely find that the team worked well together, everyone knew what he or she was responsible for, everyone met his or her deadlines, and everyone was valued and supported. If you take a step even further back, what were you, as a team, believing in order to help this happen? You likely believed in your team, believed the team members were capable and could get the job done, and believed you could count on one another.

Two scenarios, two outcomes, two very different sets of beliefs.

Sometimes in order to move forward, you might have to adopt or borrow a belief that serves you for a while so you can gather evidence that it's true.

Sometimes in order to move forward, you might have to claim a negative belief and do some work around it to either create peace with it or shift it.

Sometimes in order to move forward, you might have to choose a new belief.

So check your beliefs. Check your cultural beliefs. And check your beliefs about others. They count.

Decide

The word *decide* is one of the most powerful words we have in our vocabulary. It's a leadership skill. It's a true super power. Your results, personally and as an organization, to this point in your life are an outcome of all the decisions you've made. What have you decided?

Any kind of behavior change, any kind of breakthrough, any kind of transformation, anything you want starts internally with you *deciding* to make it happen.

The process of becoming a better leader, becoming a better culture, becoming a better team, becoming a better anything begins with you deciding to become it.

People think they've decided to be successful, but they're stuck or not getting the results they want as fast as they'd like them. It's often because they're busy and haven't fully committed. It may mean they don't really want it, they need more information, or deep down there's something much bigger at play. Success could mean giving up relationships, being judged by others, being more exposed, having to say "no" more, having to say "yes" more, or having to do the hard work to actually get to success.

What do you do when you, or you and your team, realize you're stuck or you've not fully decided? Breathe. Acknowledge why, without making it wrong. There's information in the hesitation.

That product you keep stalling out on? The corporate initiative that keeps getting postponed? The person you said you want to hire (or fire), but it's not happening? There's a place you haven't decided. And there's wisdom in there.

Explore it, discuss it, own it, and then either truly step into the decision, find a decision you *can* align with, or decide *not* to make a decision at all right now. Deciding *not* to decide is a powerful decision in itself.

True leadership requires consciousness about what you are deciding and why.

Complaints, Requests, and Dreams

Complaining is likely one of the most energetically contagious and exhausting activities you've got going on in your organization right now. You have an employee who complains all the time. People complain to you, to others—nothing gets done. Complaints become the norm. Or maybe it's you. You have a complaint. You air it, revoice it, and keep bringing it up, but nothing is getting done.

Can we agree that the person complaining the day away (whether it is your employee or you) is not even one bit compelling, inspiring, or productive? And if people do respond to your complaint, they're likely doing it out desperation, obligation, and wanting you to go away, not because they were compelled by your awesome presence? This is not exactly the energy you'd like to project and definitely not the energy you want pervading your culture.

So what do you do? The solution is incredibly simple. You flip your complaint into either a request or a suggestion.

Underneath every complaint is an uncommunicated or unidentified request or suggestion. And underneath that is likely an unrealized or very tender dream. Identify what's what, get your energy back, and get stuff done.

Here's how we do it:

COMPLAINT	REQUEST OR SUGGEST	DREAM / TENDER AGENDA
It's hot in here! So hot. Hot, hot, hot.	Will someone please turn up the AC? How about if I turn up the AC?	My body dreams of comfort and safety.
You are a slob. I'm always picking up after you!	Will you please pick up your socks?	I dream of order and cleanliness and respect.
You're so slow to respond, and I don't even know if you got my stuff!	Will you please let me know you got my note within 24 hours?	I'd like us to work together better and provide top care to clients.
You're always late. It's disruptive, and you don't care. It really sucks.	Please be on time. Would it be helpful if we met later for these meetings?	I dream of us being productive and honoring one another's time.

Note that just because someone comes to you with a great request does not mean you're now on the hook for making all these dreams come true. You might say "No, but here's something we could do." Or "How do *you* want to make it happen?" When you give people the opportunity to turn a complaint into a request or suggestion, you give them their power back. When you look for the tender dream or wish underneath that request or suggestion, you create intimacy and connection.

Of course the most important thing in this communication is your intention toward them, the energy you bring, and how you show up.

What You Focus On

Whatever you focus on, you'll find.

Whatever you focus on, you'll attract.

Whatever you focus on, you'll create more of it.

If you focus on how bad people are, they get worse.

If you focus on the three weakest people on your team, you will lose sight of the 30 who are rock stars and hungry to grow.

Instead, shift focus.

Focus on the five pieces of helpful feedback instead of the one piece of mean and personal feedback.

Focus on what you are grateful for instead of what you don't have and what's not working.

Gratitude and acknowledgment are two of the most powerful states you can stand in for your own energetic field and also for your impact on others. Focus there. (Bonus: start a Gratitude and Acknowledgment Journal and use it every single day.)

Whatever you focus on will expand. You'll gather evidence for it. You'll create more of it. The world is your oyster.

Full Range Emotional Authenticity

Throughout this book we're talking about being contagious in a positive way. I'm offering you tools and ways of thinking about IEP, frameworks for taking accountability for your impact, ways to author your personal and cultural story, and ways to look at how you contribute to positive or negative contagions in your organization.

But here's something you need to know.

And it's super important. It's key to your emotional energy, and it's key to having an authentic culture that allows for vulnerability and realness.

Nowhere in this book am I suggesting that you squash your feelings, become a robot, or obliterate any negative emotion. I'm not suggesting that at all. Nowhere am I saying that you should shut someone down for where he or she is. In fact, I believe that the more responsibility you have as a leader, the more important it is to have *facility* with your full range of emotions, knowing how to be with them and navigate them.

The more you're able to do this for yourself, the better you'll be able to do it with those you lead. Part of leadership and creating a healthy contagious culture is in being able to be with what is: the good, the bad, and the ugly. You must find comfort in the discomfort to be with a full range of emotions.

This starts with you being able to be with yourself first.

So, yes, sometimes it is hard. Sometimes this weather is a bummer, this guy is making you crazy, that coworker was really mean, your employee really blew it, or the company had a bad quarter. Sometimes it's hard.

Allow yourself full permission for authentic emotion. Experience the rut, the disappointment, the fear, whatever is going on—wallow in it for days if you wish—and then, when you're done, come on out and focus on what you want instead. And know this:

1. As a leader you don't always have the luxury of melting down in the moment and losing your temper, so knowing how to reboot and shift your state is essential.
2. You can choose when, where, and with whom to express your emotions.
3. You don't have to become your emotions and get stuck there. The more present you are to them, authentically, the easier it will be to move through them.

The more you know joy, the easier it is to know pain; the more you know dissatisfaction, the easier it is to know what "Yes!" feels like. The more you know the "ick," the more you can experience the "oomph"—they all relate. Your ability to hold space for the dark or difficult emotions is directly related to your ability to hold space for the light and wonderful emotions—so have them all. Full authentic emotion enables full authentic living. Full authentic living allows for full-range leadership.

Don't cut yourself off. Show up and thrive.

Reflection: Putting IEP into Practice

Internal IEP

Time for more reflection!

Again, work your way through this chapter and write yourself a note for each section with how you're doing (0–10) and what your next step would be (a little one and a leapfrog) to optimize that area of your Internal IEP. When you've done that, come to this page and give yourself a clean and prioritized path to address each section.

Quadrant 2: Mental and Emotional Energy

- List your top three areas that could use some TLC.
- How do you see these things impacting your leadership?
- What's the cost?
- What would the benefit be of partnering with them to make them better?
- What are your next three steps?

What was the most important thing that stood out for you in regard to Internal IEP? What do you want to make sure you take and integrate from Chapters 7 and 8?

CHAPTER 9

Showing Up for Success

Vibrational Energy

You radiate. You emanate. You instigate.

How you show up is often reflected by what people say about you behind your back. If you're lucky you'll get this information directly; if not, you may have to work for it a bit.

Charlie, a leader in a consulting firm, had been given feedback that he was doing well in a couple of areas—organization, resourcefulness, and content—and that he needed to elevate his game in a couple of others—being more connected with his team and communicating objectives more clearly. The feedback was good, and Charlie felt empowered. The plan was in motion. At a meeting that afternoon, without Charlie in the room, his colleagues discussed him further: "I like him; I think he'll do well if he follows the plan. I just really wish he had more presence and gravitas in his leadership. He's a nice guy, I just don't know if he really has what it takes to be in front of the clients we need to put him in front of." They all agreed. Ouch.

This would have been good information for Charlie to have. He had left the meeting thinking he was doing okay and working on his plan. But the stuff his leaders were too afraid to share with him because they didn't want to hurt his feelings is the stuff that's going to slow Charlie down. The issue of giving or not giving that feedback directly is addressed in Part 3 of this book, but for now, the point is this: This was how Charlie was showing up.

A big part of how you Show Up is in the feeling people get from you: It's the intention they sense, the energy you bring to the table, how grounded you feel, the "vibe" you put out, and your overall presence. Charlie's vibrational energy indicated that he wasn't a confident leader. And his colleagues questioned whether they could count on him. Of course this ties into the other quadrants of the IEP Model as well. In Charlie's case, his Mental and Emotional Energy was impacting his Vibrational and Relational Energy resulting in a lack of trust and credibility.

Just like Internal IEP in the last two chapters, External IEP has its own two quadrants. The third quadrant, Vibrational Energy, is about the energy you bring to the table and how people experience you (Figure 9.1). The final and fourth quadrant, Relational Energy, is about how you show up in relationships and how you create healthy relationships.

Sometimes making a small tweak in one of these quadrants can be the difference between creating trust, getting a standing ovation, getting a promotion, or people simply not being afraid to approach you anymore. In Charlie's case, he made conscious changes. The first shift made the biggest difference: He *decided* he *did* want to be the guy leading those clients and therefore that he'd show up and do whatever he needed to do to strengthen his presence and credibility. From there he did a couple of things: (1) he adopted the belief that he was the right guy to be leading and in front of the room—that he had tremendous value to offer, (2) he focused on being a contribution to the room instead of just looking good, and (3) he practiced the Five Steps to Intentional Impact (Chapter 5) and did Presence Reboots (Chapter 4) before he walked into any room. Notice that the majority of these shifts fall under Mental and Emotional Energy, yet they all had big impact on his Vibrational and Relational Energy.

Little shifts go a long way.

Vibrational Energy

So let's dive into Vibrational Energy.

FIGURE 9.1   Quadrant 3: Vibrational Energy

Your third quadrant for nourishing and optimizing your Energetic Presence is depicted in Figure 9.1. This quadrant is part of your "external energy." While you have little control over how others "experience you," you have a ton of influence in how you set yourself up to show up well.

There are three questions to ask about your vibrational energy: "Is my presence hurting or helping the impact I want to have? Is my presence adding to or detracting from the quality of the energy in the room? Will my presence make others—and myself—feel better or worse?"

When you walk into a room, how do people feel? Excited, inspired, safe? Or anxious, annoyed, bad? Do you elevate the room or conversation with your presence, or do you deflate it?

The answers and solutions to these questions lie in your Vibrational Energy and Presence. How you navigate and lead your presence significantly determines how effective you'll be in leading others.

When it comes to presence, know this:

1. You are always having an impact, and that impact is entirely up to you.
2. What you put out there is constantly being cycled and reflected right back to you. You create your impact and experience.
3. People may forget what you say and do, but they'll remember forever how you make them feel.
4. The minute you walk into a room, onto a stage, or into a meeting, you're being assessed for your presence: how you look, how you feel, and how you make people feel.
5. If you think Vibrational Energy and Presence don't apply to you, it's highly possible you have the most to gain from playing with it.

Your Vibrational Energy and Presence follows you wherever you go. Whether you're in a room with 2 people or 2,000, your presence has impact. Let's look at some of your highest leverage ways to optimize and shift presence as needed.

Your Default Presence

It's helpful to notice what you default to when it comes to presence. Without even moving a muscle right now, I want you to notice how you're sitting, breathing, even your facial expression. That's likely a default.

You're in a meeting and you have that guy who's sinking the room with his presence. There's the person whose facial expressions and demeanor reflect that she's ticked off. You have good news, and you're hesitant to tell your teammate because his lack of presence and excitement has a way of bumming you out.

On the flip side, you have the guy who walks into the room and you breathe a sigh of relief and comfort. You have the gal you love speaking with because she exudes presence and championing. You have news (maybe it's even really bad), and you're cool to tell your teammate because no matter how tough the news is, you know he'll be present to it and meet you where you are.

We all have a default presence; it's the presence we hold when we're not being intentional, when we think no one is paying attention to us, when we're simply not present. Furrowed brows, crossed arms, slumped shoulders—they all portray irritation or disinterest, and so often this is not reflective of what's going on. It's the default. This is pretty easy to address. Just being aware of it can often change it.

Your Vibrational Energy is contagious. Remember, the lowest vibration will win, unless you lead it. Play with this in a meeting or conversation. Notice what's in the room, check out everyone's presence, and then intentionally shift your presence, shift your face, shift your intention, and "beam it" at the person or people in front of you. Nine times out of ten, it will shift. When you shift your presence from default to intentional, it's contagious.

This all starts with intention. Intend your presence, do a Presence Reboot, or do your Five Steps to Intentional Impact. Simply decide to shift how you're showing up. And pass it on.

But what about when it's hard? What about when you can't or your presence is in the ditch? What do you do then?

The Energetic Xylophone

You're heading into a meeting and you've just had a huge fight with your spouse.

You have to give someone feedback, and you're just not feeling like it.

You have to go to work, and you just don't want to.

You have to present to your board, and you are wildly nervous.

In all of these your energy is low, your presence is not where it needs to be, and it's all very real. But you have to show up. As a leader, you've got to lead.

What do you do?

You have a couple of choices. You can skip it, do it poorly, go in a foul mood, fake it till you make it, or you can reboot.

What do you choose?

Cathy was leading a meeting in Dallas. She'd done her prep, her Five Steps to Intentional Impact; she was ready to roll. Ten minutes before she headed into the session she got into an argument with one of her colleagues. They'd been working on something together for a while, and it'd been a painful process, but they were close to the end. Cathy learned that her colleague had made a crucial decision—a bad one—without her and it was going to cost them in time, energy, and money. She was not happy. And she had to lead a meeting in 10 minutes.

Her Vibrational Energy was of blame and frustration. If she went in and led this room from this place, it would be painful for all of them. She had a couple of choices: (1) reschedule—which would also have negative impact on the team, (2) pretend it didn't happen and fake "Mary Poppins"—they'd sense her inauthenticity, (3) call her boss and complain—not productive, (4) call one of her advisors or girlfriends and get support—no time, or (5) shift her state—and lead.

Shifting her state was the most powerful plan. But to shift it, it had to be authentic. So she used the Energetic Xylophone, did a reboot, walked in, and led.

A quick state shifter, this tool can come in handy when you need to shift your energetic presence—authentically. Plug yourself in to create your own version of the Energetic Xylophone (Figure 9.2).

FIGURE 9.2 **The Energetic Xylophone**

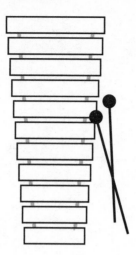

Authentically Shifting Your State

The Energetic Xylophone assumes that you have different energetic and emotional states, and that they run on a spectrum. A zero is the lowest vibration you might bring into something. A 10, at the top of the xylophone, is the highest.

We all have emotions that specifically affect our state and cause us to vibrate at different frequencies. For example, blame, judgment, and superiority might all fall on the lower end of your spectrum. When you're feeling them, your vibration may be low and not helpful. If you were to walk into a room or engage with someone from that state, he or she would feel it and respond to it. You'd likely create more of it in your interaction—thereby validating and creating more blame and judgment energy.

On the flip side, joy, love, and gratitude might all be on your high end. If you can tap into and embody these emotions and the energy that goes with them, you're probably golden. But to jump from blame to joy can be a stretch—especially for Cathy in the state she was in. Had she gone in and jumped to the top, the participants would have sensed it, and she'd have felt unsettled. She had to move with integrity.

Cathy knew that curiosity, appreciation, and contribution are higher on her personal spectrum (if she was using numbers, she'd give them a 7 or 8). To shift her state, she didn't need to go all the way to joy or to a 10, she just needed to shift to something a bit higher than her current 3 or 4 that she could stand in authentically.

Cathy chose her favorite trifecta: curiosity, appreciation, and contribution. What was going to happen today? Wow! I'm in Dallas working with this amazing group of people! I can't wait to serve and contribute. As she felt into these three states, her energy started to shift organically. And she was soon at a solid, authentic 7. From here she could walk into that room, show up well, and lead. What's great is that once you're authentically at a 7, it's a small step to a 10. It gets exponentially easier. (It works the opposite way as well, if you're at a 4 and you foster that, you're not far from a 1.)

But there was a catch. In order for her to do this without being fake or not honoring her own emotions about what had happened with her colleague, she had to promise herself that she'd take care of herself later. She'd revisit it again after the meeting when the space was right. She promised to contact her advisor that night and to follow up with her colleague so they could have a heart-to-heart and figure out a solution. She also promised to explore where she'd helped create all of this: How was she accountable? This allowed her brain and heart to relax and know they'd be tended to later. But for now, she had a session to lead and needed to be there for her people.

They had a great session.

Of course, at the end of the day, she had more perspective on the event and she and her colleague were able to navigate their issues much more productively. That's the Energetic Xylophone! You have your very own unique xylophone—play with it. Note that being at a 10 does not mean that you're bouncing off the walls and a cheerleader—that could actually be a detriment to the room if it's inauthentic or inappropriate for the needs of the room in that moment. The 10 is the *quality* of presence you bring into the room. The xylophone and its various anchor points serve as a tool to tap into different levels of vibration that will fill your field and enable you to shift your Vibrational Presence as it serves.

Directing Energy Intentionally

Another version of how the Energetic Xylophone plays out is in range of energy and vibration. Just because you're at a 10 on the xylophone doesn't mean you're going to be a contribution to the room. You can walk in full of energy and completely tank the room because you aren't meeting the group where they are. Likewise, you can be sad and serious and melancholy, maybe putting yourself lower on the xylophone, and you can still be a contribution to the room simply through your presence, being intentional about how you're showing up, and being in service of the room.

Carrie

Carrie was a powerhouse. Rock star. Ready to dive into *anything* at any time.

She was smart, she cared, and she had great presence. She'd walk into a room and the room would light up. People felt safe and inspired being with her. Her humor was bold, her tone right on, her heart—so good. All good. Only one little challenge . . .

As she put it, "I feel like I'm in a room with these people and trying to communicate and I'm just not 'getting them.' I feel like I lose their attention quickly or they can't absorb me, or maybe they don't want me in there. Maybe they don't respect me. It's kind of a bummer because I'm really excited to be there and I really want to help. What do you think?"

This is common, and you've likely seen it before. Most of us have had the experience of clobbering a room with unintentional mismatched energy. I flashed back years ago to walking into a room, pumped up, only to be met with quiet stares, tension, low energy. I tried harder to bring the room up, "Okay, ready?"

It didn't work, and it actually busted my rapport with this group before we even got started.

I'd failed 100 percent at *reading* the room and then *meeting* the room—leadership skills that are both energy driven. Apparently, unbeknownst to me the team had just received bad news and was understandably upset. I didn't know. At first I blamed the fact that I didn't know what had happened, but that wasn't the problem. If I'd read the energy of the room, I'd have picked up on it. I was missing three skills at that time: (1) read the room, (2) meet the room, and (3) Bottle and Point. If you put these three skills together you can shift the room, or at least have more intentional and helpful impact.

Like myself at that time, Carrie didn't have the challenge of not having enough energy or positivity; she had the challenge of channeling it intentionally.

In order for Carrie to be authentic and to have impact, she'd need to get better at reading a room and meeting the group where it was. She'd need to be able to have all her great energy, harness it, hold it, let it fill her field fully, bathe in it . . . and then very consciously and intentionally decide where and when to direct it. She needed to "Bottle and Point."

Of course she ran with this experiment.

Her meetings became a game of Bottling and Pointing.

She'd do her Five Steps to Intentional Impact before she walked in, getting really clear on her intended impact, how she wanted the group to feel, and how she'd need to Show Up.

She'd "Bubble Up" and set her own space.

And then she'd walk in.

Reading the energy of the room, she could still keep her own firecracker energy and enthusiasm, without having to lower her own vibration, and she'd "bottle up." Then she could direct her energy in the right place and "point." She found that sometimes the room needed a jolt, sometimes it need soothing, sometimes it needed empathy, sometimes it needed a kick in the pants—whatever was needed guided where she directed it. This expanded her range and became a natural part of her being.

Bottle and Point

Here's how you do it.

> **Step 1. Intend.** Before you head in, set your intentions for how you want to show up, how you want to feel, and how you want the person or group to feel. This will give you more "reserve" to pull from. (If you have time, do your Five Steps to Intentional Impact.)
>
> **Step 2. Bubble Up.** Give yourself the gift of your own space and get grounded in your own energy. Fill yourself up.
>
> **Step 3. Greet.** Once you're "in there," greet the room. This may be verbally or just energetically. Notice the energy of the room: the feel, the mood, the texture. It could be a room of 250 people or 2—it doesn't matter. Notice the vibe and presence of the people in the room. Notice how your body feels walking in the door. What's going on? Where's the energy set? If you have the luxury of doing an Energy Check live with the group (more in Chapter 13), this will help too, but you won't necessarily have that.
>
> **Step 4. Tune in.** Notice the difference, if there is one, between where your energy is and the energy of the room. And breathe. Hold your space. Give yourself a little flash of gratitude for having your own energetic field and let your energy fill your space up even more.
>
> **Step 5. Decide:** What do you want to do? What will best serve the room? Where do you want to direct your energy? How much? How fast? How loud? What's the tone, the pacing, the presence you need to bring to meet this room (or person) where they're at? Lead from there.

You'll find that when you Bottle and Point, you'll have more facility with being able to shift the conversation, shift the energy, and at a minimum create the space for safety to do what needs to be done.

Intention and Regard

As you know, intention is at the core of IEP work. How you intend to show up, what you intend to get done, how you intend to feel, what you intend for others, it's all key to setting intentions and to making what you want to have happen, happen. Intention is one of your super powers. You can feel the energy of intention in people. You'll likely experience it as deliberateness, hunger, drive, or simply just organized presence. You can also feel the energy of regard in people.

How you regard another human being speaks volumes. This regard impacts your Vibrational Energy and Presence; it also impacts your Relational Energy. People feel it. And they respond to it, or they resist it.

Consider someone who gives you feedback, but the entire time, despite gorgeously crafted feedback, you feel the energy of blame, judgment, or apathy—so you don't take the potentially valuable feedback to heart, you don't get the benefit, and now you just feel bad.

Consider the client you don't like but are able to give a great presentation to. You do it beautifully, but underneath that presentation is your distaste and poor regard for the client. And unsurprisingly (or maybe you are surprised because you think you covered up your distaste with your brilliant presentation) the client doesn't hire you again.

Consider the acknowledgment you might give your partner, but infused in the acknowledgment is the energy of manipulation, frustration, or simple superiority. You're really hoping your partner will do whatever you want him or her to if you "throw him or her this bone." Of course, your partner doesn't.

These are all examples of actions and behaviors well done, but the vibrational energy, presence, and regard underneath them is abysmal.

How do you regard others? That feedback meeting you're going into, the presentation you're about to give—how do you *see* the people? Do you see them as human beings? Do you see them as inferior or superior to you? Or simply not important, just not worth your time? Just notice. (For more on this, please check out the Arbinger Institute's body of work as mentioned in Chapter 8. Their work is inviting and brilliant in helping people get to the core of "regard.")

However you regard the humans in your life, it's showing up in your presence. No doubt about it. Identify your regard, breathe into it, get curious with it, do your own work, shift it, and you're on your way.

Got it? At the end of the day, we're really talking about your "vibe." How you regard people impacts your vibe. Your Mental and Emotional Energy impacts your vibe. Your physical state impacts your vibe. And your vibe speaks louder than anything you say or do. Of course this all plays big in Relational Energy, which is where we're headed next, but first, let's lock it in.

Reflection: Putting IEP into Practice

Optimizing Your External IEP

Quadrant 3: Vibrational Energy

- Reflecting on this chapter, please list your top three areas that could use some extra TLC and optimization.
- How do you see these things impacting your leadership?
- What's the cost?

- What would the benefit be of partnering with them to make them better?
- What are your next three steps?

Exercise: Energetic Xylophone

Build your Energetic Xylophone right here. What are your top three easy "go-tos" for state shifting?

CHAPTER 10

Showing Up for Success

Relational Energy

Your presence is your impact. You set the tone.

Just as food coloring blends into water, your presence blends into everything you say and do. Just as you have your own unique energetic field and presence, so do your relationships. Your IEP plays a big role in the energy of your relationships. You set the tone.

Your fourth quadrant for nourishing and optimizing your Energetic Presence is depicted in Figure 10.1. Part of your "external energy" (just as in the third quadrant, Vibrational Energy), you can't control how people experience you, but you can certainly set yourself up to show up well.

At this point, your vibrational presence is awake and intentional and you have a stronger internal foundation. How you Show Up in your relationships is stronger from working the IEP principles we've explored to this point. I intentionally put the Relationship Quadrant as the last one because it's so beautifully supported by the others. This doesn't mean you have to work

FIGURE 10.1   Quadrant 4: Relational Energy

them linearly—there's tremendous value in jumping directly into Relational Energy. That said, keep in mind that I've found that when people are clear and clean in the Essential You and the first three quadrants, Relational Energy is easier to identify and navigate.

When it comes to relationships, practicing your IEP in all four quadrants and focusing on being in service of the relationship (or the person you're in a relationship with) is the most effective and purest way to create genuine shifts. Relational Energy, like everything else, is contagious, creating ripple effects from you, to your peers, to your team, to the organizational culture, to your clients, to what your company puts out in the world. It's big. So do your personal work on this one. The questions to ask yourself here are: "Are you setting yourself and your relationships up for success by the way you show up? Do your relationships contribute to or detract from your energetic field? Do your relationships inspire you to be bigger, stronger, better? How are you creating the quality of dynamics of your relationships?"

And, of course, who the heck are you hanging out with? These are all questions you can tap into to optimize Relational Energy. In this chapter we'll dive into some of the most common things that get in the way of positive Relational Energy and what to do about them.

Awareness and Desire

Every relationship you're in qualifies as a "system"—your team, your organizational culture, your partnerships, your marriage, family relationships, and friendships. Each system has its own energy and dynamics. I find that 70 percent of leadership is in awareness and presence. The same goes for looking at the energy of each of your relationships.

Consider the relationships you have that make you soar; you feel amazing when you leave a conversation, you feel seen. Feel into *that* energy. Now consider the relationships that when they pop up on caller ID, or they walk into the room, you feel your heart sink. Feel into *that* energy.

While you have people who have that impact on you, you are also that person for others. Which person are you?

The energy and dynamics of relationships are happening all the time. There's the "elephant in the room" energy you and your team all work around. There's the "thing" you can't or won't say to your spouse or best friend or colleague because it's a hot spot and you don't want to aggravate it. There's the hurt feeling "scar tissue" from the event that happened three years ago that you override and ignore in service of keeping the peace. There's the truth your team doesn't want to speak to because it's a hard truth, and it will mean making hard decisions. So you continue to work around it, creating tension and wasting energy.

You likely see these types of dynamics in your organization every day. They're contagious and expensive. And the energy of these relationships has huge impact.

Remedying the challenging relationships starts with *awareness* and the *desire* to make it better. To address this by going straight to "fixing the culture" is a spiritual bypass. We want to address this individually, and in the different relationships that make up the culture. As always, it starts with you.

If the relationship is rocking it, name it, thank it, and let your person or team know how much it means to you. Give it extra love and gratitude. Saying, "Thank you, I see you, you're rad" creates ripple effects—the good stuff is contagious.

If the relationship is *not* rocking it, it needs more TLC, more intention, more truth telling and self-reflection, and ultimately more work. This will be as easy or as difficult as you *choose* to make it.

Naming It and the Purple Pen

The simple intention of wanting to make a relationship better and to clean up anything that's getting in the way can do wonders. Naming it, putting it on the table, even if you don't know exactly what it is, is even more powerful.

"Hey Mary, I'm noticing that we seem to have something going on, and I'm making up all sorts of stuff as to what it might be, but I realize I'm not sure. I value our relationship, and I'd like to clean it up so we can be better together. Did I do something? Have I missed something? Am I making stuff up?" And then Mary can step in.

Or, perhaps more specific, *"Hey, Claire, I have this sense I may have made a mess with you at last week's meeting. I'd love to clean it up."* Or it might be *"You know, this was the impact of X for me, and I don't think it was your intention. Can we explore?"* And sometimes naming it is just bold: *"We messed up. I let you down. We failed. Let's fix it."*

These scenarios work best when the IEP is clean, present, and "in service of."

Sometimes, in naming it, you'll be way off. You've both been making stuff up, gathering allies to be on Team Mary and Team

Claire, feeling stressed, losing sleep, focusing on drama versus creating great results, and you're both wrong.

This is where the "Purple Pen" comes in handy.

Mary and Claire, figuratively or literally, stand together side by side (not face to face), "put the problem right in front of them" (not between them), and get curious. In this case, the "pen" is the problem.

"So, Mary," says Claire, *"I think this pen is green."*

"What??" says Mary, *"Oh, no way, this pen is blue."*

Ah—Mary and Claire aren't on the same page with what the actual problem is.

Now that they've identified they're not even clear on what the problem is, they'll either explore and work it out together, or they'll call in John, who will share that *"Actually, the pen is purple."*

Make sure you're partnered on figuring out what the actual problem is and what you're bumping up against. Once you have alignment, you can work toward resolution.

I've seen relationships and teams exhaust themselves because they weren't clear on what the problem was and instead were caught up in assumptions, being right, and navigating drama.

Curiosity, care, and looking for the positive intent all work well here, as does the intention of collaboration and ease. Of course it only works if you've truly decided to have a good relationship.

The Decision of a Relationship

TJ and Margaret, business partners for three years, had a contentious relationship. Everyone knew about it and worked around them. No one could do anything about it. They worked "fine" together, but you could feel their tense energy in the room. They went for coffee, talked about it, apologized, tried to take accountability for their prospective flaws, even had a bit of mediation to support them. Each time they did it, they were "better" for a bit, but ultimately, they'd take three steps forward and two back.

Both were frustrated. But both also got some mileage out of the drama. Every time they fell backward, one or both of them felt validated for how difficult it was to be in that relationship and how hard they were trying to be a "good partner."

One day I asked Margaret if she *wanted* to have a good relationship with TJ. *Yes.* Had she decided to have it? *Of course!*

Really?

We sat for a bit, and then she said, "Actually, no."

She'd "decided" on the surface, had even done everything "right"—but energetically, deep down, no, she hadn't decided.

Jackpot. Much as I discuss in Chapter 8, the power of decision is not only a game changer for making things happen, it's a game changer for relationships.

Margaret realized she could change the relationship, *if* she chose to.

There were a couple of indicators that let her know she hadn't fully energetically decided. Checking in with her body and intuition was a good first start. She felt her misalignment. This awareness alone could have been plenty to create a shift, but as she continued to explore, she found more.

She realized she'd gotten a bit of a charge out of "trying so hard" and TJ "just not getting it." She'd been more committed to being "right" than collaborating with him and even meeting him halfway on accountability. And she'd watched for him to do things wrong. A snide glance, a delayed response, a forgotten agreement—all of these were proof and validation for how impossible he was. She'd subconsciously looked for him to mess up.

Any of these could have been worked through beautifully if she'd truly decided to have a good relationship, but until now, she'd been fed well by not making that decision. Now that she saw it, she had a choice to make.

So she decided to have a great relationship with him. She didn't even tell him. *She just decided.* Her focus shifted to being a good partner and having his back. This shift—being contagious—rippled out. She looked for him to do things well and to show up as a good partner. She let go of being right and looking for struggle. When stuff would hit the fan, instead of taking it as evidence of his incompetence, she looked for how to make it right together. She relaxed. He, not even knowing what was up, sensed the shift, and he relaxed. Their relational energy shifted. He still doesn't know what happened.

It's worth noting here the cultural implications of *deciding* on people and relationships. Organizations energetically decide about people all the time. They decide that person is awesome, or that person is not going to cut it. This decision is contagious.

Even without saying a word, people feel it and catch on. That decision often becomes a self-fulfilling prophecy. The decision is validated often only by the energy that was projected upon the person they made the decision about. (For example, *"This guy is a dope"* leads to people seeing this guy as a dope, treating this guy as a dope, and now this guy, responding to this, obediently becomes even more of a dope.) This works for the positive as well—*"We've decided we believe in this guy and he's worth supporting"* gets energetically communicated as well, and lo and behold, he becomes a rock star.

What are you deciding? What have you decided? Make sure your decisions support you and your culture.

Using Jealousy as Fuel

Even with the best of intentions and decisions in place, every once in a while the "green-eyed monster" is going to be at the core of your relationship and cultural woes. It may be subtle, or it may hit you like a ton of bricks. But it will be there.

Jealousy gets a bad rap. But you can use it as fuel.

Max was charged up about one of his colleagues, *"He's doing this thing, it's taken off, everyone loves him. I think he's a jerk. I've tried to work with him, but he's arrogant."*

He went on, *"People think he's so great, he's all fired up about the stuff he's working on, but he's not even that good."*

Deeper. *"When I look at what I'm doing, I feel like it's not enough. What* am *I doing? I should be further along in my career, I'm trying really hard. I feel like I can't keep up—it's just not fair."*

Bingo.

Underneath jealousy is often what I call the "Tender Agenda"— the thing that's really on your mind but that you cover with anger, irritation, or judgment toward others. If you sort through jealousy, or any negative emotion, there is something to be learned.

But often people have an emotion and either they bypass it and "get over it," or instead of using it and learning from it, they make someone else "wrong" for creating that emotion in them.

What if instead of ignoring, repressing, and writing off people and emotions, we partnered with the emotion to find the magic?

What if the negative emotion is just a wake-up call to have you show up bigger to "go get it"?

Jealousy can be a gift. It often points you toward something you really want in your life or career but haven't created yet, or maybe weren't even aware of in the first place.

It can point you toward the realization that you need to show up bigger, get into action, and get out of your comfort zone.

Jealousy as a Cultural Contagion

Jealousy is at play in cultural issues all the time: *"They" get to do this, "they" won't let me do that, "they" are shining brighter than I am.* It's a contagious energy that results in scarcity thinking, competition, and withholding in collaboration.

In organizational dynamics, leaders often think jealousy is bad; they try to alleviate it or eliminate it altogether.

But they could use it for good.

What if when you sensed jealousy in your organization, you used that emotion to help get clear on what was next? What if you used the wisdom that can come from jealousy to leapfrog and tap into purpose and desire? *"Ah! This is what I really want, here's what I'm going to need to do to make it happen."*

Nemesis Love

Sometimes, despite great intentions and decisions, doing your work around what's triggering you, and cleaning it all up as much as you can, you're going to have a "nemesis," or someone who's just making your life miserable.

If you have this special someone in your life, thank him or her. He or she is going to teach you a lot. Your work here might just be to love this person up, get in there, get curious, own what you want, and work your way through it. If the idea of "nemesis love" pushes a button, this could be the most valuable part of this book for you.

Get curious. Find gratitude. Be generous. And, of course, be accountable.

You can't help but shift perspective and broaden your awareness when you come from curiosity, gratitude, or generosity. And you can't be victimized by "them" if you take accountability and look at how you *might* be contributing to the situation.

Imagine . . . your colleague does something that hits you wrong. It stings. You flare. You have choices here. Whatever you choose, trust that it will be contagious.

If you choose curiosity, consider . . . What was the positive intent behind his actions? What might you be misunderstanding? Why would he do or say that thing? What's he struggling with?

What might he not know that led him to do or say that? Curiosity creates space. When you feel yourself shut down or flare up, get curious.

If you choose gratitude, consider . . . What can you appreciate about this person? What can you be grateful for? What's the gift of your relationship (good, bad, or ugly)? How is he, and even this thing that's just happened, a gift in your life? That gift might simply be that he's pointing you toward a value or boundary that's really important to you, or he's pointing you to something that's a big *no* for you.

If you choose generosity, consider . . . How can you contribute here? It's likely going to be the last thing you want to do when you're all hot and charged up, but it's good stuff. How can you contribute to making this situation better? How can you contribute to helping the conversation move forward more peacefully and powerfully? How can you contribute to this guy?

And in your accountability, consider . . . How did you contribute to this situation? Did you not make a request? Did you let poor treatment go on for too long without holding a boundary? Are you getting a bit of mileage out of suffering this difficult relationship? Just notice. Anything you can claim will give you power and perspective. Stand up for yourself *and* make sure you're clean and clear as to where you might have played into the creation of said nemesis.

Who You Surround Yourself With

In the Physical and Environmental Quadrant we talked about how the people you surround yourself with impact who you're becoming. If you hang out with mission-driven people who take care of themselves, you're more likely to be mission driven and taking fine care of yourself. Hang out with people who complain, focus on the "ick," and don't take care of themselves, and you're more likely to follow suit.

Matt

Matt was struggling with his career. He was overwhelmed, busy, trying to do a lot, and not clear on where he was going. The three guys he hung out with most at work were not helping. The four of them would wrap up work, go for beers, and talk about how busy they were and how difficult it was to work in the organization. Their conversations centered on the company's shortcomings and gossip about who wasn't "cutting it." For extra flavor, they'd exchange stories about their difficult relationships.

Nowhere in the conversation was a focus on what they were working toward, what impact they wanted to have, how they could contribute to shifting things that weren't working, or even what they appreciated about anything. These meet-ups were not only unproductive, they made things worse.

Matt noticed that he'd become more critical of the people he worked with and the culture for no reason except that his friends were contagious and he was on a slippery slope. When he was in the office, instead of focusing on results and impact, he found himself gathering stories of "they" (again, contagious). His struggle and feeling of being overwhelmed increased.

He didn't like it. So he did two things: He worked on his awareness and ownership of how he was showing up and contributing to all of it (because he was), and he worked on his Posse.

His awareness of this information alone was an instant energy and accountability shifter and put his attention on the right places. He did parts of the Essential You work (Chapter 6), unpacked values and purpose, played with vision, and then gave himself a bit of an IEP reboot to clear his own field.

Then he looked at his Posse. The five people Matt was spending the most time with were his wife (good), his best friend (good), and the three guys on his team (not great).

Matt was terrified he was going to have to ditch his friends. But, fortunately, this wasn't about ditching them; this was about awareness—awareness of how he was showing up, and awareness

159

of the impact of the people in his circle. From here, he could decide what to do. He could bail on these coworkers, or he could own up and energetically invite his Posse to step into a higher plane.

Over a short series of meet-ups, he unfolded his plan. First, he stopped colluding and piling on with the negative conversations. (This didn't stop them, but it helped.) Then, he talked about things he appreciated. (That had impact.) Then he declined beers one night, saying that he wanted to work late and explore some next steps on a project. (That was new.) No one got "ditched," shamed, made wrong, or rejected—Matt simply took account-ability for his behavior, held his space, and modeled what he wanted.

One night he got together with his guys.

"I've been thinking. I'm noticing when we get together, we're focusing on a lot of what's not working and how irritating and hard it all is. I'd love to focus on something else, like, what solutions do we see, what's inspiring about the work we're doing, where do we all want to be a year from now, and how can we support each other in getting there? What do you think?"

Two out of three of them were inspired. One of them, Adam, was not. He thought Matt was being self-righteous and dove right back into the dark side. The other two were intrigued and climbed on.

These four guys are still on the same team, but the dynamics have shifted. The conversations are different. Adam doesn't go out with them as much anymore; he's found new friends.

Your Posse

Consider the five people you spend the most time with, person-ally and professionally.

Think of this core group of people as your "Posse." You might have a personal Posse, a professional Posse, a parenting Posse, a little of all of the above. Your mission? Make sure your Posse is optimized and nurtured as much as possible.

There are two things to consider here: First, who you're spending your time with. Simply put, are these people a good influence on who you're becoming, or not? And second, you have an opportunity to be incredibly intentional and craft a professional Posse or advisory board. Whom do you want to surround yourself with?

So consider your current Posse, the people you hang out with. Do you share common values? Do they support and nurture who you are becoming? Do you feel seen, championed, challenged, and inspired? Do they believe in you and hold a large "container" for you to step into? Are these relationships life giving? If yes, fantastic! Nurture them and make sure you're contributing to them as well.

And if not, it's okay—you've got some work to do.

Crafting an Intentional Posse

Your Posse can be as big or as little as you wish it to be. I've found that five people—a close group of five—is really powerful.

I'll often give clients the assignment of creating their own personal and professional advisory board. I want them to be incredibly conscious and intentional about whom they surround themselves with.

Every time they do this, it results in accelerated growth as well as more internal peace, support, and connection. This can be one of the most valuable things they can do for their careers.

The right Posse will provide you with the following benefits:

- **Community.** Being a leader or an entrepreneur (or parent, teacher, human being, etc.) can be a very lonely venture; don't do it alone.

- **Support.** Having people around you to champion what you're up to and believe in you will be priceless, providing wisdom and courage when you need it most.
- **Possibility.** Seeing what your peers and colleagues do, how they generate, how they lead, and how they navigate obstacles exposes you to new possibilities, ideas, and opportunities you won't see alone.
- **Growth.** Having people in your sphere committed to your being your best and rocking it with your work in the world provides you with great feedback and acceleration.
- **Care.** Your Posse will love and support you through thick and thin. They'll see you as big, even when you're falling down. And they'll catch you, help you brush yourself off, and then send you back out there to get bigger.

You're not going for easy and cozy here. You want safety and connection and care, but truly, if you have the right Posse that is truly helping you grow and become into the next level, you will sometimes be uncomfortable.

It's powerful if you can form a group that keeps all five of you together and has you meet regularly in a structured manner, a mastermind of sorts. If that's not possible, you can still have your Posse; it just becomes more of a one-on-one arrangement. Be clear about why you want this person in your Posse, make clean requests, and make sure that you contribute back to him or her. Having a Posse is a two-way street of reciprocity; the power is in connection, complementing skill sets, and learning together.

You don't have to ditch anyone. Make requests, give feedback, invite your people to step in, proactively search out people you want to surround yourself with. And with this new level of intention, enjoy as you find people serendipitously start to drift in and out of your sphere.

Ready? Who you're becoming depends on it.

Reflection: Putting IEP into Practice

Optimizing Your External IEP

Quadrant 4: Relational Energy

- Reflecting on this chapter, list your top three areas that could use some extra TLC and optimization.
- How do you see these things impacting your leadership? What's the cost?
- What would the benefit be of partnering with them to make them better?
- What are your next three steps?

Exercises

Awareness and Core Relationships

List your core relationships on a piece of paper. Rate them 0–10 (0 is bad, 10 rocks). Notice if you've truly decided to shift or optimize. If yes, identify a next step.

Naming It and Purple Pens

Identify a relationship that's out of whack. Name the issue from your perspective and then from the other person's. What's the next step?

Using Jealousy as Fuel

Identify someone whom you're jealous of. Notice whether you're coming from the mindset of scarcity (there's not enough, I hate this person) or abundance (there's plenty, I'm happy for this person). Look for the "Tender Agenda": What is this telling you that you want? How will you have to show up to make it happen? It may be one little next step, or it may be a huge leap.

Loving Up Your Nemesis

1. What's got you so riled up?
2. What do you love about your "nemesis"? What can you learn from him or her?
3. How are you like your nemesis? What's it like for this person to have *you* in *his or her* life? How might you be making the situation worse?
4. What's your next step?

Build Your Dream Posse

Who do you want your five people to be? They can already be in your Posse, or they may be new. Get clear on who, why, and what . . . and then ask them. Make sure to contribute to them as well!

PART 3

SHOWING UP FOR OTHERS

You lead others.

Getting your IEP set up right helps you serve others better—much like on an airplane, in case of emergency, passengers are advised to put their own oxygen masks on first before taking care of others. With a stronger energetic field and ability to create more intentional impact, you can "pay it forward" and play an even bigger game.

Now that we've built your own personal internal foundation, we shift our focus to leading and Showing Up for others. You'll notice that the tone, pacing, and depth of personal exploration shifts throughout the rest of the book. This is because you now have a deeper understanding of how to optimize your own IEP so that you can be better for your team, for your culture, and for your organization.

Your highest leverage *leadership skills* have been sprinkled throughout this entire book in stories and in exercises for you to apply personally for yourself and in your relationships. These include skills like presence (at all levels), defining and recognizing values, clarifying purpose, creating your energetic field, creating intentional impact, and many more. These are all translatable to business and culture. In fact, the more you've grasped and embodied them for yourself as a leader, the more powerful they'll become as you use them in service of your organization and culture. Bottom line, any leadership skill will be more impactful when you're showing up and your intention, energy, and presence are in alignment.

The chapters in Part 3, "Showing Up for Others," focus on optimizing leadership and cultural mindsets, exercising your leadership skills through your presence, and creating life-enhancing meetings and agreements. I'll offer you additional essential leadership skills in this section that need to be applied individually and culturally. In Chapter 11, we'll hit up navigating "busy," burnout, and being overwhelmed, choosing one's story, accountability, and being in service of others. In Chapter 12 we dive into growing people, holding large (or small) "containers," giving and receiving feedback, and setting your people up for success (even if that means you're letting them go). Finally, in Chapter 13 we dive into leading effective and energizing meetings, creating agreements as a team, and optimizing virtual presence.

By the time we get to Part 4, you'll already be logistically and intuitively doing much of what is needed to Show Up for culture.

For the rest of this book, bring *all of it* with you. Bring you, your team, your contagions, your fate, your IEP, your super powers, and everything you've learned. We have more good work to do—in service of others.

CHAPTER 11

Out-Gracing "Busy" and Burnout, and Other Leadership Optimizers

There is no finish line. Keep driving and enjoy the ride.

At this point in the book, if you've been applying some of these principles and tools to your life, you're likely experiencing the effects of showing up more intentionally. You may be finding that you've become more in tune to your people's IEP, to what's happening in your culture, and to how you can contribute to shifting and optimizing it. You're also likely doing a great job at modeling and paying forward what you've learned for yourself. Your presence and newfound super powers have likely followed you home from work, and you may be seeing ripple effects beyond your professional life.

Any minute now, you're going to think your IEP is "handled." You'll want to put it on the back burner. You might start getting hyperfocused on others and their IEP and how you can contribute to them. This is common; just remember to stay the course. This is a lifelong practice, so keep working your stuff. Your leadership and culture will be all the better for it.

In this chapter we're taking a quick pause to hit up some extra-special leadership optimizers. These optimizers contribute to creating an even more beautifully contagious culture. For every personal leadership principle I share, there's a cultural version. For example, do you have a *culture of busy? A culture of overwhelm? A culture of "they" or victimhood or storytelling? A culture of "I have no choice"? Or the opposite?* Address these opportunities first for yourself, and your culture will be more bound to follow suit.

The results of applying these principles will be highly contagious and can have a huge impact on your team. I recommend that you work this chapter *with* your team or a colleague. Since these are high leverage game changers and are highly contagious, the more the merrier.

Let's start with one I'm sure you'll recognize.

Deglamorizing "Busy," a Leadership Energy Sucker

"How are you?"

"Busy! Busy! Busy! Oh! Sooo busy!"

The download of self-importance and overwhelm follows.

Next time you hear someone say this, pay close attention to your energetic state. Feel the lifeblood drain out of you. Spirit gone. Compelled to stay in the conversation no more.

Rarely does someone say, *"You know what? Life's full, and I'm good. What's up?"*

Busy. It's killing culture. And you want to talk about contagious? Oh boy.

What's your organization's relationship with busy?

We buy into this idea of being busy like it's a badge of honor. We've turned busy into the new "fine." We compete for who's the busiest of us all. We infect with busy.

Often we don't even realize we've been infected until someone, in a moment of care, presence, and curiosity, asks, *"Really? What are you so busy with?"* And then we get to get present to what really is.

Having a lot going on is not going to go away. You likely have more to do than ever. And you can do it—maybe even *all* of it. It's not about being *less busy*; it's about being more intentional.

John had learned to use "busy" as a default to avoid saying no to people. If he was "busy" enough, even if he projected the energy of busy, they wouldn't ask, and he wouldn't disappoint them.

Carolyn used "busy" as social currency with her busy colleagues. She'd so adopted this stance that she'd forgotten why. Her team had started to avoid her because they didn't want to burden her.

Organization "Gusto" had created a culture of "busy." The people were exhausted by it, wanted to change it, but continued to emanate it. Why? The executives unintentionally underlined the value of busy—starting with their own complaints—in a way that made busy an unspoken expectation. If you were *truly doing your job*, you were busy. And if you weren't busy and overwhelmed, then you must not care as much or have enough to do. The executives were exhausted as well. Nobody loved being busy. It had become a habit. They wondered why people were burning out and jumping ship.

It's rarely inspiring or energizing listening to someone talk about how busy he or she is.

Yet it's one of the most common conversations in our culture today.

Busy doesn't make us better, more important, or more awesome. It just makes us exhausted. And exhausting. It's an epidemic.

But never fear, because you already have the antidote. The antidote to "busy" is presence and intention.

Your first ninja move is to ditch "busy" and replace it with something delicious.

You can start with low-hanging fruit: Notice your language, and your relationship with "busy." If it doesn't inspire you, change it.

Perhaps you're "richly scheduled," "well used," "on purpose," "on track," "on fire." Find language that serves you and your physiology and creates more mental space. Everything else will follow suit.

Personalize "busy," and treat her as a friend. She's here to inform you of when you're feeling overwhelmed, when you need a reboot, when you need to be more intentional, and when you need to reevaluate if you're spending your time and leveraging yourself as optimally as possible.

Busy can teach you to ask for help, to delegate, and to intend better.

Christine was overwhelmed with the energy of busy. She evaluated her time and found that if she cut her meetings to 50 minutes, she'd get seven hours a week of her life back. Done.

Dan coordinated with his partner to divvy up what meetings they *truly* each needed to be in, along with a system of keeping each other up to date on the most important details. This opened up a lot of space.

"Team Grace" made an agreement not to use the word *busy* for one month. This created new levels of awareness and intention, shifting the energy of the team. They also stopped competing for "busy." The badge of busy lost its appeal.

None of these are huge things; little shifts go a long way.

The Seven Factors of Burnout—They're Not What You Think

Burnout usually gets attributed to people working too hard or too long. But that's just a piece of the puzzle. There are bigger factors at play, and all of them are addressable.

Jack was burned out. He was exhausted and lacking "oomph." He needed a break, and there was no break in sight.

Six months ago he'd been on fire, humming along.

Here's the rub. In the work he was doing six months ago, he'd been traveling more, was more "richly scheduled," and had more demands on his time and leadership. Long days and weeks were his life, and his self-care practice was minimal. But at that time, he felt alive and on purpose.

The last project ended, and it was wildly successful. He came off that and moved straight into something new—with less than a week of "downshift time."

The project he was on now was not using him well, he didn't care much about the content, and he didn't feel connected to his team.

The irony was that he now had more time, no travel, was leaving work at normal hours and able to get home to his family, and had time for consistent workouts again. This was all good, but now he felt burned out.

Sure burnout comes from not taking care of yourself and burning the candle at both ends, but, more often, burnout comes from one or a combination of the following:

1. Lack of connection to purpose in what one's working on, resulting in boredom, disinterest, and apathy
2. Lack of connection to people; not feeling seen or cared for, and not having a shared sense of purpose
3. Lack of celebration, appreciation, and acknowledgment for wins (little or big)

4. Lack of safety for vulnerability, creative expression, and authenticity
5. Lack of a reboot and recovery between projects or trips
6. Lack of empowerment and accountability, and not being and feeling well used
7. Lack of intention, presence, and therefore boundaries

These are all ingredients for burnout, each one exponentially increasing the chances that you, or one of your people, will need to do a significant reboot. These components alone are powerful, but put them all together and you have an epic recipe for disaster: burnout, attrition, and losing your best people.

On the flip side, reverse these, attend to them, be intentional in making sure they're happening for you and your organization, and you have a recipe for magic.

Sure, sometimes we have to do something that isn't totally in alignment with our bliss for a project: the business needs it, your people need it, or you have to "keep the lights on." No problem. Don't make it a habit, be conscious of what's what, and make sure to address the other factors so that you make that project or task as life giving and rewarding as possible.

Your next ninja move is to practice your IEP (the stronger this is, the easier it is to recover from anything that even sniffs of burnout), work your Essential You, intentionally match your purpose and values with what the organization or task needs, and codesign your relationships. And if you see your people approaching burnout, don't just write it off to working hard. Get curious—what else is going on? Get in there.

Being the Author of Your Life: What Role Do You Play?

Jackie was a team lead on a project. Her team was great but the project was tough and the team members were struggling—a lot. So Jackie saved the day. She sent the team home on time, took care of business, and worked until three in the morning. The project got to the next phase. This happened a few more times. Each time, Jackie "Showed Up."

Jackie was a hero. Or so she thought.

At her team's meeting, Jackie ~~whined~~ shared: *"I'm working until three in the morning, I have more e-mail than I can handle, I can't make all these meetings, and I'm taking care of a ton of stuff that I really shouldn't be doing. It's been really hard."* Her team sat in silence. The team members had their own stories to go with Jackie's.

In their eyes, Jackie swooped in constantly, disempowered her team, made them feel inadequate, and then turned into a martyr at sunrise. It didn't feel good.

Let's play it out. Jackie had unintentionally written herself into the role of *hero* in that *no one else could do the job but her.* (But the team was actually highly capable—the team members just needed clear communication and direction.) She then quickly stepped into the role of *perpetrator*, energetically blaming and judging the team for not being capable, and taking opportunities away from team members. (They felt small, judged, and robbed of experience.) And then she fell *victim* to being overwhelmed. Because she was so overwhelmed, she was often late to meetings, didn't respond to e-mail, and left meetings early. Her team members felt she thought she was more important than all of them.

By not speaking up, the team members had played right into the cycle with their own story, making the cycle even stronger.

The fix was simple. The team members gave feedback (with care) and then made requests. Jackie owned her impact and made amends. Then they all redesigned agreements for how they'd move forward together. There was no drama. Just accountability.

We write ourselves into roles every day. We do it on our teams, in interpersonal relationships, with clients, you name it.

These roles are contagious and pervasive in organizational culture. Perhaps you recognize them:

There's the *Victim* who holds that "it's totally out of his control, it's not his fault, everything happens to him, and he can't do anything about it."

There's the *Hero* who holds that she's "going to save the day, they need her, they can't function with out her, she'll handle it for them, she's the only one who can do it."

There's the *Perpetrator* who holds that "they're bad, they're to blame, they're incompetent, they're irrelevant, they owe me, who cares how they feel!"

And then there's *taking ownership*, which means coming to the situation clean and clear with requests and an intention to lead, show up, and contribute to helping things go well.

The trick is to be aware of when we're playing a role and why, and then to be accountable for shifting it to something more productive. If you can identify your role and the energy that goes with it, you can clean it up.

Dancing with Overwhelm—Best Practices for Intending, Designing, and Honoring

If your team or organization is suffering from *feeling overwhelmed*, it's likely that what you're really experiencing is a lack of presence, intention, boundaries, and clear agreements.

Being overwhelmed is contagious. And it usually leads to chaos. If not stopped, it infuses itself into organizational energy until no one even knows how it got started. The group now has a culture of chaos and overwhelm and everyone feels it. Finding a foothold would be nice, doing a reboot would be great, but often they're too busy and overwhelmed to see where they could even pause to do that.

If this is you, do it now. Don't make it hard. I've found that making even small tweaks in how a team addresses things can provide a reboot that reaches far.

Let's take two teams with different leadership and cultural agreements. Everyone on each team is brilliant, has great intentions, and wants to do good work.

The difference between the two teams boils down to the following:

- How they hold their boundaries
- How they teach people to treat them
- How they take accountability for showing up and honoring agreements
- How they design their time together and apart

TEAM PAIN AND CHAOS	TEAM PRODUCTIVITY AND GRACE
Late for meetings, no reboot time, everything is back-to-back. They spend the first 15 to 20 minutes of each meeting "getting there" and then updating one another on what they missed.	Meetings always start on time (often intentionally at 10 minutes after the hour so everyone can be there and have space). No updates; if someone is late, they keep rolling and the late person catches up later.
Unnecessary players in meetings. People not sure why they are there. Often partners on the same project will both be there when only one is needed.	Intentional about who needs to be in what meeting and why, and how to bring people up to speed. Partners divide and conquer to cover more ground rather than double up.
No intentional outcomes. Often they aren't even sure what the meeting is about until they get in there.	Intentional outcomes set for meetings ahead of time with a request for everyone to come in ready to rock with whatever prep needed.
E-mails are responded to in the middle of the night. It's not uncommon for them to be interacting at 11 p.m. and on weekends.	The team agreed: no e-mails late at night, and if someone *must* e-mail, it doesn't mean he or she will get a response that night or weekend. It will wait.
This team goes back-to-back on projects with no downtime in between. Work comes first. One person hasn't vacationed in two years.	Team members have a life and take vacation. They honor one another's personal lives, encourage time off, and celebrate "out-of-office" autoresponders indicating reboots.

TEAM PAIN AND CHAOS	TEAM PRODUCTIVITY AND GRACE
This team has doughnuts and pastries brought in for breakfast, and chips and popcorn and processed breakfast/snack bars for snacks in the afternoon.	This team plans meals and snacks intentionally for fuel. Instead of pastries, sodas, and processed wares, they offer whole foods, nuts, fruits, vegetables, water, teas, and good chocolate (because everyone needs chocolate).
This team reacts to "fires." Drama rolls. They are deep in the "victim/hero/perpetrator" cycle, and all are getting some good mileage out of it.	This team reacts to fires with intention and communication. It also has a commitment to accountability and no drama but rather "accurate reporting" so they can get the situation assessed and act accordingly.
Team members talk a lot about how busy they are and how hard it is.	Team members talk a lot about impact and results and how much they enjoy working together.

Which team can you relate to? Which choices do you want to bring to your team?

All of these cultural behaviors are contagious. It all starts with you and your team. Be intentional about how you want to show up together and what kind of guidelines and cultural agreements you want to honor.

Being "In Service Of"—Your Most Important Super Power

Are you "in service of"? Check yourself, check your intentions, check your heart. Whatever you're about to do, say, or be, is it "in service of"? If it is, you're golden; if it's not, breathe . . . you have some work to do.

That difficult feedback you have to give, the employee you have to let go, the uncomfortable conversation you have to have with your child, the decision your team needs to make—if it's in service of the bigger picture, the other person, or the greater good, your energy and presence will convey it, and the other person or people involved will be better able to receive it.

On the flip side, if it's not "in service of," it will make things worse.

For example, in a meeting, is the intention behind your input, words, or actions to serve the room? Or is it about making yourself look good and seem important? You can be in a room, say nothing, and be completely in service of—if that's what the room needs. You can also be in a room, say a million brilliant things, and be of zero service—if your intention was crooked.

Do you want to be in service of, or do you want to be brilliant? You can have both, but not if your agenda is driven by the intention to "look good." Serve.

Reflection: Putting IEP into Practice

Let's optimize! By yourself, with a colleague, or with your team, explore the following issues:

Busy. What's your relationship with "busy"? Mark it out here, and do whatever you need to do to feel at peace with this word and this stance.

Burnout. Of the seven factors of burnout, which ones are you strongest in (meaning you're solid and feeling great), and which are you shakiest on? What's the smallest thing you can do to strengthen that factor?

Authoring. What's your story? Consider a painful scenario or relationship in your life right now and reflect on what role you're playing in it. What are you getting out of it? What do you want? What do you need? What's the littlest thing you can do to shift it in a more accountable and healthy direction? It might just be a request. Or an apology.

Overwhelmed! Looking back at this section, consider things that are happening right now that you do not love. What boundaries will serve you here? What can you clarify or put in place to support you? The sky's the limit. Intuition works well here.

Being in service of. Consider a conversation you want or need to have that is creating anxiety in your system: Is it in service of? Connect with service and contribution, lead from there, and let your system relax.

Your choice. What else in this chapter seems important to you? Run with it.

CHAPTER 12

Growing Leaders

It's All About the "Container"

How many leaders have you created?
And how many are better than you?

Your job is not just to lead, it's to make others around you even better leaders than you are. Besides looking at a leader's skills, presence, and "hunger," I assess leadership on three primary things: (1) How do you make people feel? *Do they follow you because they want to or because they have to?* (2) How effective are you at forwarding the vision and purpose of your charter? *Are you and your people creating positive impact?* (3) How many leaders are you creating and activating? *Are you catalyzing and nurturing growth, setting people up to be even more successful than yourself?*

In today's business climate, doing good work, growing cool companies, and putting good stuff out into the world is not enough anymore. In order to lead, innovate, and create impact like we want and need to, we have to be growing even stronger and more purpose-driven leaders.

This means you have a tremendous opportunity—and responsibility—to Show Up, create space, and hold a powerful "container of potential" for the leaders you lead. With strong and positive intent, solid energy and self-care, and an authentic and powerful presence to lead people with, people will want to follow you. You can grow them.

The size of the container you hold for the people you lead is a big deal. It influences who they become, what they believe, what they'll step into, and how they'll show up.

What's the size of the container you hold for your people? What's the size of the container you hold for yourself?

When people in your organization know that you believe in them, you're committed to helping them grow, and you hold large containers for them, they thrive. And it gets paid forward fast. Containers, and even the intention behind them, create magic.

Cody and Rose

Cody was a business leader in innovation. He was hungry, caring, loving, and smart. Rose was a partner in the firm. They worked on a project together for six months. Cody learned a ton, and so did Rose. At the end of the six months together—despite the project requiring a ton of energy, bandwidth, and travel—Cody was energized and inspired. Why? He'd been "well used," seen for who he was, led well, and asked to step into bigger and bigger "containers" throughout the project. At the end of the project Rose had a new goal for him.

"Cody, I see what you've done with this project. I see how you show up, and I see there's more for you. Would you be interested in stepping into a new role guiding and directing others in this work? We could really use your leadership here."

Cody was shocked. He'd been inspired working with Rose and the rest of the team. He'd had a great experience. He'd felt stretched—possibly to his edge. And he hadn't seen this coming. This would be a leap from what he thought was possible at this point in his career and leadership. But because of the way Rose spoke to him, with a presence of belief and championing, he believed he could do it.

Cody's focus shifted. Just the year before he'd been focused on exploring his next career move. Now, he was focused on the impact he wanted to have, how to serve best in his new role, and how to pay Rose's leadership and inspiration forward with *his* team.

There is another powerful element in this story.

When Cody told his colleagues about this invitation to step up, their responses surprised him. His teammate responded with jealousy—*"Cool. Why didn't they ask me? Aren't you nervous about what'll happen if you blow it?"* When he told his boss about this invitation, his boss responded with concern—*"That's a big deal. Are you sure you're up for it?"* Cody's reaction? Deflation. He didn't feel seen, believed in, or supported by his colleagues or his boss. He shared, *"I don't know how to work with people who don't believe in me."*

Holding Containers

Rose held a large container for Cody. His colleagues did not. Rose was *impact* focused, coming from presence, abundance, and belief. Cody's colleagues were more internally and self-focused, coming from scarcity, jealousy, and fear. Note that this is not because his colleagues were bad people—they just responded from a personal space, not a leadership space. The way they held Cody in this opportunity was more reflective of where they were internally than it was about Cody or his abilities. But the impact it had on Cody was powerful.

This happens a lot. On the receiving end, you see something for yourself, step in, and claim it, and then someone either disregards it or champions it. The response may be verbal or it may be energetic, but the impact is similar. If it's positive, you may elevate and gain momentum. And if it's not, you may deflate and halt.

This is where it's especially helpful to have your Posse in place, your energetic bubble intact, and your connection with self solid. All three of these pieces are essential components in helping us hold our space so we don't get knocked over by others' beliefs in us—positive or negative.

It's also valuable to consider intrinsic versus extrinsic motivation. Where is your drive coming from? Is it extrinsic, coming from wanting a promotion or a raise or an ego boost or approval? Or is it intrinsic, coming from wanting to do well, to create impact, to thrive? The more intrinsic our motivation, the easier it can be to hold our space when extrinsic forces present. (This doesn't mean extrinsic motivation is bad—it's just useful to know where you stand.)

From a leadership perspective, it's important to recognize that not only can holding a small container happen *to* us; we *do this* to others as well—most often completely unintentionally. How we show up as a leader in this special moment, in holding that container, will so often make the difference between whether that person stumbles or soars. We have a beautiful opportunity—and responsibility—to be a contribution.

Checking Your Container

Rarely does someone set out to knock the wind out of a person's sails or to hold a small container for someone else. When it does happen, there are usually a couple of things at play. If you can identify what's going on for you, you can shift it and serve.

1. A lack of presence in the moment. I'm just not tuned in to what this guy is telling me and how important it is to him. Maybe I'm really "busy."
2. This news triggers some emotion or vulnerability in me, and I can't see past myself to truly see and support him.

3. I'm unable to hold a large container for myself, especially in this domain, so it's really hard for me to do that for anyone else.

4. I just don't like this guy, but I don't know what to do with him—I can't get rid of him, and I can't promote him.

5. I really don't think this is the right move for this person at this time. This will not serve him.

With the first four issues, there's good work to do there. Get present, explore your triggers, own your challenge with your own container, and own your resistance to this guy. You don't have to do any of this alone; you can work through it responsibly with a partner.

But let's look at number five. Let's say you don't believe that this is the right move for the person at this time. You can still create space for him to share what's up. You can still support him, have that conversation in a way that is caring and curious, *and* be open to having your mind changed.

The main question becomes, what's the size of the container you *truly* hold for him? And are you *willing* to be surprised and expand that container?

The Container

So let's look at the container. When I use this language people often think of it as something restrictive or confining. Held intentionally and with purpose, it's not. I've found it provides two things: energetic fuel and more space to grow safely.

The container is what you believe is possible for this person (people often can't see it for themselves) and the energetic space of potential you hold for him or her to step into. It's an intention.

When you point people to what you see is possible, and the intention you hold for them, they get the gift of seeing their reflection in your eyes. They're seeing what you believe they're capable of.

You don't even have to tell them you're doing it. Energetically holding this space of possibility and authentic belief enhances your regard and presence, which in turn shifts their experience of you. More important, this can shift what they believe is possible for themselves.

You've likely been in the conversation or had the colleague or friend whose belief and intention and support you could feel. It's almost palpable; such a person sees you as even bigger and more capable than you can see yourself.

Here are some examples of bigger containers:

- Mark writes an article, and his editor says she believes he can rock that article into a meaningful book.
- Eileen gives a talk, and her colleague says she needs to be on the TED stage with that message.
- Henry is leading a case at his firm (he loses the case but plays well), and his boss tells him he'd like to see him in partnership in 18 months.
- Margaret wants to be a mom, and her mother-in-law *holds* that she'll be an incredible parent. (Margaret *feels* this.)

Some of these are big, some small; some you'd tell the person, some you'd just hold energetically. The game is to hold it, and hold it well.

The size of the container you hold for yourself has a huge impact on what you can see for another human being. Jealousy, assumptions, beliefs, your Essential You, your IEP, your relationships—these all impact the size of the container you can hold for yourself. So if you notice you're having a hard time holding a container of potential for someone else, do your own work. Likewise, if you're having a hard time holding a container for yourself, hold one for someone else. Nine times out of ten, when we're struggling with our own stuff, the best way to move through it is to go and contribute to another human being.

Creating Trust—and Leaders—Through Feedback

You want your colleague to do really well. And there are a couple of things she needs to get better at in order to move to that next level.

Or, your employee or colleague has a habit that's wrecking him. It may be a bit uncomfortable to speak with him about it, but it's essential to his success.

In both of these cases, you hold great power and responsibility to contribute. The feedback you have for your colleagues could change their lives, accelerate their careers, and save them a ton of time, pain, and energy.

This is where you as leader *getting comfortable with discomfort* and *being in service of* come in handy. This is also where you as leader provide helpful feedback.

Feedback done well, and truly in service of another human being, is a gift. Ironically, while people think giving hard feedback is what creates tension, it's actually *not giving* it, withholding truth and wisdom, that creates the tension. Giving good solid productive feedback creates trust—and better leaders.

It's commonly thought that these conversations are *only* for negative or critical feedback, giving feedback even more of a bad rap. But positive feedback and acknowledgment are equally as important for growing leaders as the "tough" stuff. They're contagious accelerators. Make sure you have a healthy balance of both.

Giving Productive Feedback

Now that you've decided to give feedback, how are you going to do it?

Step 1: Prepare Ahead of Time. Who is this person? Connect with the person's heart, empathize, consider what he or she is up against and dreaming about.

Step 2: What *Is* the Feedback? Be clear about it. Here's a little equation I like to use to craft powerful and clean feedback.

Intention for Service + **Quality Feedback and** *Good IEP* ➜ ☺

The intention has to be "in service of."
Quality feedback includes:

- Context and when it happened.
- What you observed happened.
- The impact you perceived.
- The next thing you think the person could do instead to make it better.

And then stick around. Stay and be responsible for your impact and the feedback you just gave, and help the person craft a plan. Remember, good IEP is mandatory.

Working your feedback through this equation will help keep it clean. If you can't get it through the equation—you find you have no "next," you don't want to be responsible for doing it well, you can't be in service of, or it's just personal feedback—don't give it.

This being said, if you truly feel it will be "in service of," but you just don't have it "right," you can still give the person the feedback—if you're clean and intentional about it. For example, if it's a personal preference, own that.

Step 3: Set It Up. Lay the groundwork so you have a good place to have this discussion in.

1. Ask the person for permission to give the feedback.
2. Set the space for the discussion; make sure the Environmental IEP is right.
3. Be intentional about the timing; if either of you is not in the right state to give and receive feedback, hold off. Wait for the right time (but not too long).

Step 4: Dive in with Good IEP. Since you've prepared and set the space, it's up to you, your IEP, and your leadership prowess to take it home now.

- Your *intention* should be to serve, care, contribute, and help the person feel seen and inspired.
- Your *energy* should be clean, clear, and helpful.
- Your *presence* should be there with the person, right now. Your physical presence should be helpful, engaged, and facing him or her. (The rules of presence apply on the phone or on video too.)

And then you work with whatever comes up in that conversation.

Cultivating a Culture of Feedback

In a perfect world this all comes together beautifully, and the person feels inspired, cared for, and excited to move forward. But sometimes it doesn't go down that way. And this is when you'll be called to a new level of leadership.

Cultivating a culture of open feedback requires safety and modeling. If people resist, you'll want to tap into care and curiosity about what's going on for them. Be present with them—don't get defensive. As a leader, your job is to "walk with them" to work through this together.

On the flip side, one of the best ways to support your people in being open and comfortable with feedback is to model asking for it, receiving it well, and putting it into action. *Proactively* ask for feedback. Let them see you and your peers actively exchanging feedback. Make it safe for people to give it directly to you. Be helpful to them in laying it out. And above all else, receive it with grace and gratitude. (The good stuff too—"receiving" is a leadership skill.)

Done well, and with the intention of service, feedback is one of your greatest super powers. Feedback can come in the moment with intentional shorthand if you have rapport and an agreement with your colleague to deliver it that way. It can come more formally, like an annual review. It can come in the format of the formula offered above for specific event feedback or growth feedback. And it can come in the form of the Container Game, which I've included in the Reflections section for this chapter. However it comes, use it in a way that is authentic to you, use it consistently, and use it to acknowledge the great stuff too.

When You Just Can't

When you can't hold an honest large container for another human being—especially someone you're responsible for leading, growing, and nurturing—it's time to get help. First, check yourself as leader. Explore if and what you might personally be bumping up against with this person, what you're feeling triggered by, and where you're making assumptions. And then explore where it's clean—where you really *can't* see the bigger container and it's *not* personal.

If you can't hold the container, and you're not willing or able to have your mind changed or help get a person to a better place, you're not the right leader for him or her. It's time to move the person to another business lead, find another creative solution in service of everyone, or exit the person out of the company.

Holding a Large Container *and* Letting Them Go

George wasn't working out at his company. Despite shifting his role several times, putting him on a performance plan, and having several conversations to help him be more successful, it wasn't happening. His business lead, John, was frustrated and found that when he tried to play the Container Game, he couldn't see anything bigger for him.

John went to his leadership team for a last check-in. *"Do we want to move him again in his role?"* (No.) *"Does anyone want to take over as his business lead?"* (No.) *"Have we done all we can to set him up for success?"* (Yes.)

It wasn't that George wasn't trying; he was. Everyone liked him. But it wasn't a fit, and trying to make him fit into something that didn't work was making everyone, including George, miserable. They had to let him go.

John set his intentions for impact before he and George sat down for the final conversation. In setting his intentions he played the Container Game, but not for George *in* the company, but rather *outside* it. He found he could authentically hold that George was a good guy; he'd taught them a lot, he had potential and a good heart. He also believed that George would thrive in the right position with the right culture—they just didn't have that position or culture at this organization. The conversation John had with George was caring, compassionate, and powerful. George left with his dignity and feeling supported. And John completed with his integrity and feeling clean.

Everyone deserves to have a large container held for him or her—regardless of the person's skill level, prowess, presence, and impact. If you truly can't do that for your people, do the right thing by finding the best way to be in service of them.

Reflection: Putting IEP into Practice

The Container Game

Play this game for yourself and for your people. It also works well for kids, partners, friends, and your boss. (Bosses and mentors need containers too.) You can do this solo, you can do it with a partner, or you can do it with your team. Just do it. First, ask the following questions:

What's possible for this person?
Who is this person becoming?
What's getting in his or her way?
What's the next littlest step the person can take to move forward?
How can I support him or her?

And ask yourself:

How big is the container I hold for myself?

Sometimes people may not want what you hold for them, so it's helpful to be aware of what they hold for themselves. Have the person you're working with answer these questions as well. Then have an exploratory conversation around what's next.

CHAPTER 13

Life-Giving Engagements, Agreements, and Meetings

Your meetings and agreements are where culture shows up.

Your mindset is solid, you're growing leaders, you're holding containers left and right, you're creating a culture of feedback. And now you have a meeting. It might be with 2 people or 200. It may be for two minutes or 12 hours. And you might be with them *in* the room or a thousand miles away doing it virtually. Either way there will be impact. Your quality of IEP, how well you prepare, and the agreements you create together will determine what kind of impact you make and how much your team loves your meetings, or not.

What is your culture's relationship with meetings?

Do you walk away from meetings feeling clearer, more connected, and more inspired than you were when you walked in? Or do you feel ambiguous, frustrated, and validated that meetings are a big waste of time?

In the land of impact and culture, meetings and live engagements are some of the most powerful places we have to ensure that our interactions are life giving, forward moving, and, at a minimum, meaningful. Even a two-minute encounter can have positive ripple effects on someone else's day—*if* it's done intentionally and you Show Up.

How do you make every interaction you have with people a positive contribution to their day, leaving them feeling better than when you started? And how do you set your meeting up so that even if it's rough, people still feel honored and connected? The short answer to both of these questions? Work your IEP, be intentional, and use the content in this chapter to build upon the tools you've learned in the first part of this book.

Showing up for Meeting Success

You have a Google Hangout scheduled with your team to discuss next quarter's strategy. You rush in from the last meeting. You're aware you're late and hope everyone else is too. But they're all there waiting for you.

Three things go instantly wrong that set you on the slippery slope for a bad meeting before it's even started.

1. You're late. And you're the team lead.
2. You're not exactly "present," and it shows. Your brain is still processing the last meeting you came out of.
3. The background on your Hangout is dim, messy, and distracting.

You now have a very loose "container." I call the meeting space a "container" as well; instead of growing individuals and expanding potential, we're creating a safe space for a group of people to do their best work together. The way the container is set up and held throughout the meeting is foundational for ensuring it supports your team's energy and outcomes.

Then your meeting gets worse.

Still distracted, and now feeling bad because you're late, you continue the Hangout meeting. And you multitask: Your eyes shoot to the upper right-hand corner of your screen, checking alerts. You check your phone. You do a quick IM—click clack. You're all over the place. You think no one notices.

But they notice.

Your presence and impact are contagious. The others on the call were originally present and in good shape. But as you get further into the meeting, they start to "check out" too. You've given them energetic carte blanche to "disappear" as well.

If you want to get anything done, you're going to need a reboot. Stop. Start over.

1. **Name it and take accountability.** Speak to the quality of the container of the call and your contribution to it. Apologize for being late and for your lack of presence.
2. **Get present.** Invite everyone to "take a minute" and get present. Do a quick *Energy Check* and *Presence Reboot* with the team. How is everyone, anyway?
3. **Intend and agree.** Revisit your agenda and the *Five Steps to Intentional Impact* to give it a breath and get everyone on the same page. Depending on how your team is set up, you might create agreements here or just revisit old agreements to presence them. (More on this later.)

This process will be well worth the five to seven minutes it will take you to get aligned. Now you can begin.

Meeting Glory

If meetings are an energy sucker in your organization, you can change that. There is no need for a huge overhaul or organization-wide initiative. If you're not happy about how meetings are unfolding, or people hate them, you can change it.

In this scenario, we took a virtual meeting going bad and flipped it. But how do you "get in front of it" so your meetings start out right in the first place?

Laying the Foundation for a Solid Life-Giving Meeting

In order to create the best meeting possible you'll need to consider the following:

1. The logistics and venue
2. The intentions for the meeting
3. The container you and your team create
4. Safety and matters of the heart
5. And of course, how you personally show up

Logistics and Venue

You can have the best agenda and the best presence, but if the environment is weak, the food is not nourishing, or you all show up exhausted, you've lost a huge energetic opportunity.

Be intentional with your meeting space, the location, and the food you serve. If you're providing food and beverages, fuel and hydrate yourselves well throughout. Encourage people to take really good care of themselves: to sleep well beforehand, eat well during, and do whatever they need to do so they can show up fully. Consider whether the meeting is best done on location at your office or off-site to provide a separate and safe container to connect and work in. And if this means you're traveling, give your team time to acclimate.

Clear Intentions

Before you even plan it, get clear on the why, the what, the how, and the who. What do you want to get out of this meeting? Who should be at it—truly? What do you need to set yourselves up for success? Use the Five Steps to Intentional Impact framework to prepare and help you set it up right. (Review Chapter 5 for the five-step framework as well as real-life examples of how to apply it.) In the meantime, here's a quick refresher:

1. What are the *outcomes* we want to create?
2. What is the *emotional impact* we want to have?
3. How will we have to *show up* to create this?
4. What will we have to *believe* to show up this way?
5. What will we have to *do* to make this all happen?

If these are addressed ahead of time as a team, not only will you have the right people in the room, you'll have energetic alignment, which means a stronger chance for people feeling good, being productive together, and saving a lot of time.

Your Logistical Container

For the actual meeting, there are logistical and energetic things you'll all want to do.

Logistical Peace and Alignment

1. **Show up on time.** Period. (Set this up in your agreements beforehand.)
2. **Create clear, unfettered space.** Give yourself the gift of full presence. Put an "out of office" autoresponder up, put your phone on "do not disturb," turn off your instant messaging and alerts—whatever will allow you the mental and emotional space to give this engagement your full attention.
3. **Set your *personal* intentions before you even get in the room, on the phone, or on screen.** Yes, you're clear as a team, but you'll want to do this personally as well. What's the impact *you* want to have? What do *you* want to get out of the event? How do you want people to experience you?

Virtual Alignment

If you're having a virtual meeting, have everyone show up 5 to 10 minutes *before* the meeting begins to create virtual alignment and make sure the following items are set up right.

1. **Connection.** Make sure your Wi-Fi and phone connections are clean.
2. **Your sound, background, and lighting.** Your environment speaks volumes; make sure it speaks well.
3. **Your camera angle and screen span.** Make sure the other participants can see you, not just your chin or your forehead or your dirty socks.

Building Blocks for Leading a Solid, Life-Giving Energizing Meeting

It's now time to dive in and bring it home with matters of the heart, creating safety for everyone to show up fully. Here are some core building blocks for your meeting. I've listed these in the order I like to do them—you can do them in whatever way feels best for you and your team.

1. **Kick it off with gratitude. Set the tone.** Connect and honor these fine humans for being there. Acknowledgments, presence, and gratitude are key.
2. **Do an Energy and Presence Check before you start**. Check everyone's Physical, Mental, and Vibrational Energies. Get the participants present in their bodies and to their impact. There's no "wrong" answer here, by the way, and you can all reboot as you please. It's your choice. (A full Energy Check is described in the Reflections Section.)
3. **Do a Presence Reboot.** If needed, and at any time throughout the meeting, use the Presence Reboot to support people in showing up and having the most impact.

4. **Revisit the intentions and outcomes for the meeting. Do a "time integrity check."** See if anything has changed or needs to be revised. Put up a "parking lot" on your whiteboard or flip chart to capture ideas as they come up and if they're out of the scope of this session. Confirm the timing of the meeting, review the timeline and agenda, and make shifts as needed.

5. **Create or revisit agreements.** What agreements are you going to need to have in the room and as a group so that you can all show up well, take risks together, and create the outcomes you've set as a team?

6. **Dig in.** Content and connection time is what you came for. With solid intentions, agreements, and presence supporting you throughout, this should be a productive and energizing space. During a long meeting—if you must have a long meeting, make sure to take breaks at least every 90 to 120 minutes.

7. **Close.** Compile all actions and next steps so everyone knows what they're being counted on for and where to focus. Do not leave without this. Just as you led your meeting intentionally, you want to close it intentionally.

Creating Life-Giving, Innovation-Supporting Agreements

Agreements are one of the most powerful things you can do as a team, as a culture, as an organization, even personally as a couple. The point of having agreements set up is so that everyone can show up well, be safe, and do their best work together.

When a team has clean agreements in place, it creates a safe container to play in. You might think of these agreements as codes of conduct or rules of engagement or simply guardrails. Either way, when you do this well, you've set the tone for truth telling, clean engagement, and optimal productivity.

There are several types of agreements. Cultural agreements are implicit in your cultural values. Organizational or relational agreements are generally set as a location, as a team, or in partnership and are operating at all times. And special agreements may be set for a specific meeting or conversation. In the guidelines above, I'm speaking to setting up agreements for a specific meeting, but if you already have team agreements in place, those can be your general operating guidelines.

Creating General Agreements

Team agreements will often change over time. The agreements are generally a reflection of what the team values and also any challenges or tensions the team may be experiencing. For example if the team creates an agreement for *direct engagement*, it means no talking behind one another's backs and taking issues to one another directly. If a team has an agreement of *time integrity*, it may be because they all value timeliness, or often, it's because lateness has been an issue in the organization.

To create agreements, do it with your team. Start an open conversation. *"What are some of the agreements we'd love to have in place to support us in being our best together?"* Whether it's for your location, team, or relationship in general, or just for a specific meeting or point in time, the idea is the same. Dive in.

Here are some of my favorite agreements.

- Direct engagement—no colluding or gossip, no back channels, go direct.
- Be present—be here *now.*
- Phones off—create space for being present.
- Time integrity—be on time.
- Be prepared—do your work, do your five steps.
- Ask for what you want—don't suffer silently.
- Turn complaints into requests or suggests—contribute to the solution.
- Be responsible for your own experience—own it.
- Be responsible for the energy you bring into the room—own it.
- Let go of looking good—be "in service of" rather than "brilliant."

- Be prepared to be surprised—look for new learning.
- Assume good—posit positive intent.
- Get curious—seek to understand.
- No judgment—make it safe.
- Be helpful—help, don't criticize.
- Be in service of—check your intentions.
- Ask for help—celebrate needing help, don't make it wrong.
- Timeouts are okay—take care of yourself.
- It's okay to be a "4"—when your energy is low or you're having a bad day, be kind to yourself.
- Be responsible for your impact—even if you're a "4," take care of yourself, ask for help, be responsible for how you show up.

There are literally hundreds of agreements you can play with. Work with your team to figure out which ones will serve you most. And then revisit them. I think of agreements as living partners to help us connect, learn, and do our best work together. Agreements grow as you do.

When Agreements Go off the Rails

Sometimes agreements get broken. Not often, but it happens. In my experience, 70 percent of the time it's unintentional, 15 percent of the time it's because the agreement wasn't really an agreement, 10 percent of the time it's because it needs to be redesigned—it was unrealistic, and 5 percent of the time someone just messed up. When this happens, stay away from blame and let curiosity kick the conversation off. Come back to your agreements as a team.

1. Acknowledge that the agreement was breached. Name it.
2. Get curious as to why. Is the agreement not necessary? Unreasonable? Was there not really agreement? Does it need to be changed?
3. Make amends. Yes, the agreement got breached, it was intentional or it wasn't, here's what we're going to do about it.

4. Redesign as necessary.

5. Reboot and move forward.

The way you lead your meetings and the way you create your agreements for showing up well together has a huge impact on the energetic presence of your team, your culture, and even how your clients experience you. The clearer and more intentional this is, the better you'll all be.

When It Gets Sticky, Address Things Directly

Despite great intentions, a thoughtful container, solid agreements, and everyone showing up the best they can, stuff is going to come up—especially if you have a team that's up to big things. This is an opportunity to work through issues and build trust. Here are three high leverage skills to try in service of keeping your meeting productive and energized.

1. **Name it.** If the meeting starts to get off track, or presence gets fuzzy, or you stumble upon an "elephant" in the room, call it out. Maybe there's something big happening on the team or in your organization—speak to it. Don't work around it.

2. **Allow for curiosity and safety in service of.** If there's tension, or if you hit an obstacle, address it with heart. You might have a code word as a team for when there is a problem. You might get curious: "Hmmm, . . . what just happened here?" You might take a timeout. No blaming. Care, get curious, use all of your personal IEP skills that you've been so beautifully working on, and move through—together.

3. **Stay high vibe.** That guy sinking the energy in the room? Don't get sucked in. The lowest vibration in the room will win unless you're good at holding your presence and energetic state. So hold your space. Ask the person a question that will

invite him to "step up" a bit. If it continues, and you're not able to shift it by modeling and giving the room space, get curious. *What's going on for him? Does he need anything?* This will often open up space and shift the state. If it doesn't, take a break and address it with him privately and directly. That conversation, done well, will consist of curiosity, feed-back, and/or a request.

Play with the ideas and tools in this chapter. Use your super powers of curiosity, connection, and care to lead through any challenges. And create the space for a meeting that will leave people feeling honored, valued, and well used. Your most life-giving meeting might just be an intention and agreement away.

Reflection: Putting IEP into Practice

Whether you're in person or online, set yourself up for life-giving engagements.

The Current State of Your Meetings

- How would you rate the quality of your meetings right now?
- What's your culture's relationship with meetings?
- Identify three things you can do differently, personally and as a team or organization, to optimize your meetings.

Your Team Agreements

Go back through the agreements section and create agreements with your team.

You can jump right in as a group. Or, you can start this pri-vately, just for yourself: *What would you love to see?* An interest-ing experiment is to have everyone create their dream agreements separately, and then share back with the group what they'd like to have. The themes that come up will tell you a lot and will help you create healthy agreements as a group.

Create a general team agreements list, and then, if needed, additional specific agreements for different meetings. The more you do it, the more natural it will become.

Energy Check

To bring everyone present, check in at the beginning of the meeting and rate the following from 0 to 10:

- What's your Physical Energy? How do you feel?
- What's your Mental Energy? How present are you mentally?
- What's your Vibrational Energy? What's the vibe or energy you're bringing to this meeting?
- What's the Collective Group Energy? How does it feel in here?

Shift whatever needs to shift and dive in. If needed, move into a more formal Presence Reboot (see Chapter 4).

IEP Meeting Assessment

Rate the quality of your meeting from 0 to 10 based on the following factors:

1. We were all prepared for the meeting.
2. We all showed up and finished on time.
3. Our space or virtual platform supported the energy and quality of the meeting.
4. We did an Energy Check. The team average for energy was ____ at the beginning of the meeting, and ____ at the end.
5. We did a time and agenda check.

6. We connected as humans.
7. We practiced IEP and were intentional about how we showed up.
8. We crafted and agreed upon next steps.
9. We are glad that we had this meeting.
10. We're looking forward to the next one.

These ratings will serve as an assessment tool to point you back to your highest leverage areas for improvement as well as get you collaboratively focused on the right things. The goal of course is to continuously improve the quality of your meetings.

Here's to your next meeting!

PART 4

SHOWING UP FOR CULTURE

You create the culture.

So you've got a strong foundation, you're Showing Up for yourself, you're Showing Up for others, you have some serious leadership wisdom, you're rocking and rolling, and if you've been doing this work with your team—you have an even stronger team. At this point in the book, whether you realize it or not, you've already done a lot of work to shift culture. Whether it's your organizational culture, your family culture, or the culture you carry within yourself, you are the culture. You emanate the culture wherever you go.

We spent the first half of this book giving you tools to show up well and unlock more of your own leadership potential. For the rest of the book, we'll apply what you've learned to culture.

The word *culture* gets tossed around a lot. When I think about culture, I look at it on two levels: what the company is doing for culture and who leaders are being. The doing can include things like how leaders manage schedules, do training and feedback, set up their environment, manage HR policies, conduct onboarding and exiting processes, and lead meetings, how much fun they have, how they support connection, what kind of food and perks they have in place. What you do is important. All of it provides structure and support for your culture.

But when I look at the heart of culture, which is what's creating the positive energy, I'm even more interested in the being and the intention behind it all. I've found this carries way more weight and is a higher leverage area to focus on: (1) the being, who they're being in creating and emanating the culture, and (2) the intention, where they're coming from and how they want people to feel and be impacted.

The being includes things like organizational values and purpose and how a leader shares them (or not). It also can include how each person shows up as a leader, how leaders regard one another, how they deal with conflict or challenges, and whether they assume good in one another or the worst. The being is in how every single person (especially you) Shows Up.

You can feel the being in the energy of the culture as well: the energy you feel when you get off the elevator or walk in the front door, the amount of care, comfort, and integrity you feel just in sitting in the room. The feeling people get from the vibe is the culture. The unspoken agreements and ways of being that people have with each other is the culture. How people feel is the culture.

The being trumps the doing. If an organization does all the great things listed above for the doing side of culture making—it's got the cool stuff, neat schedules, awesome hot lunches—but the being and the vibe and the intention of the culture are not clean or healthy, people won't feel safe, seen, or inspired. You're basically putting good stuff on top of an unsustainable foundation.

On the other hand you could have great being, great intention, great ways of showing up, yet not have all the fancy perks or the cultural things figured out just right, and people will feel better about the culture because they feel connected, seen, and inspired. The doing can build on top of it.

Make no mistake, the doing is essential—it provides great structure and opportunity for people to bring their best selves to the table and feel good at work. The structure can be incredibly helpful, in fact crucial. But you want to be aware of what lies beneath and the subtle nuances and energy of how that impacts how people show up.

In this section we're diving into culture. First, we're going to look at the seven things you want to consider to cultivate a healthy culture. Then we're going to look at some best practices and common pitfalls that contribute to making or breaking culture. Finally, we're going to look at how you make sure you have the right people in place. Since your people *are* your culture, we want to hire (and yes, sometimes fire) for the energetic good of all.

Ready? Let's take it up a notch and explore the Cultural "Super 7."

CHAPTER 14

Organizational Needs for a Healthy Culture

Culture requires nourishment.

Your culture is alive. And just like you, it requires nourishment and TLC. How well you *intend* to it will determine how alive and healthy it feels. What you focus on and measure will influence the results it creates. Who you are and how you show up will become a part of its DNA, fast.

Because as we all well know, we're contagious.

Culture rarely happens overnight. A conversation here, an event there, a broken agreement, a huge act of contribution, a leadership misstep, a major client win, a rumor, a great hire; good and bad cultural contagions all happen quickly, often quietly, and then build upon one another. As leader, how you celebrate and navigate will determine how quickly and solidly culture gets created, for better or for worse.

Elaine witnessed part of a conversation between Nate, a leader at the company, and Trevor, an employee. The conversation *seemed* intense. She couldn't hear all of it but sensed Trevor was upset. That night on the way home, she tells two of her colleagues what she saw without knowing the actual details. When they get home, they tell their spouses, adding a bit of color to the story. By the next morning, they've taken on Elaine's assumptions and the energy that goes with them. Now Nate is the *bad* guy. They become careful around him. The story continues to evolve and catch on. Nate can't be trusted; he was really rotten to poor Trevor. This is how gossip works.

Nate has no idea. When he sees them he senses something's off, but he doesn't know why. Contagions are spreading.

What actually happened? Trevor had taken a risk in a meeting, and it had gone badly. Nate had helped him figure out how to remedy it. Trevor *was* embarrassed and upset, but Nate was supportive. He held space for him, was honest, acknowledged his risk taking, helped him mine the learning, and then held Trevor accountable to shift the situation so it was right.

Later that afternoon, Trevor, who'd had a great experience of Nate, told two of his colleagues. He shared he'd felt horrible, he'd been nervous to talk about it, and the conversation was amazing! He'd felt seen, supported, able, and held accountable—not coddled. They'd created a solution together. Now he was jazzed to climb back on and swing out again. His colleagues, inspired by Nate's leadership, told two of their colleagues he could be counted on. A different kind of contagion spread.

Here's where this went really well and kept things at a high and clean vibration. Trevor took *ownership* of what happened and *asked for help*. Nate *provided a space* for *vulnerability* and got *curious* with him. Nate came from the *energy of contribution*, asking how he could help. He held Trevor *accountable* to move forward and *show up*, holding a big *container* for him throughout. When Trevor felt bad, Nate *didn't coddle* him or hold him small, he *heard* him out, *provided safe space*, was *compassionate*, *celebrated* him for taking a risk (even though he failed), and held him as *capable* to clean it up—and get back up.

Though this could have gone badly, it worked out. This was partially because this organization had a lot of what we're going to talk about in this chapter. But it was also because of how Nate and Trevor showed up. Despite Elaine and her colleagues getting hooked into a bit of drama, because of the way Nate and Trevor navigated the situation, and because of Nate's integrity, strong Bubble, and solid leadership presence, the drama fizzled out. All is well.

In this chapter I'll share seven components for cultural health. In the reflections section, we'll look at your own organization and do an IEP Cultural Assessment. Later in Chapter 15, we'll look at some additional best practices and actions to build upon all of these.

The "Super 7" for Cultural Health

The seven core components to build trust, create positive energy, and create an environment where people can show up authentically and powerfully (at work, at home, and in any of your relationships) are:

1. Shared values, vision, and purpose
2. The intention of contribution and service
3. Safety to show up, speak the truth, and take risks
4. Curiosity and vulnerability
5. Accountability and ownership
6. Reciprocity
7. Conscious measurement and rewards

For best results, all of these should be infused with good personal IEP.

Shared Values, Vision, and Purpose

In Chapter 6 we explored your personal vision, values, and purpose. Those principles and exercises transfer directly to organizational work and exploring the core of your culture.

Shared values, a meaningful "why," and an inspiring vision will save time, energy, and money in building a positively contagious culture. Having these in place will also help you attract the right talent from the beginning.

Your *vision* guides you on where you're all going together; it provides leadership and direction, an inspiring opportunity for collaboration, and something for everyone to hook into and say, "Yes. Let's go there!" The vision may not always be crisp or perfectly clear, and in some cases people choose to opt out of formal visioning. That's okay. If you have values and purpose grounded, when the vision is bumpy, ambiguous or even a bit off track, you have the heart and soul to keep you going.

The following are examples of companies using values, purpose, and vision really beautifully. These are just snippets of their stories. None of them are terribly difficult or complex, and all of them are aligned with what feels right for that organization.

IDEO, a global innovation and design firm committed to *creating positive and disproportionate impact through design*, holds the power of values and purpose core to just about everything it engages in. In a collaborative, values-driven effort, they created the "Little Book of IDEO" as a meaningful and fun way to share their culture and values, and what's important to the company in how everyone shows up together. This little book supports their people in nourishing themselves and their culture and in bringing on the right people.

IDEO's core values and purpose are infused into its talent, performance, and business processes in almost everything it does. This includes looking at how to serve and grow their people, their leadership and development plans, and their team agreements, as well as the kind of work they take on, their annual goals, and the clients and partners they engage with.

IDEO's purpose is one of the core reasons these passionate people all come together to do meaningful work. Regardless of what location they're at around the world (each location has something it's extra passionate about), as an organization they're devoted to *creating positive and disproportionate impact through design*, making the world an even better place, solving real challenges that make people's lives better, and having fun while doing it all. This is what nourishes them together. Spend five minutes in a room with any of these guys and you can feel values, purpose, and intention at play.

Zingerman's, a community of businesses in Ann Arbor, Michigan, involves all partners and employees in the visioning for the company in order to cultivate more positive energy, get everyone's best thinking, and create more ownership and participation in the vision. Ask any employee where they're going, and they'll tell you.

This organization uses visioning—with all the energy-building benefits it brings—in every element of its work. The Zingerman's 2020 vision is nine pages long and describes the future of the organization overall. Each business in the community also writes its own long-term vision (compatible of course with the 2020 vision). Additionally, visioning is used for every new project, new product, and new position that's created.

The power of visioning infuses the organization creating more great energy, remarkable customer experiences, and a lot of engaged and delighted team members running around the Zingerman's campus.

Companies like Tasty Catering, a catering business in Illinois (and sister company to many others), Nuphoriq, a marketing company in Illinois, and The Whole Brain Group, a strategic branding and marketing firm in Ann Arbor, live their purposes by having a commitment to their clients' well-being, experiences, voices, and impact in the world. These organizations also have beautiful ways of nourishing values throughout the company.

Displaying core values prominently throughout the location, referring to values at the beginning of every meeting, using them in their performance evaluations, using them for criteria in onboarding and exiting employees, sharing them with their clients, and displaying them on their marketing materials helps people stay connected, inspired, aligned, and accountable to honoring values.

Tasty Catering and Nuphoriq have even assigned numbers to their values (*"Hey! Is that number 2?"*) to make it easier for a quick recovery and a reboot if someone's out of alignment or heading to the "dark side." Whole Brain Group has built values into its "appreciation" sessions, making it really easy for people to honor and acknowledge one another for demonstrating company values and the impact they have.

Regardless of industry or vision, in all of these organizations shared purpose and common values are a huge part of what drives them, enabling them to do high-impact work while fueling their tanks and putting an extra spring in their step.

The Intention of Contribution and Service

"Is this in service of? How can I be a contributor? Is how I'm showing up helping things go better or worse?" When led through the lens of contribution and service, participation, and simple one-on-one conversations, there is a shift for the better—making gossip, back channels, and bad behavior completely unnecessary (and less rewarding).

So how do you make this happen?

First, model the behavior you want to see in others. Then, discuss intention and contribution as a team and create agreements around it. There's no one in your organization who does not want to contribute. (And if there is, check out Chapter 16 for how to exit this person with grace.)

Safety to Show Up, Speak the Truth, and Take Risks

One of the most powerful ways to energize your culture is to make it safe for people to show up fully, take risks, and even fail. The quickest way to shut it down is to do the opposite. If you say you want innovation, risk taking, and authenticity in your organization, sanction it: Make risk taking, and even failure, something to be celebrated.

If you say you have an "open door policy," keep your door open. If you say you're committed to people, commit. If you say you have a "nonhierarchal organization," behave in nonhierarchal ways. If you say your organization is "transparent," keep people posted and include them.

Reward the failures as well as the wins; acknowledge the initiative and bravery, give solid honest feedback to build from, help people capture the learning, talk beautifully about them behind their backs, and continue to believe in them. Their next failure might be your greatest learning and innovation yet.

Curiosity and Vulnerability

Creating a healthy culture requires curiosity and vulnerability. Vulnerability requires trust and space. Curiosity creates trust and space. They all work together.

Curiosity, one of your most powerful resource states, creates connection, builds rapport, and broadens horizons all at the same time. The state of curiosity provides the receiver the gift of inquiry and reflection. It provides the giver the gift of more information and understanding. And it provides both with new awareness.

It also creates space in the face of tension, confusion, fear, and vulnerability. Have curiosity about *What's just happened? What was the positive intent? What's going on with this person? How can I help?* These are all questions that open up more possibilities and create space for vulnerability.

In order for people to tell the truth about who they are, to connect intimately, and to tap into their deepest levels of creativity,

215

they have to have that space for vulnerability. Dr. Brené Brown,[1] a researcher on vulnerability whose work has had a profound impact in the areas of vulnerability, creativity, leadership, innovation, and so much more (she is one of my most favorite people in the world), says that *"Vulnerability is the birthplace of innovation, creativity, and change."* She also says it's the birthplace of love, belonging, courage, authenticity, and so much more. It's a big deal.

As a leader, one of the most powerful things you can do to create more safety and connection is to share your own vulnerability. To share your brilliant, flawed, beautifully imperfect, scared, tender, awesome self.

I recently witnessed a leadership team, meeting with their community about a significant initiative, tell their people that they, the leadership team, did not have it figured out—at all. They needed help. Their people had been in resistance and storytelling mode thinking leadership was keeping something from them, when in truth, leaders had felt bad that they didn't have a solution. When they named that, the room relaxed. The two "opposing" sides blended. Curiosity emerged. And the quality of intimacy, connection, and "we're in this together" amplified significantly. The conversation elevated.

Accountability and Ownership

In Chapter 11 we talked about authoring your story and taking ownership for your results. This principle has a big impact on culture. Accountability and ownership at its core boils down to this: Be responsible for your career, your choices, your behaviors, and your actions. Owning that we are the *captains of our own ships* and can *decide* how we *choose* to show up in life may be one of the greatest leadership stances we can pass on.

There are three types of accountability. *Personal accountability* takes us back to basics as mentioned above. I take responsibility for my life and the impact I'm having. I own my part in creating situations and solutions. In the extreme opposite of personal accountability, I blame everyone else and become a victim to all circumstances. Basically, I say, *"Nothing is my fault and there's nothing I can do about it."*

Both stances are contagious. My degree of accountability will often invite that level of accountability in others as well. The more accountable I am, the cleaner my leadership, and regardless of the "pickle" I'm in, the more power I have to *choose* to shift it.

Organizational role accountability takes us into the land of jobs and roles. What am I accountable for in my role, and what can I count on my peers for? My boss? Leadership? Where does the buck stop? Who owns what? When we have clear roles and everyone knows what to expect from each other, we're simply more efficient. Even more important, we've now reduced a ton of the anxiety, ambiguity, and opportunities for the slippery slope of blame and abdication that create more negative contagions.

Finally there is *leadership and behavioral accountability*, which is about how people show up. If people behave in a way that is culturally toxic, hurtful to others, or simply out of alignment with your organizational values, will they be held accountable? If someone says he or she will do something and then doesn't, then what? If someone leaves "dead bodies behind" (more coming in Chapter 16), will he or she be held accountable for this behavior, or will the organization tolerate it because the person brings in great revenue or is an essential part of the business?

These three types of accountability are happening at all times. They maybe subtle and energetic, or they may be right in your face. In any case, for *personal accountability*, your highest leverage is to model accountability, take responsibility, and lead. When you see it slipping in others, point them back to their power and what they can do about it.

For *role accountability*, sit down with your team or your boss and get clear about your role. What do you *want* to be held accountable for? What does the organization *need* you to be accountable for? Map out timelines or goal dates to support you in making accountability more solid and complete. This is not a perfect science. For some organizations, especially large ones with a lot of infrastructure, this is often clearer and very distinct with KJRs (key job responsibilities) and a solid career path mapped out. For other organizations that are smaller, more start-up oriented, highly complex, or have a high value around freedom and creativity in role creation, this may be fuzzier. Get it as clear as you can.

Finally, for *leadership and behavioral accountability*, work with your leadership. Clear agreements will help create a code of conduct with one another. Organizational values will help guide behaviors. Be clear on what you measure and reward, what's most important to you as an organization, and the behaviors that are "deal breakers" (and how you'll handle them when they occur).

Reciprocity

Conscious healthy giving and receiving are two of the most important leadership skills you can cultivate in your organization—the ability to give with generosity, openness, and care and to receive with grace, gratitude, and vulnerability. When this cycle is healthy, relational and organizational energy flows.

When the cycle is out of balance, tension, resentment, confusion, and burnout occur. An overemphasis on either is neither sustainable nor healthy. In order to fuel others and contribute from abundance, we want to be able to fuel ourselves and be fueled as well.

Reciprocity in relationships occurs in any system. It might be between two people, with a team, or with an organization as a whole.

There is *reciprocity with yourself*: the agreements you create with *you* to honor your needs and be in personal integrity.

218

There's *reciprocity with others* (your team, family, and friends): the intentions and clarity you hold for what you can be counted on for, what you want to give, what you want to count on them for, and what you want to receive. The clearer these are on both sides, the cleaner the relationship.

Finally, there's *reciprocity with your organization*: what you contribute to the organization and what the organization contributes to you. You and your employees contribute your creativity, energy, brilliance, time, and service. In exchange, the organization gives you all a paycheck, benefits, meaningful work, shared purpose, growth and mentoring, and culture to contribute with. The clearer you are about what each of you will contribute and what you want to receive, the cleaner and more powerful the reciprocity becomes.

The more everyone in your organization comes from this place, the more contagious it becomes as others feel it, are inspired by it, and are invited to step into it as well, creating a life-giving cycle.

Conscious Measurements and Rewards

The culture and impact you have today are a result of the decisions you've made, the work you've done, who you've been, and what your organization *measures* and *rewards*.

For example, if you're finding your culture has a lot of competition or that people are more focused on making money and their professional stature than they are on collaboration, quality results, and treating one another well, you want to look at how you're measuring and rewarding your team. It's possible your organization is focused more on financial outcomes, profit margins, and titles than on innovation, people, and culture.

However, if you've been prioritizing collaboration, growth, people, and impact *and* have metrics for financial success and quality results in place, you'll likely find you have more people considering how they show up, how they represent organizational values, how they impact others, and how they do their best work together, all while keeping business results in mind.

What you focus on, measure, and reward influences the behaviors, energy, and mindsets of everyone around you.

Sometimes an organization will seemingly prioritize *financial* values over *people* and *cultural* values. It's rarely because the leaders don't care. If you ask them, they'll tell you, *"Of course our people and culture are number one, but we have to stay strong financially in order to keep the doors open so we actually have a culture to nurture."* Absolutely.

Your organization needs to have a strong financial foundation—*and* you want to be aware of the *cost* of how you're making that happen.

Getting clear and intentional about what, why, and how you measure and reward will help optimize your costs. The goal is to inspire and support people to collaborate in service of creating outcomes *together* that are bigger than they could ever create *alone.* If they're rewarded on revenue and outcomes over people and impact, this won't happen. They'll likely be more concerned with winning their *own* game than they are with collaboration and helping others be successful.

The solution is simple. Keep your financial metrics *and* build in *intentional* measurements and rewards that focus on people and values. Make all metrics important, and then decide: *When you have metrics competing, what will you prioritize and how will you proceed?*

Measure the tangible stuff: the timeline, financials, pipeline, client and employee satisfaction ratings, attrition and retention, and any other business metrics you care about.

And measure the less tangible stuff. Identify criteria for what makes something culturally and holistically successful from a people and energy standpoint. You might measure impact, energy, and collaboration from a couple of angles. For example:

- How energized and positive did the team feel coming out of this experience?
- How well did they help set one another up for success?
- How many people grew from this and now have new skills?
- How many like their jobs *more* now because of this experience?
- What were their energy levels throughout?
- How many risks did they take?
- How many failures occurred? What was the learning and recovery from those failures?

If you want a healthy culture that provides the optimal playing ground for solid collaboration, peak innovation and creativity, and also bottom-line success, you want to measure and celebrate both the hard and soft skills.

What will you measure and reward? Why? This component of the "Super 7" alone could be a cultural game changer.

Putting It All Together Plus One

How are you doing with these? Where are you rocking it? What would you love more of?

Speaking of love . . . Just like IEP is infused throughout all of these, love is another best practice. Because especially in business, love conquers all. It's not always a perfect game, sometimes it hurts, and sometimes you'll be way wrong . . . but if you come from love—love of self, of one another, of the organization, of your clients, and of the work you're doing and the impact you're creating together—you will be a force.

A high-impact, energizing, positively contagious cultural force.

Reflection: Putting IEP Into Practice

IEP Cultural Assessment[2]

Have everyone on your team do this individually first. Then share results. Identify themes and next steps together.

Rate

Review each section of the "Super 7" in this chapter. Give yourself a rating (0 to 10) for how well you're doing with each component.

Reflect

1. How would you describe your organization's culture?
2. How are *you* contributing to creating the *current* culture?
3. What kind of a culture do you *want*?
4. What can you do to create *that*?
5. What are your cultural values?
6. What behaviors do you reward in your organization? Are they in alignment with your organizational values and the culture you intend to create and nurture?
7. What do you want to do more of? Less of?

Reflect and Assess (0-10)

Give yourself a rating (0 to 10) for how well you're doing with each of the following.

1. The energy and effectiveness of your meetings
2. Your general feeling of joy, hope, and inspiration when you walk in the door (*and* how you talk about work when you go home)
3. How honest—and direct—people are with one another
4. How inspired people feel to bring their best thinking and creativity to the table
5. How valued people feel by one another

6. How connected people feel to the vision and bottom line of the company
7. How inspired people feel by the organization and by the work you're all doing together
8. The quality of connection and collaboration your clients sense when they work with you
9. The level of ownership your team feels in creating culture
10. How much your team members trust one another

CHAPTER 15

Creating a Culture People *Want* to Catch

The littlest things you be and
do determine the health of your culture.

Are your culture and the work your organization is doing inspiring people to stay, grow, and create more impact in your company? Or does it have them seeking other opportunities? The answer to these questions is another strong indicator of cultural health. If people are pumped and thriving, you want to look at why, then nurture and optimize. If people are fried and leaving, you want to look at why, then heal and build.

When people are looking to unlock greater leadership potential and create more impact, at some point in the process they're also going to look at if they're in the right organization to do this. Is their organization a good fit for them in terms of their values, their purpose, and what they can contribute? And does it feel good? If it's not feeling like a good fit, it often boils down to three things: (1) the organization's not right because it's not doing work that's meaningful enough for them, (2) they don't feel they can make a difference and impact what they care most about, or (3) the culture doesn't feel good; they don't fit, they feel unappreciated or unseen, or they just feel exhausted by the dynamics.

A Tale of Six People, Two Cultures, and Contagions

Melody was a senior-level executive at her entertainment company; she'd been there for 18 years. She was a rock star. John was a senior-level executive in his banking organization as well; he'd been there for 8 years. Sara was a mid-level manager in her food and hospitality company; she'd been there for 4 years.

Despite their roles, levels, industries, and genders, these three leaders had several things in common:

- They were all responsible for leading others, leading the company, and creating results.
- They were all really good at what they did and wanted to have a bigger impact.
- They were all experiencing burnout and trying to exit their companies to find something more meaningful.

Why? They each shared a similar story. They felt they couldn't have the impact they wanted to have where they were. They'd disconnected from purpose and meaning. They didn't feel seen and appreciated as people. The culture they worked in was negative with complaints, blame, a clock-punching mentality, and high attrition.

In all of their cases, since they weren't feeling inspired themselves and were out of energetic alignment, they couldn't hold a big and inspiring container for others. They continued to cultivate the negative culture and issues they complained about. The morale and energy were low. A heavy energetic haze blanketed their teams, which just made it all worse. The cycle was in play.

Mark, Julie, and Jack

Mark was a supervisor in a tech firm; he'd been there for three months. Julie was a designer at a firm; she'd been there for six years. Jack did business development for his consultancy; he'd been there for nine years and was in a senior leadership position.

What did these three have in common?

- They were all responsible for collaborating with their teams and clients and creating results.
- They were all really good at what they did and wanted to have more impact and contribute big in their lives.
- They were all energized to learn more and be more so they could better serve the organization, create more impact, and contribute to others.

They all loved the cultures they worked in, were really proud of their tribes, and felt good about their lives and work. Their cultures were rampant with connection, curiosity, safety for taking risks, authenticity, honoring and even celebrating of differences, going the extra mile, flexibility for schedules and personal needs, contribution, and helping one another do well.

How were these three so different from the first three? The different roles and industries have nothing to do with the differences in satisfaction and purpose between these two sets of people.

The first group were all in companies that had negatively contagious leadership and cultures. The second group were all in companies that had positively contagious leadership and cultures. And they each contributed to how the culture rippled out just by how they showed up.

So what happened? Mark, Julie, and Jack continued on the path of optimization and paying it forward with their teams. Melody, John, and Sara had different work to do.

Melody realized she truly wasn't in alignment with the organization and that she didn't want to be, so she left. John realized he'd disconnected from his team, his "Posse" had disintegrated, and he felt isolated. So he decided to build stronger relationships and be more intentional. And Sara realized she'd been focusing in the wrong spots, allowing herself to get overwhelmed and disconnected from purpose. She reconnected with her core values, the company's values, and why she'd signed on with the company in the first place.

These three were lucky. Things weren't working out, and they were willing to look at why and how they were contributing to it. And then they got into action. *Often when people are not happy, they need to leave. But more often, they just need to Show Up.*

Positive and Negative Cultural Contagions

What's the difference between a company that creates positive contagions and one that creates negative contagions?

Here are five main indicators to consider:

1. The degree to which people feel they can honor their core values and pursue meaningful, purposeful work.
2. The degree to which people feel seen, heard, valued, and connected.
3. The degree to which people feel they can make an impact.
4. The degree to which they can grow and be challenged and the size of the "container" people hold for themselves, their clients, and one another.
5. The level of intentionality of every leader (and employee) in that company in how they show up and lead.

Notice that nowhere on this list is there the amount of money they make, or the hours, or the food perks. While these are important, and often indicators of a good culture, these are not primary drivers. As long as people's basic survival needs are taken care of—and they have enough to live on—the motivation is about something much larger than money and perks. It's about making a difference. It's about freedom. It's about mastering one's craft. It's about *living* a life well lived. Some of my favorite research on motivation has been shared by Daniel Pink,[1] who's done gorgeous work on exploring what *really* motivates people and shares that "autonomy, mastery, and purpose" are where it's at.

I agree. I see it every day. I'll bet you see it too. People want to contribute, they want to know their life matters, they want to get really good at stuff, they want to grow, they want freedom, and they want to have an impact. Nurture these desires—these needs—in your organization and you'll have a self-propelling culture driven by happy impact agents.

Culturally Energized or Exhausted?
Best Practices and Common Pitfalls

Building upon the five main indicators, let's look at some of the things you may be doing personally or as a team to either make your culture hum and be positively contagious, or to stall it out and be negatively contagious. Of course, since this all starts with you, I'm putting this one on you as an individual versus looking at it as your whole culture. When working with this, if you prefer, you can look through the lens of your team or your entire organization.

Here are several scenarios I see that people do with their presence and leadership that contribute to being either culturally exhausting or energizing. Some are obvious, some are subtle, but all have big impact. Where do you fall personally? How about your culture? Pick one, three, five, or ten you want to shift (personally or with your team), and dive in. These are all fixable with intention, action, and care.

EXHAUSTIVE *WHAT'S HAPPENING*	ENERGIZING *WHAT TO DO INSTEAD*
You focus on "lack"—what's *not* working. It's never enough. Whether it's the 5 people out of 100 who are having a hard time at your location, or what you don't have, but want. Perhaps your focus is on your shortcomings, or someone else's. Or how bad your culture is. Instead of leading, you're driven by pushing and forcing things to be better. You forget to honor what is, appreciate it, give it space, and acknowledge what is great. The energy of "lack" is contagious. Your people follow suit.	**Focus on what *is* working and acknowledge it.** The 95 people who are thriving? Make sure you're acknowledging them and helping them grow. That thing you want? Go after it, and be grateful for what you have. Your shortcomings, okay. Great! New places to step into. Love your strengths and what you're doing well, while you grow yourself. The one thing that guy did poorly, while he rocked the rest? Acknowledge him for who he is, what he does, and how he shows up. Your culture? What does work? Nurture it. Get grateful.
You complain about the "they," your culture, and other things that stop you from having the job, role, and environment you want.	**Pivot.** Turn complaints into requests and suggestions for making things better. Your dissatisfaction is a gift for optimization.
You wait for the culture to be created around you; you wait to be told what to do. You wait.	**Get rolling.** What's the littlest thing you can do to start moving things forward?
You collude with your peers, family, colleagues, and friends about how awful the culture is.	**Stop it.** You're feeding the fire. If you must vent, vent responsibly for a moment, and then figure out what to do about it.
You judge. When someone does something to contribute in a positive way and you think it's lame, you criticize (if only energetically), crushing spirits and creativity all around.	**Find the glow.** Your job as leader is to support, encourage, and give productive feedback. Find the thing you can build upon. Contribute. Shift it with care.
You leave no room for *your own* feedback or vulnerability. In fact there's a wall of "can't touch this" around you. You could learn so much, build your credibility, strengthen your connections, and accelerate your growth if you'd just let down that bridge over the moat.	**Time to "get naked."** Time to allow for some vulnerability and humanness. Your people and peers need to see you in your humanity. Ask for feedback, share what you're working on, being willing to say, "I don't know," and "I'm scared," or "I'm weak here." It's okay.
You can't hold or make space for the dark. When there's a problem, you instantly jump to "look at the bright side!" People feel slighted, invalidated, and that they can't trust you to lead them or hold space. You start seeing people get careful, holding back on their truths.	**Allow room for the negative.** Honor the hard stuff. Hear it. Give people space to complain and feel. Your ability to be comfortable with discomfort in someone else's pain (or your own pain) is directly related to the quality of leadership and trust you will build with that person.

EXHAUSTIVE *WHAT'S HAPPENING*	ENERGIZING *WHAT TO DO INSTEAD*
You are a Debbie Downer, always looking through the lens of what won't work and why. People pivot on their heels when they see you coming. You might even get a little bit of a charge out of this. "That's just who I am. I tell it like it is" may be your mantra.	**Be in service of.** Your knack for seeing where the problems are can be a tremendous gift used intentionally and with care. Point to what might not work, suggest solutions, and be willing to have your mind changed.
You gossip, give feedback through other people, talk behind people's backs, withhold feedback that's tough, and criticize silently.	**Direct engagement.** No gossip, give feedback directly—especially the tough stuff, go straight to the source.
You're not present. You slide into meetings and conversations still living in your previous meeting or conversation. Your body is "here," but your brain, heart, and spirit are still "there."	**Get present.** Take three minutes between meetings to do a Presence Reboot, to set your intentions, to capture any loose ends to address later, and then get "in" that room with those people.
You're chronically late, delayed, or canceling meetings. You usually have a great excuse. (If you're a leader in the company this is especially bad.)	**Practice time integrity.** Do what you say you'll do, be where you say you'll be on time. Keep your promises. If you're chronically late, redesign. Show up.
You're a victim to whatever's going on. When you're wrong, you cover it up versus owning it. You blame. There's always a reason it didn't work, and it's rarely on you.	**Own it.** Lack of accountability is an exhausting habit that is well worth breaking. Own your part, even the littlest way you made this happen.
You're not clear with people on what your requests are, what you want, or what they can count on you for.	**Be clear** in your requests, timelines, action plans, desires, and what you can be counted on for. Clarify and communicate.
Your physical presence is bad. Your body language, facial expressions, posture, and tone of voice portray you as terrifying and unapproachable, or simply miserable.	**Reboot.** This one is all about awareness and intention. The better your IEP the easier this is. Show up well. Intend your presence and impact. Recover and reboot.
You're unprepared for conversations, reviews, and meetings. You do them on the fly, leaving the person on the other side of the table feeling unseen and unimportant.	**Prepare.** This person is giving you their time, energy, and attention. This could be the most meaningful conversation of his or her life. Give it the time it deserves.
You have little rigor or intention in your meetings. People come in (or often saunter in) 5 minutes and 10 minutes late, and walk out feeling unclear about outcomes and like they've just wasted another hour of their lives.	**Create a clean agenda** before the meeting. Use the Five Steps for Intentional Impact. Demand presence, hold time integrity and rigor, and don't leave without next steps. Make that meeting count.

EXHAUSTIVE *WHAT'S HAPPENING*	ENERGIZING *WHAT TO DO INSTEAD*
You're not inspired or inspiring. You feel the need to be inspired, and you're bored. The more you focus on it, the worse it feels. You see others who inspire and wish you could too. The energy you spend in jealousy (or admiration) takes away from where you truly should be focusing—on reconnecting with yourself and leading.	**Inspiration comes from purpose.** Connect to purpose again: What's exciting to you? Why do you do the work you do? Why do your clients do the work they do? What do you want to change or make obsolete on this planet? Find a way to impact that.
It's all about you. You're in a conversation with someone and your attention is on you—how this applies to you. You're more invested in saying something brilliant than being connected. You're simply not present. (And they feel it.)	**Listen. Get curious. Get present.** If you're not listening, you're missing out. Focus your attention on the person talking. Be with them. (Bonus: If you're really attached to your idea, look for evidence you're wrong.)
You're entitled. You deserve the moon and back, people *should* respect you, you're hot stuff, maybe even too good for this task or this company or this culture.	**Get in there. Get grateful.** You may be hot stuff, but don't let that get in the way of focusing on results, leaning in, getting your hands dirty, and contributing.
You scar them. You go to give critical stretch feedback to people who've fallen down, and your feedback is simply *"Hey, this didn't work, do it differently next time."* You've given them nowhere to go, they just know they didn't do it well. You've evoked fear and deflation, not inspiration and growth.	**Point with love.** This will make the difference between them feeling inspired or deflated. Be specific as to what didn't work, the impact, and why. Give them something to do to make it better *next* time. Craft a plan and be responsible for the impact of your feedback. Check in. Did it land? Can they use it?
You feel hopeless. You're not having the impact you want to have. You're having a hard time leading your team. You're not loving your clients. It all feels impossible. You trudge through, and people feel it. This energy ripples to other areas of your life.	**Create something beautiful.** If your current situation is not ideal for the impact you want to have, find other ways in your current role to address it. Revisit agreements with your team, make requests, and ask for help.
You're focusing on the wrong things. You're more focused on whether or not you're doing a good job, excelling in your career, or looking good than you are on creating impact and results. People feel it and are uninspired.	**Focus on results and impact.** Of course!! Make sure you're having the impact you want to have and that you're on track and on path. *And* for longer-term impact, focus on results, your people, and the impact you all want to create together.

EXHAUSTIVE *WHAT'S HAPPENING*	ENERGIZING *WHAT TO DO INSTEAD*
You've disconnected from your Essential You. You've lost connection with purpose, your values, and where you even want to go with this work, leaving you in the land of ambiguity and sleepiness.	**Go "home."** Go back to the Essential You, reconnect with *why* you do this work in the first place, your core values, your dreams for where you want to go with your life, and the impact you want to have.
You're not working your IEP. You're burned out, you're not taking timeouts for self-care, you're busy and tired, you feel disconnected from family, and you're constantly on the go. You are hanging on by a thread.	**Reengage your practice.** Unfortunately for people like you who care enough about leadership to have read this far in a book like this, this area is often the easiest one to skip in service of others. Get "selfish" here. It's important.

So there you have it. Twenty-four things that you may or may not be doing to make your culture one that people want to catch. Of course, this list is not all-inclusive. What would you add? What did I miss? Capture it for yourself and hop to.

Reflection: Putting IEP into Practice

Inquiry

As a culture, how are you doing? Healthy? Thriving? Exhausted? Why? What's *one* thing you can start doing today that will contribute to optimizing or healing your culture? Consider that *one thing* personally, as a team, and as an organization.

Rate Your Five

In regard to the five indicators for making a culture hum, how are you doing? Rate yourself on a scale of 0 to 10. Identify the gaps, and put a next step here.

- The degree to which people feel they can honor their values and pursue meaningful, purposeful work.

- The degree to which people feel seen, heard, valued, and connected.
- The degree to which people feel they can make an impact.
- The degree to which people feel they can grow, and the size of the "container" people hold for themselves, their clients, and one another.
- The level of intentionality of every leader and employee in our company in how we show up and lead.

Exhausted or Energized?

Dive into the table of cultural exhausters and energizers and pick your priorities! First, pat yourself on the back for where you thrive and rock it. Then, pat yourself on the back for where you see you need some TLC.

Choose 1, 3, 5, 7, or 10 things to work on and do them individually or as a team.

CHAPTER 16

Hiring and Firing for the Energetic Good of All

Your people are your culture.
Hire them well. And release them with care.

Karen loved Mondays. Her team had been working on some great stuff, clients were happy, things were humming along. But as she drove to her office that morning, she felt a deep, sinking sense of dread. Her employee would be there, and things were tense.

She'd hired her employee four months before, had set him up with a great role, great benefits, and a solid salary and comp plan. They'd created a great environment to support their cultural IEP that included purpose-driven work, codesigned job descriptions, healthy clean food, good coffee, gym memberships, and time off. She felt happy, aligned, and really proud of what they'd created.

Only there was one problem. Her new employee wasn't the right person for the job.

Despite a great résumé, a strong desire to work in the company, and solid references—it wasn't working out. If Karen was being honest with herself, there'd been glimpses from the start, even in the interview process. However, anxious to fill the role, she'd overridden her intuition, blown off red flags, and hired him. As she got closer to the office and felt her energy sink even more, she knew she needed to decide what to do about it—and at the same time she hoped it would correct itself.

She didn't want to let her new employee go. She'd invested time, energy, and money into this guy. He was a good person. She cared about him, she wanted him to be happy, but she also cared that he did his job well. At this point, the team members had become dependent on him for just enough that losing him would set them back. She didn't want to blow it all up; she wanted to find a way to remedy it. So they got to work.

When she got into the office, they dove into refining his role. Again. As they refined his role, Karen continued to ignore her intuition and the strong sense that it just wasn't the right fit.

Three months later, she was in the same spot, only more frustrated. And now her team was in a more precarious position— and frustrated as well. She was painfully aware that she would need to let him go. Energy was being drained, and many things had gotten "stuck" in the business because of the misfit, including some of the team dynamics and even projects. Letting him go was the right thing to do for him, for the team, and for the business. She'd let it go on too long. As she looked back, she could see where she'd created this. She'd overridden her intuition from the start.

You likely have your own version of hires and fires gone beautifully and badly. You may have hired wrong, you may have hired for loyalty or potential instead of competency or drive. You may have hired in a rush, and you may have hired from hope instead of knowing. You may have fired too late, fired from frustration, and fired with or without grace. You might think that if you had known then what you know now, you'd have saved time, energy, money, and painful lessons. True. But then you wouldn't have the wisdom you have now to hire and fire well and surround yourself with energetically aligned people.

Whether you're part of a large organization or a small three-person shop, I've found that no matter how well intended, versed, or trained you are, in the land of business, hearts, and hiring no one is immune to bad yet hopeful hires and well-intended but painful fires.

As a leadership advisor, I'm often brought into a company at the outset to help companies create the culture they want and to build upon that culture with their hires. As a result of this front-row seat, I can attest that hiring and firing is one of the most important things you'll do in your organization—period. People create your culture. And every single person on your team is contagious.

In this chapter, I'll share some of the most common pitfalls and best practices I've learned in hiring and firing, and how you can get out ahead of them in your own organization to create a positively contagious culture. Every person counts.

Creating a Culture Intentionally

As with everything we've discussed, IEP plays a big role both in the hiring and exiting processes. If you're part of a small organization, or just getting started, you can lay this out foundationally. You can hire intentionally, consciously integrating IEP from the beginning so that it naturally becomes part of your culture and just who you are, saving lots of headaches.

If you're part of a large organization with an established culture and maybe even in triage mode, it's never too late to start. It could be as simple as gathering a small group of people (ideally a combination of senior leadership, talent people, and some core employees), deciding you'd like to make IEP a part of your everyday life and organization, and doing it.

Regardless of your organization's size, stature, industry, and years in business, it's never too late—or too early—to optimize the way you build your culture. How complicated it will be is up to you. Starting now, who and how you hire and exit will be essential components to creating a culture that thrives.

So let's first look at hiring for the energetic good of all.

Hiring Well

Your company is growing, you're excited, and you want to create more impact and work with people you love working with—people who'll inspire you, challenge you, make great stuff, and *be* and *do* whatever else is on your dream team list.

How do you make sure you get the right people on board?

From an IEP standpoint, there are a couple places to look. These inquiries will give you information that often gets missed in traditional hiring practices. Integrate these into your own processes, take what serves, and make it work for you.

Explore Intentions

Hire people because all hearts and intentions are in the right place—including yours.

Explore *Their* Intentions:

- Who is this person?
- What are his or her core values? Do they align with the organizational core values?
- Why do they want to work *with* and/or *for* you? This language and their frame is important.
- What gets them out of bed in the morning? What's their heartfelt connection to their profession, their "why"?

- Where do they shine? Where are their opportunities for growth?
- Are they willing to be vulnerable? Where are they preoccupied with "looking good"? Will they put the organization's results and the success of their teammates ahead of their own agenda and being a super star?

Explore *Your* Intentions:

- What do you stand for as an organization? What are your core values? Being clear on your own "why" will help you spot it in others. When you get clear on your "why," you attract the right people.
- Are you hiring them because you're desperate? You need someone in that role, now? This may be so, be conscious about it. Despite the short-term gains, this often costs more in the long run.
- Are you hiring them because they're your sibling or your close friend or brother and they need a job? Don't—unless they are hands-down the very best rock star for this position and you're going in with clean agreements and eyes wide open.
- Are you hiring them alone? Don't—get your Posse involved for hiring.
- Are you hiring them because you want them to like you or you don't want to hurt their feelings? Oh, that's sweet. Stop it.
- Are you hiring them because your boss wants you to, but red flags fly high? Look into that one. Sit down with your boss and explore the reasons.
- Are you hiring them because you're simply moving too fast, you can't do the work and take the time to make sure they're the right hire? Slow down. An ounce of proactiveness is worth 20 pounds of cleaning this up later.

Hire for the Right Reasons

Hire them because they have great energy and because they can create impact. Great energy does not mean they're bouncing off the walls and being a cheerleader or Energizer Bunny. It simply means their presence says, "I'm here, I care, let's go." Their posture and body language say they are paying attention, and they're someone you'd be proud to put in front of clients (or have in whatever role you're hiring for). They feel good, they listen, they make a contribution to the room just by showing up. And they can balance this with creating impact. They have a record of creating results.

Ideal hires should want to contribute to your organization: the cause, the clients, their peers, and you. They speak from a "we" stance rather than a "me" stance. They're driven, good at what they do—maybe not even the best, but they're committed to growth and are accountable for their impact. They listen and ask questions, they're curious; they're also focused on helping others do well too, not just themselves. They care holistically about people and culture, *and* about the bottom line and results. They want this job as a vehicle to contribute, be in service of, and create results through—*not just* because it's a stepping-stone in their careers, it's great for their ego, or the money is hot.

Crafting Questions and Exploring Visions to Get at the Goods

You can craft questions that are congruent with your organizational values and language to help determine if people are a solid fit.

For example, the question *"Tell me about something difficult you went through this year and (1) how you navigated out of it, (2) where you fell down, and (3) what you would do differently?"* is going to help you unpack their levels of resiliency, accountability (do they blame or take ownership?), and ability to learn and move.

The question *"Who's better than you at your job? And why?"* is going to get at their level of humility and connection to what they want to grow into, their willingness to give credit to others, and their inclination to come from abundance or scarcity.

And the question *"What are you most excited about this past year?"* is going to get at values, what they've been up to, and hopefully, who else they've helped be successful and grow.

In all questions and answers, pay attention to presence and congruency; you're sorting for authenticity. You're also sorting for if they're going to be a contributing, energizing, and solid match for your organization—both for your culture and their own well-being.

Visioning Exercise

Visioning is a powerful exercise that can be blended into the interviewing process when it feels right. It's often an intuitive call whether or not to integrate this piece, and if you do and it doesn't work out, that is great information to get up front.

Where Am I Going? Before the interview, ask people to share their vision for where they'd like to be one, three, or five years from now. Ask them to make it as specific as possible. *What are they doing day to day in their jobs? How do they feel coming to work? What are they known for in the organization? What impact have they created so far?* These questions will underline core values and give you a sense of internal and external energy.

Where Are We Going? Have them write up a vision for your organization or your team. *What do they see is possible one, three, or five years from now? What's the company doing? What's the impact it has in the world? What's something that's happened in the last year or so that the company created but didn't even see was possible? What's the culture like?* These questions will give you a sense of what they see as possible for your team or organization, why they're attracted to working with you, what they may want to focus on, and what they're looking for in a culture.

If the visions and values are way out of whack, if their energy is incongruent, or if you see red flags—pay attention to the "do not pass go" sign that will either be subtle or smacking you over the head.

There are three factors that can make this exercise work especially well, and they're all *intentional and energetic*: (1) hold the intention that the experience will be positive for both of you (you as interviewer and your candidate) no matter what the outcome, (2) intend that this experience provides value to their life in whatever way serves them, and (3) be fully present and totally unattached to them being the "right" candidate. Be open to whatever shows up.

The *actions* that make this process work well are having a clear plan, asking candidates to prepare ahead of time (and to be as specific and thorough as they feel compelled), and a good set of open-ended questions swimming in the energy of curiosity and presence.

This does not need to be a crazy intense process. It has three primary components: the initial screening to see if you should go further, the prework of writing the vision, and the debrief and interview. For me, this process takes about three hours of my life and is worth every minute.

Firing Them (and Freeing Them) for the Right Reasons

Keeping employees motivated, inspired, performing at their best, and being positively culturally contagious happens as a result of doing much of what we've discussed in this book. And if you've done a good job on hiring, you're 10 steps ahead.

But what if it's not about keeping them? You've done your work, you've involved the right people, and now you've decided that letting this person go is the right thing to do. What do you do?

Here's what you *don't* do: Don't avoid it, lose sleep over it, commiserate with your leadership team about it, and hope it will all go away. Or the favorite—wait for it to work itself out!

These choices rarely work out well for anyone. At least not with everyone's happiness, credibility, and respect intact.

Let's be real: If you have players operating on your team who are bringing their B and C game rather than their A game to the table, sinking the ship, or simply bringing everyone down, your other employees know it. And they're not loving it. Instead they're resenting that it's not being handled and they're having to pick up the slack, suffering the drain of negative teammates. Those B or C players? They sense it too and don't feel great about it either. They're likely feeling isolated and frustrated, especially if they're not being given direct feedback.

Bottom line, you've got to clean it up. But what do you do?

Address It Head On

You address it directly. But before you do, self-awareness is essential. Identify what's driving you in any avoidance you have to letting someone go. In my experience there are five primary things that drive people when it comes to fear of firing:

1. They feel hopeful that it will somehow just correct itself if they give it time.
2. They want to be nice and definitely don't want to hurt anyone's feelings (besides, that's an uncomfortable conversation to have).
3. They're afraid of morale issues and don't want to rock the boat.
4. They feel responsible because they've moved this person from another company or location to be in this position.
5. They feel hostage to the situation, almost hopeless. Will the business be able to survive without the person?

All of these are completely understandable and worth acknowledging. The goal is to be conscious about who's driving what and what's driving whom.

Who's Driving? Fear, Love, or Service?

When a company is avoiding a difficult decision about someone because of what *might* happen if they let that person go, you have what I call a "hostage" situation. The company is the hostage. Often unconscious, this common and very human scenario unfolds and gains momentum, resulting in the contagious energy of fear, carefulness, and paralysis.

It's totally understandable. You've hired this person, you're a good human being, you don't want to hurt him or her, you don't want to freak others out, and if the person happens to be a solid performer—especially around something that generates a lot of revenue or is core to your business—you may be genuinely afraid to lose him or her. Plus, this person is a human being. But if the person is having a negative impact, and not caring to shift his or her IEP or performance or even give it a try (because, at this point, you've given the person feedback, offered him or her support, and put him or her on a plan, done everything you sense to do is right—and the person is still not *willing* or *able* to create the shifts), you're not left with a lot of options. As we talked about in the last section, the damage of keeping such a person on becomes exponentially worse. For all of you.

In service of what's best for your company, your team, your results, and the person in question, you *must* be willing to make the harder choice. You have to be ready to let someone go, and even mess you up completely, if it's truly the right thing to do. If you find peace with this, coming from your own power and knowingness rather than a place of fear, you're no longer held hostage to what *might* happen, and now you can make a clean leadership decision. Ironically, from this state, you may find a different solution that results in you keeping the person on in a different way. Who knows? But coming from "love and service" creates space and clarity and inspires that the best outcomes for everyone unfold. Coming from fear, you're all in the sludge.

Regarding Hostages

You have someone in your organization who is "leaving dead bodies behind" in the way he or she treats people. But because the person is a "top performer," "bringing in great money," or you'd "be lost without him or her," you step over the dead bodies and continue to give the benefit of the doubt. In the meantime, morale, creativity, and trust take a dive.

The energetic chaos that infuses your organization when people don't feel led, don't feel leadership has their backs, or don't feel leadership is aligned is what I call *leadership confusion*. It is dangerously contagious and will spread like wildfire, gathering evidence and speed as it goes.

In this scenario, the focus is now no longer on doing good work or bringing in revenue; it's on surviving this negative person's impact and leadership confusion. At best, it's a distraction. At worst, it's all-consuming. This will cost your organization way more in the long run than whatever revenue or benefit your toxic person is bringing in in the short term.

There are choices to be made here. There are three things you can do about this immediately.

1. Decide as an organization what you want to stand for. Is it cool to be awesome at your job but make people feel bad? Even setting this intention and making the declaration will have impact as a leadership team and culture. The energetic decision alone seems to create shifts. Play with it—but mean it.

2. Don't put yourself in a situation where no one else knows how to do this person's job, leaving you vulnerable to negative business impact. Make sure you have junior (or senior) people who can step in and carry *some* of the load until you can replace the person.

3. Look at how your organization and what it rewards may be contributing to creating these scenarios. For example, do you reward and value financial results over people and impact? That has impact on behavior (as discussed in Chapter 14).

No matter how many times I've seen "hostage" scenarios, and no matter how long they're tolerated, the organization usually lands at this: *Great results do not excuse toxic impact, especially when you want a culture that thrives.* How long it takes people to get to that stance determines how exhausted they'll all be by it when the situation is finally resolved and how much time, energy, and business development they'll lose in leadership confusion.

Regarding Morale and Matters of the Heart

You may be concerned that you'll demoralize your culture by firing a team member. But if you have toxic people on board who are infecting others, your people know it, they're impacted by it, and they're managing it every day. You'll want to consider what will serve everyone best here. There are a couple of ways to address this.

1. *Believe* that you can let people go *and* be loving and graceful about it.

2. *Name it.* Speak to the pain of the loss; be as honest as you can about it. Be clear about your commitment to culture and values and the level of performance and showing up you *all* hold dear.

3. *Reconnect* people to why you're all there in the first place, what's important, and how you all need to Show Up and collaborate in order to create the impact you want to have together.
4. *Share* that it's not your culture's way to just let people go. This was a conscious decision in service of everyone.
5. *Reassure* that you're committed to helping people move through rough patches if they hit one in your organization. There's compassion, support, and space to be human—and there is also accountability. It's everyone's job to Show Up.

Will you be driven by fear, love, or service? Decide and lead from there.

When a "Good" Hire Goes Bad

"Good" hires don't usually go bad—if they go bad, the person likely wasn't the right hire to begin with. Somewhere along the line, intuition got overridden, an important step got skipped, someone put on an extraordinary show, or an essential team member got left out of the process. For whatever reason, it just got missed.

Additionally, sometimes employees will get into a company, be happy for a bit, and then for whatever reason they'll shift. This could be for anything: they're not being led well or with the right style, they realize their values don't align with the company's values, they don't feel seen or appreciated, they're not feeling they're on purpose, they get bored, you name it—something shifts. When this happens, you hope first for a collaborative resolution or a peaceful resignation. But sometimes they hang on, and if they hang on and perform poorly or bring toxins into the culture, now they're dubbed a bad employee. A lot of times this just needs a bit of curiosity and attention on the manager or business lead's part.

I also believe that *for the most part*, there is no such thing as a bad employee. As soon as we start to believe there is, we set people up to show up that way. In my experience, while every once in a while, yes, someone will take advantage of the system, phone it in, manipulate, or even cheat or steal, generally speaking, people want to do well. They want to have a positive impact, they want their lives and work to matter, they want to be needed, they want to contribute—they want to count. They may just not be in the right place to do it with *you* or your organization.

The story I shared at the beginning of this chapter about Karen's failed hire has almost all of these components in it. She overrode her intuition, she tried to make someone into something he didn't want to be, she got really frustrated when he didn't show up the way she wanted him to, and she energetically held him as a "bad" employee (which only contributed to making it worse). But really, he wasn't bad. He just wasn't right for her organization or her leadership style.

Doing Your Work as a Leadership Team

Your job as a leadership team is to identify the right fit in the first place, and when you don't—when you hire the wrong person, or for whatever reason the right one goes "off the rails"—get in there and lead.

Check your style and the energetic intentions you're each holding toward the person, and make sure you've *done* and *been* everything you can to set him or her up for success.

Have you? Did the person know his or her job was on the line? Has he or she been given regular feedback? Was it clean and clear (not sugarcoated)? Have you put the person on a plan? Gotten him or her coaching or mentoring? Truly done what you've sensed was the right thing to do?

Have you done whatever you needed to do from an HR and legal standpoint to exit the person properly and with integrity? (Check with your own state and organizational policies on that one—I'm not talking legalities or policy here, I'm talking about human beings.)

And finally, for your *being* as leader: Have your mindset and heart been in the right place? Have you seen and treated the person as a human being? Have you believed the best possible? Have you shown up well and given the person space to do so too?

If your answers are yes to the queries above, and you and your team are clean and clear, you will know your next step in setting the person free to find better fitted opportunities.

Moving Forward with Presence, Care, and Grace

As you move into this final phase of completion, here are a couple of things to consider that can bring more presence and grace to a difficult situation.

This person you're about to exit was a part of your organization. You believed and cared enough about the person to bring him or her on and trusted the person enough to have him or her be part of your culture. This person may not be the right fit for you, but he or she is a human being. He or she cares, wants his or her life and impact to matter, is valuable, and is taking the experience of you and your culture with him or her.

It's your job as leader to hold a large energetic container for the person, as he or she steps into this next phase, that will honor and leverage who he or she is. Exiting someone, while difficult, does not have to be a horrible experience. How you hold yourself—your intention, energy, and presence—will determine how powerful or painful this experience is. And the person will remember it for the rest of his or her life. You have an opportunity to contribute to who this person is becoming. Show Up.

Reflection: Putting IEP into Practice

Criteria and Collaboration Are the Name of the Game

Use the questions below to help you create a hiring and firing game plan.

You

- Consider your best hire ever. What was your secret sauce? How did you show up? What criteria did you sort for?
- Consider your worst hire ever. Where did you fall down? What did you learn? How would you do it differently next time?

You and Your Hiring Team

Building upon your organization's (and state's) guidelines and policies for hiring and firing, here are some places to look as a team to make the process more energetically productive.

Get clear up front on these issues:

- What are the timelines for hiring and exiting? What's the appropriate amount of time to invest in both situations? How much time will you give decisions? How will decisions be made and communicated?
- What are your core values as an organization?
- What does good or awesome look like in a new hire? What core criteria will you be sorting for?
- What are the deal breakers?
- How will you make hiring and firing decisions? How will you agree to disagree?
- What questions will you ask if you want to integrate the visioning exercises?
- What else is important for a new hire? Build in your own priorities here.

PART 5

SHOWING UP MOVING FORWARD

You make it happen.

Congratulations! You've made it to the end. Ready to wrap it up?

Here's where we've been. In Part 1, "The Fundamentals of Showing Up," we laid the groundwork for *why* all of this is so important. In Part 2, "Showing Up for You," we set *you* up for success in optimizing your own leadership presence, influence, and fulfillment. In Part 3, "Showing Up for Others," we set you up for further success in unlocking more leadership potential while serving and collaborating with others. In Part 4, "Showing Up for Culture," we took it all deeper to build an even more positively contagious culture from the inside out and from your first hire to your final fire. And now, in this final part, we're wrapping it all up with a big bow, moving it forward and making it even more real.

If you've been applying the tools and principles offered throughout the book, for yourself, your personal leadership, your organization, and your culture, this should already be *very* real. And it's time to take it even further.

Moving forward, what will *you* do? In this section I'll give you the secret to making this all come together. I'll share some best practices and examples of how friends, partners, collaborators, and clients have built positively contagious cultures by integrating good IEP and practices into their organizations. You might wonder, or even doubt, how this can work for your organization, so we'll do a bit of myth busting. We'll create your plan, building on all the other Reflections and exercises you've done throughout the book. And finally I'll give you some of my favorite resources to support you on your journey. Ready? Let's go.

CHAPTER 17

Launching IEP in Your Organization

All of this is only as good as you be it.
Integrate, integrate, integrate.

You've launched this work in your life. You have your own IEP practice. You're feeling good and bringing it to work with you. You sense this could be helpful for others. And now you want to integrate it into your organization.

You want to be even more intentionally and positively contagious. Great.

Launching IEP in your organization—be it your business, your team, your family, or the PTA—can be as simple and easy as you choose to make it.

There are two secrets to doing it especially well. The most powerful element of launching IEP in your organization is that you practice it yourself. And you don't stop, ever.

When our presence becomes stronger, our energy elevates, and we become more intentional, we shift how we Show Up with others. Our ability to create more intentional impact increases significantly. Do your own work first, look to contribute and be in service of, keep your energetic field strong and clear, work with your team, and lead.

And number two? It's big. We've spoken about it, but not nearly enough. I want to underline it. Because it is big, and contagious. And you can have it now.

Gratitude. Gratitude for your current situation, your current culture, your current anything. To create a shift, you must appreciate the present state.

Gratitude is one of the most contagious energetic states you can generate. It is a perspective shifter, a cultural shifter, and an impact shifter. Practice it big with gratitude for your health, life, job, and kids, and practice it small with gratitude for your toothpaste, Post-its, this moment, and your pen—just practice it. Even when it's tough—especially when it's tough.

How? Say thank you. Start a gratitude journal. Acknowledge someone. Play the Gratitude Game. Build "appreciations" into your meetings. In a funk? Go on a gratitude bender. Find the littlest thing you can be grateful for and let it expand.

To apply this work in your life and organization, and to energize your culture, here are your shortcuts: Show up with good IEP and be grateful. I've given you tools and ideas throughout this book to help you clear your energetic field, work your mindset, and love yourself up from the inside out. This gives you extra access to gratitude. Gratitude is contagious, and the more you access it, the stronger and richer it becomes.

If you do nothing else—Show Up, take care of yourself, focus on creating positive impact, and practice gratitude.

There are several ways you can integrate what you've learned in this book into your organization. The most basic? Pick something, apply it personally, and try a couple of things out with your team. For more formal integration, the sky's the limit—make your own magic.

In this chapter I'll offer more ways to build this work into your life and organization *today*. I'll share stories and examples from individuals who've integrated this work into their lives and built really healthy cultures. Unlike previous chapters where I've changed identifying details in order to honor privacy, the folks in this chapter are who I say they are.

In the final Reflections section of this book we'll map your plan. Big or little, easy or intense, you'll craft your plan. From there, you're off using this book as a living resource to come back to again and again.

Integrating IEP into Your Life and Organization

Integration can be informal, or it can be full infusion and really formal. It's up to you and what your organization wants and needs.

The Informal Route

Let's take the simplest informal route first. Model it. Inspire others to show up well by the way you show up. Then, invite your team to read this book. Use it as a study guide. Work a chapter a week (or a month) as a "book club" using the Reflection sections to make it real. I intentionally crafted the Reflection sections at the end of each chapter both to be an interactive guide for you individually and also to be used to connect with your team or a partner. Through these discussions you'll find ways to support yourselves better as well as ways to make your organization more IEP friendly.

A More Formal Route

Share this work through the book and/or any of the tools I provide in the resources section (Chapter 18) to help you integrate in a way that fits you. Do your IEP Cultural Assessment (Chapter 14), start a Stewardship Team, make your own Cultural

IEP Tool Kit and Credo. Create your Organizational IEP Plan. Play with the activities and structures I've provided in the next section. If there was something in this book that stood out for you and feels exciting, run with it.

And the Most Formal Route

If you want something really structured, you can create a formal program in your company. You can do this your own lovely way, or if you want help, later in this book I've offered information on ways our organization can support you on that path.

Or Just Practice as an Individual

In this option you simply practice IEP as an individual, sharing it with your team or people as you feel compelled.

Whatever you choose, know that you can create more of the impact you want by being more intentional about how you Show Up. Period. You are contagious.

Organizational Integration Ideas

The following activities and structures need only you, your team, and the information and resources from this book to help you make this work real. This is by no means an all inclusive list.

- Share the book with your team and/or organization.
- Start an internal "book club." Hold monthly discussions and application sessions.
- Apply the model and frameworks. Plug yourself in and work it.
- Create a Personal and/or Team IEP Plan and check it regularly.
- Craft your vision, values, and purpose using content in Chapter 6 for the Essential You.
- Sponsor healthy, life-giving food at your meetings and events.
- Create space for exercise and self-care and make team agreements around this.

- Provide opportunities for coaching and mentoring to help people show up well.
- Build agreements as an organization, as a team, and at your next meeting.
- Create space for "appreciations" or "acknowledgments" in your meetings.

From the Trenches: Organizations Doing It Well

The following are organizations that've done a lovely job of nourishing a healthy culture, elevating their organizational energy, and doing really great work in the world. I've intentionally chosen a range of industries and businesses to share how this can unfold. For each of them I've highlighted different things to give you the broadest range of examples.

IDEO

IDEO, the design and innovation firm devoted to *creating positive and disproportionate impact through design* (and which I mentioned in Chapter 14) has core organizational values of *"embrace ambiguity," "collaborate," "make others successful," "be optimistic," "learn from failure," "take ownership,"* and *"talk less do more."*

IDEO is highly committed to supporting people in their growth, and we've worked together for years to help the company unlock greater leadership potential, enhance collaboration, optimize energy and presence, lead intentionally, and help people show up well, over and over again.

Through a blend of engagements and experiments that have included everything from grassroots advocacy and paying it forward in one-on-one conversations with one another, to live and virtual group experiences, to training official Global IEP Stewards who can coach and help people on the ground at their different locations, the people at IDEO have infused this content into their culture in a way that is congruent, sticky, and also contagious.

IEP has been blended into their agreements and into their performance, design, and feedback processes; they've created tools and cultural assets to make meetings and collaborations even more effective; they've brought this work home with them; they've used it to nourish themselves; and they've used it to nourish and show up beautifully for one another. All of this contributes to the impact they're able to have together and how energized and on purpose they feel.

They use IEP to help:

- Optimize leadership presence and identify specific areas and needs for growth
- Support feedback, design, and collaboration conversations
- Gauge energy and check in with teams on how they're doing during projects, during meetings, and even just in general
- Set intentions and design agreements before and during meetings and projects
- Bring their best selves to the table in service of creating the best impact possible—on each other and for their client work
- Support themselves—their communication, energy levels, and impact—in client meetings and workshops
- Create more self-awareness so they understand their motivations and intentions as they navigate leadership challenges and conversations
- At home with their families to build better relationships and dialogue
- Troubleshoot presence issues and help people fine-tune where they can shift to be even more impactful
- Serve, support, and coach other employees in their leadership development
- In their feedback and career navigation conversations

For the more "formal" integration and engagements, it's important to underline that IDEO makes this work and the internal discussions optional. People engage and apply it in way that works for them. It's not everyone's cup of tea. But it's available as people wish, it's sanctioned by leadership, and leadership also plays.

When I spoke with Heather Currier Hunt (Global Director of Learning and Development) and Duane Bray (Partner and Head of Global Talent) about how they relate to contagious culture, here's what they shared.

> As a design firm, we design for culture by meeting what comes down from the top with what's bubbling up from the rest of the organization. We have a two-way reciprocal street in showing up well for each other. Our values are how we do our work and how we show up for each other every day.
>
> **All our moments of organizational culture design begin with ourselves as individuals and what we all bring with us to our teams every single day.** In order to do this, there are many, many little moments, tiny changes, and simple intentions we employ to ensure that the culture we are in fact designing is a reflection of every last one of us, i.e., on our best days: present, intentional, well hydrated (!) and that we're clear on the outcomes we hope to achieve from the conversations we have over coffee, to the presentations we share with a client, to the speaking engagement that may touch thousands of listeners.

Dependent on people bringing their best minds, spirits, talent, creativity, and hearts to the table in order to innovate and create *positive and disproportionate impact*, having a healthy contagious culture and showing up well is essential to IDEO's success and well-being. These people are creating this every day, and the impact ripples far beyond the walls and hearts of their own organizations.

Zingerman's Community of Businesses

Zingerman's Community of Businesses in Ann Arbor (mentioned in Chapter 14) has been integrating this work into its already energized culture and spirit for quite a few years. I circled up with Ari Weinzweig (CEO and Cofounding Partner) and

Maggie Bayless (Managing Partner, ZingTrain) to see how it's unfolded and what they're seeing today.

Maggie shared that people now do personal energy ratings at their ZingTrain weekly huddles. If anyone is below an 8—or has been consistently no higher than an 8 for a couple of weeks—they ask what they, as a group, can do to help. This can be an easy opening for someone to share what's bothering him or her. This in and of itself often helps bring their energy up. The Vibrational Energy of individuals—and of the room as a whole—has become a key component in their "iZXi" ratings, which they do a few times throughout the course of any workshop they teach. The presenter or copresenters will take a "reading" of the room and assign a score to how engaged the group (or specific individuals) are, determining whether they're energetic promoters, neutrals, or detractors.

Having a common language around energy has made it easier to connect and engage with someone who is walking around under a thundercloud of gloom. Just asking *"Is everything OK? Your Vibrational Energy isn't as up as it usually is"* sends the message that someone cares and often helps the person become more self-aware, usually resulting in improved energy.

Ari offered that teaching and sharing this work has brought energy mindfulness into the organization and given people a common language around what energy is. They've adapted *"positive energy"* as their professional definition of "fun."

One of the most powerful things leaders at Zingerman's have done is that they've made positive energy a ***performance expectation*** instead of it being something they hope for. Ari says it's no different from making a cappuccino correctly or anything else that they train their employees on. And since it's a teachable recipe, everyone can learn it. Finally, one of the biggest benefits to their culture is that this is all stuff people can take home with them. Ari shared, *"Most of them end up using the same mindfulness outside work, which makes their personal lives more positive,* *which in turn cycles back to the workplace in a good way."* It's contagious.

Domaine Carneros

Domaine Carneros, a beautiful winery located in Napa Valley, California (offering some of *the* best sparkling wine and Pinot Noir you will ever have the pleasure of), hosted a two-day "off-site" for its executive leadership team to work on their team dynamics using many of the principles of IEP we've been discussing in this book.

Afterward the leaders rolled it out for the whole company. Every department—from finance, to customer service, to hospitality, to production—participated with leadership's support and sponsorship in a series of internal events. The majority of employees attended. They became more aware of their impact and worked on showing up even better with one another.

Immediately afterward, with subteams of advocates leading the charge, they began integrating different components of IEP into their organizational practices. They created assets to support them in keeping IEP alive, sticky, and congruent with their culture. They built Energy Check-ins into meetings. They created visuals (with grapes!) with IEP principles and reminders and put them up around the grounds. They created "Energy Check" boxes and distributed those as well. They also put more attention on food, placing healthy snack options in the snack room. This was just some of what they did initially, and all of it was employee instigated.

Today energy is seen as impactful. People can identify how their own personal energy affects their relationships with customers, vendors, and fellow employees. They've found that their internal and external energy can impact sales. Their interpersonal communication has improved. Their awareness of energy in impacting themselves and others has become forethought in how they function as a business.

Fifteen months after initial integration, their CEO, Eileen Crane, shared that even a year later the energy has continued to build, they have a more enthusiastic and energized culture than ever, and she marveled that something like "energy" could have such a big and lasting impact.

The reason the work has had a lasting impact is because leadership internally embodies and supports it and there are internal advocates and stewards who've made it theirs. When I asked Elaine what the impact has been and how they've gotten there, she offered, *"I could break this down into we're more appreciative, we look at the bright side, we're kinder, more supportive, and more conscious of how we show up. But in the end, we're just happier."*

The majority of this integration example has been employee driven. There was some formal implementation up front to give them official structure and training, but truly Domaine Carneros's success in integration and in creating a culture with even more energy and enthusiasm has been due to their commitment to showing up and applying their own IEP over and over again. Cheers!

Bulletproof Executive

Another approach to supporting your employees' IEP and creating a positively contagious culture is by supporting employees in optimizing and nurturing their own well-being. Who better to discuss this with than the Bulletproof Executive himself?

If you've heard of butter coffee, Bulletproof Coffee, or biohacking, you likely know Dave Asprey, the Bulletproof Executive. His organization is devoted to creating high performance in human beings through nutrition, self-care, biohacking, and all sorts of great stuff.

Knowing that Dave cares very much about his people, impact, and their culture, he and I discussed how they optimize their collaboration and work together. We talked about three primary areas of focus for his organization that contribute to creating a healthy and contagious culture: *self-care and performance optimization, cultural criteria, and job matching.*

The first was self-care and performance optimization. Dave shared that his organization spends more money on proactiveness and optimization than some companies spend on healthcare because they believe so much in the power of performance and optimal brain function.

To support their people in this domain, full-time employees are given a variety of Bulletproof products to nourish their energy and brainpower every month. Employees receive unlimited vacation time and are directed to take "rejuvenation time" as needed, allowing them to self-manage and take care. Since they're all committed to impact, they use this time off intentionally and as needed. In addition, his direct reports participate in intensive mindfulness training ("40 Years of Zen") to support them in coming from a centered place.

These perks fuel their people well. This puts them in a better mood and helps them set intentions and make decisions from a mindset of kindness, abundance, and clarity. All of this together contributes significantly to creating a strong IEP foundation, which in turn has a huge impact on their presence, how they show up, and how they work together.

The next area we explored was their cultural criteria and getting the right people on the team. When they hire, they sort for values and criteria that honor and add richness to the culture. They sort for kindness and respectfulness, integrity, commitment to continuous self-improvement, and a person's ability to consider science and facts and also have empathy and emotion, and that they're motivated by passion, accountable, and committed to creating impact. A high level of self-awareness is also important as it enables team members to acknowledge their challenges and know their buttons so they can lead and collaborate well.

Finally, they use *job matching*. They're committed to ensuring that the jobs of all members of the team match their desired impact and purpose. They do this via strengths assessments, job description transformation sessions, and making sure that people are doing things that align with what they're excited and passionate about doing.

Tasty Catering and Nuphoriq

In addition to having great structures in place to support people in honoring values and creating an energized culture, Tasty Catering (as mentioned in Chapter 14) also uses artifacts around its office to help ground people and remind them of the importance of showing up well together.

Tom Walter, a serial entrepreneur and Chief Culture Officer for Tasty Catering, shares that in addition to the energy board (where they put their picture next to how they're feeling energetically every day), leaders repeat their culture statement before meetings, they have a crucifix on display in their office, they post motivational pictures—with their staff *in* them so that everyone can see his or her *own* face around the company, and they have their culture statement, in Spanish and English, throughout the building in public areas. With core values around *quality, discipline, respect, ethics, standards, determination, freedom, and responsibility* (all of which any customer can find on the company's website), this organization hums.

Nuphoriq, a sister company to Tasty Catering, co-founded by Erin Walter and Jamie Pritscher, also has special ways of nourishing its culture, creating positive energy, and showing up well together.

Jamie, Chief Communications Officer, shared that in addition to reciting their core values at their Monday Meetings, they also do energy checks and then say something they are proud of from the prior week either personally or professionally. This helps them start the week off on a positive note, and if someone has low energy, they work as a team to get it up. Throughout the week, team members have full permission to say, "My energy is low." From there they take responsibility to shift it and get support as needed. They might take a walk, talk it out, or even have a dance break to shake it off.

15Five

The crew at 15Five is all about culture and improving team and organizational communication. These guys, and what they're up to, support the IEP Model big time, especially in the Mental and Emotional and Relational Quadrants (I've included them in the resources section as well).

The people at 15Five walk their talk using their own tools, nurturing their environment, taking time-outs for team engagements and adventures, and having a commitment to showing up well every day.

Shane Metcalf, 15Five's VP of Customer Success, offered, *"Perhaps the most powerful and simple thing we've done is doing IEP check-ins at the beginning of team meetings. Having awareness of the IEP Method combined with simply bringing awareness to how we're feeling in the present state reorients us toward how we want to feel.*

We've also led the company through the process of identifying our core desired feeling states (powerful, creative, awake, competent, etc.), and this has proven to be extremely powerful in helping people intentionally feel the way they most want to feel. It all comes back to asking questions on a regular basis—How do you feel? How do you want to feel? The questions are the key."

Again, this is simple integration boiling down to awareness, intention, and showing up.

Bringing It Home (and to Work)

Which examples resonate for you? What ideas do these stories give you? If you were going to implement one thing right now, just one thing, what's the easiest thing to get you and your organization started?

For all of these, regardless of who these leaders are, what they do, how they're integrating IEP, how they're nourishing and building culture, and how they're creating impact, there is a common theme woven throughout:

Treat people well, bring your best self to the table, take excellent care of you, manage your energy, be responsible for your energy, be accountable for what you create . . . and do it all in service of having big impact, being a contribution to people, and feeling good while doing it. Show Up.

And now it is your turn.

The last Reflection section of this book is geared toward helping you craft your plan. Don't worry about getting it right. And if you're doing it for your organization, don't do it alone.

We have a lot of great work to do together. We have organizations to grow, problems to solve, great things to create. We have lives to contribute to, children to love and raise well, and future leaders to mentor, lead, and inspire who will also have positive impact on this planet.

It is time, now more than ever, for us to Show Up. To Show Up well. To shine. To be grateful. To take care of ourselves. And to be the biggest contribution possible in this big, beautiful world.

Please take this work and apply it to your life and organization as it best serves and supports you. Pay it forward. Show up, lead, and be contagious.

To you and your impact,

Anese

Reflection: Putting IEP into Practice

What's Your Game Plan?

It's your turn. Map it out. You can do this any way you like. A powerful way to do it is simply to go through each chapter and pull the most resonant pieces for you. The Reflection sections in each chapter have specific exercises to help you lock it in. Even those alone hold valuable pieces of your plan. And here are some more places to look as well as some examples of what you might plug in.

Consider:

- What do I/we want? What is my/our dream impact for this work?
- What's missing? What is my/our biggest most urgent need to address culturally?
- What's the dream?
- What organizations do I/we admire and respect? What's their IEP like? What kind of contagions do they spread? Identify three things I/we want to adopt, or one next step.
- What are the examples that resonated for me/us in Chapter 17 and the components I/we'd like to adopt (from any of the lists or stories)?
- What is my/our cultural vision? Include how it feels, what we do, what we're known for, what we measure, what we value, why we rock. What is our story?

Create and gather:

- My game plan.
- My allies and partners to make it real.
- My next three steps. (Feel free to go deeper here.)

Sample Plan

My game plan. Share this with five people. Create a team. Start integrating IEP now.

My allies and partners. Izzy, Sue, Mike, Tim, Michele.

Our next steps.

1. Give one another feedback on how we can each optimize our own presence. Ask for help and support one another in personal integration.
2. Complete the IEP Cultural Assessment.
3. Go through the integration section in this chapter and pick three things we can do right now. (At a minimum, run our team or culture through the IEP Model and see where we are now.) What's one thing in each section that would start shifting cultural IEP?

Here are a couple of *examples* of things you might do in each section for cultural or team IEP support:

- **The Essential You.** *Create our vision and our organizational values and identify our purpose. Have everyone do his or her own personal set as well, and share it. This will strengthen organizational IEP.*
- **Quadrant 1: Physical and Environmental Energy.** *Make sure everyone has healthy food options in anything we sponsor, put water coolers around the location, put flowers in the rooms, tweak desk configurations in project spaces so they feel good, change our meetings to 50 minutes instead of 60, and encourage everyone to build in time for self-care.*
- **Quadrant 2: Mental and Emotional Energy.** *Create agreements as a team, identify beliefs that are holding us back, starting integrating the Five Steps to Intentional Impact into our meetings, create intentional energetic space for vulnerability,*

practice curiosity, assume good, turn all complaints into requests or suggestions, and add appreciations into meetings at the beginning or end.

- **Quadrant 4: Vibrational Energy.** *Do an Energy Check at every meeting, practice Presence Reboots, paint our door handles different colors to remind us that our presence has impact, "Bubble up" before meetings, commit to supporting one another in using the Energetic Xylophone and being responsible energy shifting partners, be intentional about our default postures and facial expressions.*

- **Quarter 4: Relational Energy.** *Create agreements as a group, name intentions in meetings at the beginning, name issues, make it safe for feedback, decide to have a healthy team and get really honest about what's getting in the way, express acknowledgments, give positive as well as critical feedback, and have each person on the team share his or her accountability with one another.*

CHAPTER 18

Resources, Apps, Tools, and Secret Sauce Super Powers

Presence is your super power. There's an app for that.

Many of the practices, tips, and principles of IEP, especially for the internal work, have been informed, influenced, and supported by the wisdom, intelligence, and hearts of experts in their domains that complement and nurture healthy IEP. For a growing list of resources that support this work, check out www.anesecavanaugh .com/ccresources/.

Your Number One Super Resource Is *You*

Take care of you, be in service of others, and create positive impact.

To Create Positive Contagions, Use Your Super Powers

1. Take excellent care of you.
2. Intend your impact.
3. Be integrity.

4. Own your story.

5. Set yourself (and others) up for success.

6. Be present. Stay awake.

7. Honor pleasure and delight.

8. Decide to Show Up.

9. Contribute.

10. Ask for help.

11. Assume good.

12. Practice gratitude.

13. Love.

To Create a (Positively) Contagious Culture, Remember

1. Use your super powers.

2. You are contagious.

3. Culture starts with you.

4. Take care of yourself to lead.

5. Work your personal IEP every day.

6. Be responsible for the energy you bring into the room.

7. Build your skills.

8. Intend your presence and impact.

9. Embrace the trifecta: people, self-care, impact.

10. Check your Containers.

11. Make clean agreements.

12. Hire and fire in service of all.

13. Make "being a contribution to" and "in service of" your default.

14. Set your environment up for success.

15. Model authorship, leadership, accountability, and contribution.

16. Model what you want to create.

17. Lead and collaborate together.

18. Have a shared vision, values, and purpose.

19. Measure and reward intentionally.

20. Integrate and stay awake: Keep coming back to basics.

Additional Resources to Support You in Building Strong IEP

The following are apps, books, and resources I personally use, refer to, and have found great wisdom in. All of these support and complement creating positive IEP, solid impact, and leading well. (This list is ever growing; see the resources page mentioned above.)

Apps and Tools

- **5 Minute Journal:** www.FiveMinuteJournal.com A journal and app that help you focus on gratitude and positivity.
- **5Dynamics:** www.5Dynamics.com Online tool suite to help you understand how you and your colleagues prefer to get things done, contribute, and communicate.
- **15Five:** www.15Five.com Web-based software that makes it easy for you and your team to uncover obstacles, opportunities, and ideas each week.
- **Work/Life:** www.WorkLife.com A software application that helps teams run highly effective and engaging meetings.

Bodies of Work

- The Arbinger Institute: www.Arbinger.com
- The Bulletproof Executive: www.BulletProofExec.com
- The Work of Byron Katie: www.TheWork.com
- The Intuitive Journey: www.TheIntuitiveJourney.com
- Intuitive Way: www.IntuitiveWay.com
- Whole30: www.Whole30.com

Books

- Arbinger Institute, *Leadership and Self-Deception: Getting Out of the Box* (Berrett-Koehler Publishers; 1st edition, 2002).
- Arbinger Institute, *Leadership and Self-Deception: Getting Out of the Box* (Berrett-Koehler Publishers; 2nd edition, 2010).
- Arbinger Institute, *The Anatomy of Peace: Resolving the Heart of Conflict* (Berrett-Koehler Publishers; 1st edition, 2006).
- Arbinger Institute, *The Anatomy of Peace: Resolving the Heart of Conflict* (Berrett-Koehler Publishers; 2nd edition, 2015).
- Dave Asprey, *The Bulletproof Diet: Lose up to a Pound a Day, Reclaim Energy and Focus, Upgrade Your Life* (Rodale Books, 2014).
- Brené Brown, *Daring Greatly: How the Courage to Be Vulnerable Transforms the Way We Live, Love, Parent, and Lead* (Avery, 2012).
- Chip Conley, *Emotional Equations: Simple Steps for Creating Happiness + Success in Business + Life* (Atria Books, 2012).
- Chip Conley, *Peak: How Great Companies Get Their Mojo from Maslow* (Jossey-Bass, 2007).
- Charles Duhigg, *The Power of Habit: Why We Do What We Do in Life and Business* (Random House, 2012).
- Byron Katie and Stephen Mitchell, *Loving What Is: Four Questions That Can Change Your Life* (Harmony, 2002).
- John H. Gottman and Nan Silver, *The Seven Principles for Making Marriage Work* (Harmony, 1st Edition, 1999) (great for teams, too).
- John H. Gottman and Nan Silver, *The Seven Principles for Making Marriage Work* (Harmony, 2nd Edition, 2015) (great for teams, too).
- Melissa Hartwig and Dallas Hartwig, *It Starts with Food: Discover the Whole30 and Change Your Life in Unexpected Ways* (Victory Belt Publishing, 2012).

- Melissa Hartwig and Dallas Hartwig, *It Starts with Food: Discover the Whole30 and Change Your Life in Unexpected Ways* (Victory Belt Publishing, 2014).
- Daniel H. Pink, *Drive: The Surprising Truth About What Motivates Us* (Riverhead Books, 2011).
- Julia Ross, *The Mood Cure: The 4-Step Program to Take Charge of Your Emotions—Today* (Viking Adult, 2002).
- Simon Sinek, *Start with Why: How Great Leaders Inspire Everyone to Take Action* (Portfolio, 2009).
- Ari Weinzweig, *A Lapsed Anarchist's Approach to Building a Great Business* (Zingerman's Guide to Good Leading series, Zingerman's Press, 2010).
- Ari Weinzweig, *A Lapsed Anarchist's Approach to Being a Better Leader* (Zingerman's Guide to Good Leading series, Zingerman's Press, 2012).
- Ari Weinzweig, *A Lapsed Anarchist's Approach to Managing Ourselves* (Zingerman's Guide to Good Leading series, Zingerman's Press, 2013).

Now go create some awesome impact.

ACKNOWLEDGMENTS: GRATITUDE IN MOTION

Nothing good happens alone. Relationship is everything.

It's taken a village to write this book, and the village has been awesome. So awesome that the first draft of this section was 4,000 words, and even that didn't get the job done. So here is the eight-word version: *Thank you. You know exactly who you are.* If I've missed you in print, please know you're in those eight words, you're in this work, and you've had impact here. I hope you've enjoyed this book you've nourished and helped come alive.

Tremendous gratitude to Donya Dickerson, Ann Pryor, Pattie Amoroso, Cheryl Hudson, Alison Shurtz, Tanya Punj, and the rest of the crew at McGraw-Hill for bringing this book to life so beautifully. Donya, special thanks for seeing the vision for *Contagious Culture* so quickly and clearly, and for your grace and partnership in editing and creation. To Scott Spiewak, thank you for helping me navigate the world of publishing and for helping connect the dots to make this book happen.

To the companies who've been mentioned in this book and to the people who've allowed their stories to be shared (whether you were identified or not), thank you.

To the brave souls and organizations who've trusted me to work with them over the years, thank you for the honor and privilege. You move me.

For anyone who's been in an IEP launch, program, event, cohort, or random heart-to-heart conversation during a break—you inspired and fed this book in some way.

Very special thanks to IDEO for years of collaboration, partnership, and participation. For inviting me into your sphere so generously in so many ways—there is no bottom to my gratitude.

Duane Bray, you are a dream partner in collaboration, impact, and delight. Heather Currier Hunt, you inspire partnership and are a model of what it looks like to *decide* to get in there and steward oh so beautifully. Fierce gratitude to you both for early reads, feedback, and delicious leaning in as this book unfolded.

Sally Clark, Britta Durtsche, Mike See, Jamie Styles, Laura Brumit, and all the IEP Stewards in IDEO, thank you for showing up, diving in, and making this content work for you authentically.

David Kelly, Tim Brown, Dave Strong, Paul Bennett, Jane Fulton Suri, Sue Siddall, Kersh, Bruce MacGregor, and so many other partners and collaborators in IDEO who've been champions and stakeholders in this work. There are so many to thank—you know who you are—so from New York to San Francisco to Singapore and everywhere in between, thank you.

Ari Weinzweig, for leaning in at "hello." Thank you for your friendship, curiosity, belief, and endless support. To the Zingerman's crew, I adore you. Thank you for feeding me in so many ways.

Dave Asprey for conversations about this book, for your support of this work, and for fueling my body and brain throughout. Your coffee and supplements basically coauthored this book.

Countless hugs from Carmel to LA to NYC go to Linda Sivertsen, Agapi Stassinopoulos, and Jesse Krieger for guidance, support, feedback, and precious heartfelt conversations on couches. You are gifts.

Mike Robbins and Shawn Murphy, thank you for sharing your wisdom so generously and making me laugh. A lot.

For support in growing me, growing this work, and getting this book done that came in so many forms this year: early reads and edits, meaningful conversations, shared stories and perspectives, feedback, friendship, guidance, meals, input, and simply helping me stay grounded, deep bows and big thanks to Alison Macondray, Kate Blake, Keather Roemhildt, Eric Newton, Anthony Lemme, Joe Graceffa, David Schonthal, Matt Clark, Tom Walter, Jamie Pritsher, Glenn Burr, Paul Speigelman, Nick Sarillo, Steven Wilkinson, Bo Burlingham, Rob Dube, Chip Conley, Eileen Crane, Shauna Sullivan, Diane Cooper, Steve McPherson, Maggie Bayless, Dave Kashen, Nick Myers, Sandy Speicher, Coe Leta Stafford, Chris Domina, John Ravitch, Margaret Kessler, Henry Cheung, Ingrid Fetell, Neil Stevenson, Jon Wettersten, Travis Lee, Mike Peng, Owen Rogers, Henry Dzuiba, Josh Pietak, Sandra Martini, Jenny Sauer-Klein, Alan Levine, Jerry Calabrese, David Hassell, Shane Metcalf, David Mizne, Lauren Lee Anderson, Mimi Lemanski, LiYana Silver, Patrick Hoban, Tom and Trish Gancer, Cheryl Perlis, Melissa Epperson, Mandy Bryant, Missy and Rob Patton, and so, so, so many more.

To Gina Petersen, Jef Lear, Marisa Smith (and crew!), Karen Sims, Bridget Wessel, Rochelle Rizzi, Jeff Ochrach, Cheryl Keller, Justin Bench, Ariel Zimmerman, and all the people who made my life and business hum this past year—keeping me solid and clear so I could write and thrive, thank you.

To my "Coven," for intentions set in a forest grounded in belief, business savvy, and sisterhood, see you on the log, witches. To Michele Serro, we've played on so many amazing levels, grab your boots, I will thank you on the mountain. To Kathryn Body, Carrie Bain, and all friends, Room Angels, and champions. Yum.

To Glen, Jake, and Izzy. Intense love and gratitude for being who you are, for showing up how you do, and for leaning in extra special this last year in *far* too many ways to capture here. I love you dearly.

To my parents and my children's grandparents, thank you for your love and support. A very deep bow to my sisters: your love, "flowers," and support this year carried me when I didn't even know I needed to be carried. I love you tender.

To all who've given their hearts, expertise, and brilliance to help me push my own edges and love myself well. To the Arbinger Institute, Coaches Training Institute, Intuitive Way, and The Intuitive Journey. To Laura Whitworth, Karen Kimsey-House, and my Morning Stars for leadership and community; to Bryan Franklin, Jennifer Russell, and the rest of the L7 Community for business and family; to the Small Giants Community for inspiration and mojo; to Anne Pearce, David Pearce, and Aimee Eoff (X 1000) for intuition, care, and even more specifically for my own "Bubble"... Thank you. Your wisdom, impact, and contributions are contagious, creating ripple effects every day that helped make this book possible.

Thank you all for showing up.

NOTES

CHAPTER 2

1. Albert Mehrabian, *Nonverbal Communication* (Chicago, IL: Aldine-Atherton, 1972).
2. Albert Mehrabian, *Silent Messages: Implicit Communication of Emotions and Attitudes* (Belmont, CA: Wadsworth Publishing, 1972).

CHAPTER 7

1. BulletProofExec.com.
2. Whole30.com.

CHAPTER 8

1. TheWork.com.
2. ArbingerInstitute.com.

CHAPTER 14

1. BreneBrown.com.
2. Assessment adapted from the IEP Organizational Stewardship Guide. Used with permission.

CHAPTER 15

1. www.DanPink.com

INDEX

ABOUT THE AUTHOR

Anese is a leadership and collaboration advisor and thinking partner to leaders and organizations primarily in the design, service, and innovation spaces. As a leading voice on intention, energy, and presence in leadership and culture, she knows what it takes to make "busy" beautiful, and helps people create the impact they want. Anese built the IEP Method to enable people to gain greater access to their own *secret sauce* for showing up more powerfully, collaborating more inspiringly, creating more openly, intuiting more bravely, and leading more joyfully and effectively.

Anese is passionate about helping people design businesses, lives, and powerful personal and professional relationships that make a positive impact in the world. Clients say she "builds creative leaders," "gets people having honest conversations" and "unlocks potential." Working with executives and organizations in different industries—design, hospitality, tech, entertainment, law, education, medical, and nonprofit—she helps people show up more intentionally and teams work together more cohesively. She has spoken around the world on stages at Stanford University, Inc., and other entrepreneurial conferences and organizational events. Top innovators and executives in companies like IDEO, Zingerman's, Cooper, Joie de Vivre, and Citigroup have engaged with Anese to strengthen team health, maximize leadership impact, and optimize company culture.

In addition to being an active entrepreneur, advisor, author, movement-maker, and speaker for the last 13 years, Anese is also a mom to two kids and three rescue dogs in Rocklin, California.

Check out www.anesecavanaugh.com/ccresources for expanded resources, interactive products, and free tools.

How Our Organization Can Help if You Need or Want More

You can do a ton with the information and resources provided in this book. A ton! Should you want or need further help, there are additional methods of support and engagement you are welcome to tap into.

Just like you, we continue to learn and evolve our own IEP and business practices every day. As the work continues to grow, we'll continue to add more stewards, coaches, and additional resources to help make it even more real and impactful for others. So at a minimum, please stay in touch. You can join our community at anesecavanaugh.com or send us an email at Info@ AneseCavanaugh.com. This will get you on our list and give you firsthand access to tools, announcements, articles, and resources as we continue to create them.

Should you wish for more, here are some additional ways our organization can support you:

- **Resources and Tools.** Our website is loaded with tools, resources, articles, and videos to support people in their IEP Practice.
- **IEP School.** Register for our online programs for yourself, as a team, or for your whole organization.
- **IEP Live! Leadership Experiences.** Attend a public session, or host one privately for your organization.
- **IEP Stewardship Training and Organizational Programs.** Put some of your IEP advocates and internal trainers through official IEP Stewardship Training.